GUERRILLA STRUGGLE IN AFRICA

GUERRILLA STRUGGLE IN AFRICA

An analysis and preview

by Kenneth W. Grundy

A World Order Book
GROSSMAN PUBLISHERS
NEW YORK 1971

To Will, Tom and Anne
Who look to the future, not to the past

Copyright © 1971 by World Law Fund

First published in 1971 by Grossman Publishers
44 West 56th Street, New York, N.Y. 10019

Published simultaneously in Canada by
Fitzhenry & Whiteside Limited

SBN: 670–35649–2 (*cloth*)
SBN: 670–35650–6 (*paper*)

Library of Congress Catalogue Card Number: 78–143536

Printed in U.S.A.

FOREWORD

War, social injustice, poverty and ecocide are phenomena which the vast bulk of mankind has participated in and accommodated to throughout its recorded history. For most of his existence man has considered these matters to be "in the nature of things." Yet in the last 200 years radical transformations have occurred in consciousness and society: the "natural" has become irresistibly amenable to social change. Human sacrifice, cannibalism and slavery, archaic institutions all, have been virtually eliminated from society. Yet other problems of great magnitude persist, and appear insoluble.

Foremost amongst these is the institution of war. It is still a conviction widely held throughout the world that war, springing from aggressive impulses in man, is an inevitable and enduring institution of human society. The pervasiveness of this conviction does not seem to be diminished by the fact that scientific data tend to undermine the belief that large-scale organized violence is a necessary outgrowth of the aggressive impulses experienced by the human species. Our understanding of the human mind and social psychology leads toward the conclusion that while man may be an aggressive animal, his aggressive impulses may take various forms, many of which are actually constructive in ways probably indispensable to the future of civilization.

In this context we should note that the attempt to eliminate war as an institution—rather than merely to diminish its horror and brutality—is of relatively recent vintage. The League of Nations aside (since neither the United States nor a large number of other states were ever members), it can be said fairly that the first major attempt to outlaw war was to be found in the Kellogg-Briand pact of 1927, where for the first time in the history of mankind, the leaders of the majority of nation-states which had the capacity to initiate international wars, renounced war as an instrument of national policy. In 1945 the creation of the United Nations, building on the League of Nations and the Kellogg-Briand pact, represented an even more significant commitment to outlawing war. Nevertheless it is true that the United Nations has had only the most modest success over the first twenty-five years of its existence. The present world political system, dominated by individual nation-states, states which refuse to surrender sovereignty on matters concerning their own security, now bears within itself the threat of such large scale violence that the institution of war has emerged as one of the great survival problems of mankind.

Inseparable from the future of war are the worldwide problems of poverty, social injustice and ecocide (by which we mean overpopulation, resource depletion and pollution). Each of these have, to some extent, different natural histories in civilizations. They nevertheless stand out even more saliently in the contemporary world as crucial problems that must be solved. Thoughtful persons throughout the planet have begun to recognize that all these problems are in complex ways interrelated and that together they constitute a systemic crisis of the greatest magnitude.

During the last few centuries two revolutions, the scientific-techno-logical and egalitarian-ideological, have brought these problems to an explosive, earthwide point. The incredible growth and tempo of the technological revolution has made it possible for one or more nation-states, acting on its own authority, to destroy much of mankind in minutes' time. The explosion of egalitarian ideologies into mass conscious-ness has led to an unprecedented situation in which demands for justice and improved conditions of material wellbeing are being made with ever-increasing insistence. The prolonged inability of nations to control the burgeoning world population, to moderate the race between the de-pletion of resources and the long term achievement of universal welfare and ecological stability, to control the eruption into violence of newborn and ancient rivalries and tensions, and to achieve minimal standards of social justice, is leading to the breakdown of structures of authority and continued widespread, pervasive suffering.

It is to the solution of these problems, war, poverty, social injustice and ecocide, that this series of world order books is directed. World order, then, is an examination of international relations and world affairs that focuses on the questions of how to reduce significantly the likelihood of international violence, and to create tolerable conditions of worldwide economic welfare, social justice, and ecological stability. In more connotative but less precise terminology, the question is, how may we achieve and maintain a warless and more just world.

The World Order Books are part of an emerging transnational effort to free the future from the past and to shape a new world order over the last third of the 20th century. The authors contributing to this series share the view that it is both meaningful and necessary to engage in analyses that lead to the solution of world order problems. Because we generally recognize that these problems are planetary in scope, requiring a world-wide response, the authors will come from all the regions of the world, thus providing perspectives from diverse segments of mankind. Whatever his national allegiance may be, each author is asked to take seriously the notion of a world interest, and must articulate policies and recommendations that accrue not only to the benefit of a particular geo-political unit, but to the benefit of mankind.

This series of books, in addition to being transnationally oriented to some conception of the world interest, will exhibit a distinctly futuristic perspective. Each author will thus attempt to build an image of the future he wishes to see realized over the last third of the 20th century. But it will not be enough to create utopias. Each author is also asked to link his image to a concrete description of whatever steps and strategies he believes are both necessary and possible to achieve the world order he wants. The creation of these relevant utopias—relevant in the sense that they permit the reader to understand what would be necessary in order for the image to become a reality—will, we hope, contribute to a much needed dialogue that will in turn lead to the creation of a preferred world in which the world order values of peace, economic welfare, social justice and ecological stability are realized on a planetary scale.

Within this broad context the World Order Books will be varied in style and tone. Some will be scholarly; others will take the form of the speculative essay; yet others may be primarily fictional; a number may reflect combinations of these genres. Many of the books will be published in languages other than English. We shall be crucially aided in the task of recruitment and in the shaping of the series generally by a small multi-national board of consulting editors already familiar with the perspective and purpose of the world order approach. It is our belief that the intellectual framework provided by the perspective of world order, particularly as it will be shaped by thoughtful persons throughout the globe, will yield new and powerful insights into man's past, his turbulent present and above all, his future.

We are indebted to Grossman Publishers for having assisted us in embarking on this worldwide enterprise. We should also like to express our appreciation to the World Law Fund for its contribution and support of this program.

Ian Baldwin, Jr. and Saul H. Mendlovitz
General Editors

ACKNOWLEDGMENTS

Like so many other books, this book was never really intended to be a book. In the winter of 1968–1969, I wrote a paper that was read and discussed first at the 1969 Annual Meeting of the International Studies Association in San Francisco and then at a session of the African Studies Round Table at New York University. My friend Ali A. Mazrui of Makerere University, Kampala, Uganda, read the paper and brought it to the attention of the participants of the World Order Models Project, one of whose conferences was convened in Northfield, Massachusetts, in June 1969 to discuss the need and prospects for developing arms policies on global and regional bases for the decade 1990. That paper, incidentally, appears in substantially revised form as Chapter Four of this book. From there the momentum was supplied by Ian Baldwin, Jr. and Saul Mendlovitz, who saw the manuscript through to completion. It was their insistence that this study conform to the standards of the World Order Series, and that it endeavor to contain normative and prescriptive components as well as descriptive, empirical, and analytical ones.

I am indebted to several other individuals and groups for assistance in my work. First, I am thankful to the Rockefeller Foundation and to the Department of Political Science and Public Administration at Makerere University for enabling me to spend the 1967–1968 academic year in East Africa. It was a stimulating stay and my colleagues and students were indispensable in providing me with ideas and insights, many of which are presented in one form or another herein. I am also deeply grateful to Professor George W. Shepherd, Jr. and to the Center for International Race Relations at the University of Denver, who encouraged and financed my trip to Southern Africa during 1969. The scores of people with whom I talked there were tremendously hospitable and generous with their time. Closer to home, my colleague Professor Don R. Bowen has discussed with me many of his ideas about civil violence. It is essentially his model which provides the skeleton for Chapter Two. My graduate students in Political Science 475, whether they realized it or not, were the guinea pigs on whom I tested many of my own hypotheses. I should single out Mr. John Breckling, who supplied ideas for the scenarios in Chapter Seven. Finally I should thank Mrs. Anne Miller whose typewriter could almost miraculously transform what often were chaotic drafts into neat finished products.

My last vote of thanks goes to my patient and loving family, particularly to my wife Marty. She suffered through innumerable readings, she "Strunked" my scripts, and she kept the boys out of harm's way while I was sequestered on the third floor. All of these people, and so many more, have a hand in the creation of this book. They deserve far more than a thank you buried in perhaps the least read section of a book.

Cleveland Heights, Ohio   K.W.G.
January 1971

CONTENTS

Preface   xv

1. SOME THOUGHTS ON VIOLENCE AND A WARLESS
   FUTURE   *1*

2. THE CAUSES OF POLITICAL VIOLENCE   *7*
   A. An Abbreviated Model of Political Violence   *7*
   B. The Focus of Systemic Frustration   *12*
   C. Political Violence in Africa   *24*

3. AFRICAN CONCEPTIONS OF VIOLENCE   *27*
   A. A Variety of Formats for Political Utopia   *28*
   B. The Role of Violence   *30*
   C. Conclusions   *36*

4. WHY CHOOSE GUERRILLA STRUGGLE?   *41*
   A. Communist Theories of Guerrilla Warfare   *42*
   B. Is Mao's Doctrine Universal?   *46*
   C. Guerrilla Training for Africans   *49*
   D. African Theories: Reliance upon the Peasantry   *55*
   E. African Theories: Patterns of Political-Military Interaction   *62*
   F. African Theories: The Protracted War   *67*
   G. Counterguerrilla Thinking in Africa   *68*
   H. Conclusions   *72*

CONTENTS

5. THE MOVEMENTS AND THE WARS   75
   A. A Typology of African Guerrilla Movements   75
   B. Wars against Domestically Democratic Colonial Powers:
      Kenya and Algeria   77
   C. An Unbending Colonial Power: Portugal in Africa   91
   D. White-Settler Regimes on the Defensive: Rhodesia and
      South Africa   107
   E. Indigenous African Governments: The Congo and Sudan   115
   F. Conclusions   124

6. THE FUTURE OF GUERRILLA WARFARE IN AFRICA   127
   A. Technological Change and Weapons Development   128
   B. The Extent of Cooperation among Guerrilla Movements   129
   C. Cooperation among Antiguerrilla Target Regimes   132
   D. Extent and Nature of External Involvement   135
   E. The Global Distribution of Power   143
   F. Short-Run Trends (Five to Ten Years)   146
   G. Long-Run Trends (Thirty Years)   149

7. TOWARDS A MORE ACCEPTABLE FUTURE IN
   SOUTHERN AFRICA   153
   A. A More Acceptable Future—1998   156
   B. Steps toward Change   161
   C. The Transitional Period   182

Appendix 1. ABBREVIATIONS USED IN THIS BOOK   189

Appendix 2. FACTUAL SUMMARY OF THE MAJOR GUERRILLA ORGANIZATIONS
CURRENTLY OPERATING IN AFRICA   191

Index   197

LIST OF ILLUSTRATIONS

TABLES

TABLE I. Estimated per Capita Incomes in African States, 1963–1967 *14*

TABLE II. Average Annual Earnings of Employees, Zambia, 1966 *15*

TABLE III. Average Annual Earnings of Employees, Rhodesia, 1969 *16*

TABLE IV. Rise in Salaries by Social Categories, Congo, 1960–1965 *18*

TABLE V. An Abbreviated Model of Political Violence *24*

TABLE VI. Africans in South African Urban Areas *57*

TABLE VII. A Typology of African Guerrilla Movements *78*

TABLE VIII. Average Annual Wages by Race, Mozambique *93*

TABLE IX. Force Levels in Guinea (Bissau) *98*

TABLE X. Sudanese Refugees, 1964–1968 *121*

TABLE XI. Military Force Levels in Southern Africa, 1966–1968 *134*

TABLE XII. Importance to South Africa of Trade with Main Trading Partners *167*

TABLE XIII. Importance to Main Trading Partners of Trade with South Africa *168*

MAPS

Map 1. Nationalist Military Activity, Algeria, 1954–1958 *86–87*

Map 2. Guerrilla Warfare in Southern Africa, 1970 *95*

LIST OF ILLUSTRATIONS

Map 3. Liberation of Guinea (Bissau)—General Situation, 1969
   100–101
Map 4. The Congo, Areas of Greatest Rebel Advance, 1964   *117*
Map 5. The Sudan, Southern Provinces   *120*

PREFACE

Any serious student of political affairs would quite naturally be hesitant to venture into the realm of futures, particularly if the time period examined extends much beyond a few years. Thus it is not without some earnest misgivings that I have undertaken this brief volume. I will attempt to make explicit some of my misgivings as well as to outline a few of the reasons why I have decided to proceed. My desire is that the reader will appreciate the problems of research and analysis and will be aware that the author makes no claim to be definitive; that this preview into the future of a particular issue—guerrilla warfare—in a particular region— Africa—is highly tentative; and that its primary purpose is to provoke serious thought about affairs that might well shape our own lives no matter how far removed, spatially and temporally, they may appear to be today.

One group of reservations centers on the current state of social science and particularly on the study of the future in social affairs. Although this is not the place for an exposition on the current state of political science as a science, it should be clear to the general reader that theories of political behavior regarding topics as complex as political violence, international politics, or political legitimacy (all of which are relevant to this current study) have hardly advanced to the stage of widely accepted causal propositions. On the contrary, there is a good deal of controversy over whether or not if-then hypotheses can (or should) be formulated, least of all operationalized, tested, and verified. There is little agreement among political analysts on the relevant variables to be dealt with or even on a comprehensive descriptive content. The specific nature of these difficulties with regard to the matter of political violence and guerrilla warfare will be sketched more carefully in the next chapter. With these sorts of fundamental disputes among those most conversant with the issues, it is understandable that one would be reticent to make projections into the future based upon questionable empirical data and debatable causal propositions. In other words, since our knowledge of the causes of political violence is incomplete, subjective, and uncertain, efforts to project such phenomena into an uncertain future must necessarily be treacherous.

Yet in recent years the study of societal futures has become a serious scholarly, and increasingly scientific, endeavor. This development grows out of a general fear that ecological and sociopolitical change might well escape the control of man. Thus the study of contingent futures is not so much a scientistic extremism born of the revolution in the social sciences, but, rather, a product of socially concerned natural and social scientists who are alarmed that the voluntaristic component might be seriously impaired unless mankind does something quickly to preview possible futures with an eye to directing its own destiny. Concerned men do not want to be caught up in an inexorable and unacceptable march of history. Therefore, futurology, in order to be really fruitful, must combine the twin components of value research as well as trend research.[1] Futurologists want not only to describe accurately the likelihood of certain developments in societies, but want to be able to erect control mechanisms so that they or someone utilizing their skills can devise control systems to warn of impending dangers in the early stages and to retard, deflect, or reverse them before they reach what Kenneth Boulding has called a "break boundary." [2]

There are problems, however, in effecting this admirable desire to avoid unacceptable futures. Perhaps the most crucial intellectual problem is that all futures research is based upon at least one unprovable assumption. Even if the researcher were to be able to offer accurate causal propositions, to describe reality accurately, and to collect relevant overtime data

1. See Johan Galtung, "On the Future of the International System," *Journal of Peace Research*, IV, No. 4 (1967), 305–306.
2. "Is Peace Researchable?", *Background*, VI (Winter 1963), 73–74.

for projection purposes, he would still have to make an assumption about the pace and pattern of future change. At this point his choices are essentially four. He can assume a fundamentally unchanged environment—a condition of systemic statis. He could assume, alternatively, that trends current at the time will continue. He could assume a sort of cyclical trend development—that the future will be like the past rather than the present. Or he could assume that the future will be full of historical surprises, essentially unpredictable other than by giving play to one's imagination based upon an educated knowledge of the past. Or the researcher could allow for some combination of these four assumptions, all of which are partially true, each of which, by itself, is false. It soon becomes evident that futurology is as much art as it is science.

Unfortunately, all of these difficulties are compounded, not diminished, as the time span under study is extended. There is a sobering note of pessimism in Saul Friedländer's article "Forecasting in International Relations." [3] There he contrasts short-term forecasting (up to two years) with long-term (ten to fifteen years). What is pessimistic is that anything beyond the range of fifteen years is implicitly beyond the range of any sort of reliability. That we are concerned with Africa thirty years hence demands humility on the part of the reader and writer alike.

It must be remembered that in the social sciences we are dealing with *human* behavior subject to some element of choice. There is little point plunging into that old debate between the determinists and the free-will proponents. But the fact remains that a prediction (or any aspect of social science observation, for that matter) becomes an element in the system, and this may lead to the possibility of the self-fulfilling and self-denying prophecies. Futurologists are not unaware of this problem and thus prefer to eschew the term *prediction* in deference to *prevision,* less associated with claims of precision and control.

A second set of reservations stems from one facet of the subject matter —the region of Africa. By their own admission, Africa's leaders regard Africa as a revolutionary continent. Certainly there is a commitment to change and economic development—both in domestic-state terms and in international terms, i.e., in the entire relationship between Africa and external peoples and forces. Africans want to be masters of their own futures

3. In Bertrand de Jouvenel (ed.), *Futuribles,* II (Geneva: Droz, 1965), 1–112.

and in many respects this demands a fundamental alteration in the current distribution of wealth and power in the world as well as in Africa. So the pace of change in Africa is as staggering as the directions of change are perplexing.

If any serious effort at preview can be undertaken, adequate and reliable data must be accumulated. This leads directly to the question of access. Understandably, Africans are supersensitive about political problems in their societies. Neither the established regimes nor those anxious to upset the status quo are willing to divulge what they know about their own sources of support and those of the opposition. The acquisition of reliable data about a sensitive political issue, even if they were existent, demands virtually superhuman efforts and unparalleled contacts. Few political analysts, regardless of race or nationality, can command such access. I am not among the select. By and large, we shall have to make do with what frequently originated as impressionistic, ideologically biased, non-comparable data. Furthermore, projections into the future can best be accomplished by over-time data. Again, the relatively recent emergence of a politically conscious Africa often renders projection conjectural. All this being said, one could expand the range of error further by suggesting that Africa's problems are not unique. The generalizations arrived at might, conceivably, be applicable to other geographic regions of the less-developed world.

Related to the subject matter problem is the racial issue that might be injected. One might ask, Can an outsider understand political violence in Africa? Actually one might respond with a further question, Is a white person really an outsider? Can he really be detached? Given the racial factors involved in so much (but not all) of Africa's political violence, particularly in Southern Africa, is it possible for a white person to divorce himself sufficiently from some sort of emotional attachment to one side or another? Although total detachment is impossible, and relative detachment unprovable, I would still answer yes. This position is predicated upon the hope, as much as the knowledge, that one may be humanly capable of a necessary measure of objectivity. It could even be argued that a non-African (of whatever race) is *better* capable of transcending psychological involvement in this emotional issue. Saying this does not make this so, of course, and the analyst must, alas, defer to the reader's estimation of his ultimate fairness, hoping that no a priori judgments are arrived at based on some corollary of the genetic fallacy. Although it is often helpful to view the situation through the eyes of the participants, it is less likely (although possible) that a direct participant could be as objective as a trained outsider. The views of participants from both sides must be understood, and the scholars must also be able to stand off to see the total picture as it "really" is. Even the best scholars cannot be thoroughly detached from the subject matter. But what makes them good scholars is their ability to recognize openly their value preferences and thence to attempt to minimize the intrusion of such values into the research process itself. Nonetheless, a relatively high degree of objectivity is still no guarantee that Africa's future, in regard to guerrilla warfare, can be forecasted with any reliability. One can easily cite numerous examples of erroneous projections about affairs in Africa. The following example pertains directly to the liberation struggle in Southern Africa and comes from the pens of Colin and Margaret Legum, analysts with a well-deserved reputation for hard work, excellent contacts, and a competent grasp of Africa's realities. But in a study published in 1964 they discussed a hypothetical point at which the Republic of South Africa would be surrounded by hostile liberation movements on the march.

> How long will it take to reach this point? Here one can only guess: perhaps two or three years before the collapse of Angola; another year for Mozambique and Southern Rhodesia—if they have survived that long. Thus one would fix the crisis point at between 1966–68.[4]

I repeat this "guess" here with no intention to embarrass or disparage the work of the Legums. My purpose is to demonstrate the hazards of prediction about events in Africa, particularly events involving a multitude of variables about which we know so little. I can only expect that in a few years someone will take glee in juxtaposing my findings with reality. I can hope at least that the reasons for undertaking this work are sufficiently compelling to offset any errors that may occur in the process.

My own interest in this topic is essentially simple. It grows out of my own value preferences, which are that each human being deserves to live in a social system that attempts to maximize his personal and economic

4. *South Africa: Crisis for the West* (New York: Praeger, 1964), p. 5.

security at the same time that it guarantees him a tolerable level of human dignity and individual justice. Thus the best system, according to my value structure, is one where there is a relatively low level of violence from outside and coercion from within the system, and where each person is judged on the basis of his qualities as an individual and, moreover, is provided with optimum opportunities to realize his full potential as a human being. Obviously, any such system would encounter manifold difficulties in societies where resources are scarce. But it is mentioned here as an ideal system—one toward which man should strive. If such a system is utopian, then I am guilty of being a utopian.

There are, however, large sectors of Africa (both black- and white-governed) where these values are not, in fact, approximated; indeed, parts where they are not even aspired to. My reaction as an individual committed to the well-being of the world community is that this is unfortunate and should be rectified. My goal as a scholar is to understand why this is so and what are the ways in which it can be changed. Although it is not the responsibility, nor would it be wise, nor feasible, for outsiders to impose their values on other peoples against their own wishes, the very act of doing nothing is itself a passive, if not an active, form of support for the existing system. Social engineering, however, is not my chief concern here. Rather, our desire is to understand the phenomenon of political violence in Africa. It is a humanistic concern for the *quality* of human life, not just its mere existence or its material security, that leads me to write this book.

Chapter One

SOME THOUGHTS

ON VIOLENCE

AND A

WARLESS FUTURE

There is no inherent virtue in the absence of warfare or violence. Its fundamental utility is that it is a necessary precondition for the fulfillment of other ends that people seek in life. Physical suffering may be diminished and human lives are preserved. Since experiencing violence is traumatic, in individual as well as in group terms, the absence of violence makes less likely the creation of intense, emotional images that may lead to retaliatory violence. President Julius Nyerere of Tanzania put it well by writing:

> Even the most successful and popular revolution inevitably leaves behind it a legacy of bitterness, suspicion and hostility between members of the society. These are not conducive to the institutions of equality, and make it difficult to build a spirit of co-operation between the whole people. In particular there is always a fear that those who suffered during the revolution may be looking for an opportunity of revenge; there is the memory of injury and bereavement deliberately inflicted, which poisons the relations between men within the society. A violent revolution may make the introduction of socialist *institutions* easier; it makes more difficult the development of the socialist *attitudes* which give life to these institutions. . . . But violence is a short cut only to

the destruction of the institutions and power groups of the old society; they are not a short cut to the building of the new.[1]

There is a good deal to be said for the maxim that each war sows the seeds of the next war. But the absence of war is not, in itself, condition enough for the enrichment of the quality of human existence. Peace is, at heart, a derivative value. Peace is only important if the established order affords one the dignity and opportunity for the fulfillment of valued ends.

It would be helpful at this point to devote a paragraph or two to the question of the priorities attached to various formulations of ultimate ends. The World Order Models Project of the World Law Fund seeks to harness social scientific enquiry to the creation of a world political and social system in which war has been eliminated as an accepted social institution and in which tolerable conditions of worldwide economic and social justice have been achieved.[2] This value model in which war prevention, economic welfare, and social justice are assigned equivalent weight is not only tantalizingly perplexing, given the transitional character of global human affairs, but downright paradoxical, given the determination on the part of some people to employ, as a means, the very negation of one of the suggested values in order to achieve the fulfillment of the other two values. No one would doubt that the ends-means dilemma is a slippery one. Every goal can also be viewed as a means to some other goal. The same set of principles might be classified as both ends and means. It makes a difference, for example, whether one posits war prevention as a goal of a people, or as an instrument for the achievement or defense of other ends. Many a people have gone to war convinced that they were fighting to make wars in the future less likely. Any resolution of this profound dilemma would have to be subjective. Nevertheless, some effort should be made to discuss the issue and, at least, to attempt to rank priorities in some meaningful way.

1. Julius K. Nyerere, *Freedom and Socialism—Uhuru Na Ujamaa: A Selection from Writings and Speeches, 1965–1967* (Dar es Salaam: Oxford University Press, 1968), pp. 23–24. Nyerere's emphasis. For a contrary view, see Kwame Nkrumah, *Handbook of Revolutionary Warfare: A Guide to the Armed Phase of the African Revolution* (New York: International Publishers, 1968); and Frantz Fanon, *Wretched of the Earth* (New York: Grove Press, 1963). Nkrumah and Fanon, particularly the latter, see a cathartic quality in violence, which can supply the exhilaration and dynamism needed in the building process.
2. For a description of the World Order Models Project, see Ian Baldwin, Jr., "Thinking About the Decade 1990," *War/Peace Report*, January 1970.

Still, all things being equal (and they are not), it would be sensible to favor a global social system—or a domestic one, in the short run—in which people (including the regime) did not resort to violence, largely because without personal security people are not able to achieve their highest forms of self-expression. We know, however, that security is a part of one's psychological environment as well as of his operational, or objective, environment. For one to be secure in his person and his property, however defined, a certain sense of satisfaction and freedom of choice are imperative. There is little security in the knowledge that others can make decisions which affect wide areas of your life, particularly in adverse ways. Thus the quality of the social system is as vital to a sense of security as is a diminished likelihood of warfare. Some of the world's most outwardly stable social systems were, themselves, established by violent means and are maintained by the constant threat and reality of calculated and controlled regime violence. The dichotomy between violence and stability may often be an artificial one.

Thus, if one ranks the absence of violence as the primary end of a system, it becomes necessary to achieve, as first priorities, the more immediate ends of social justice and economic welfare. Until they are achieved, any state of peace would merely be temporary and illusory. The ideal, stable, nonviolent society is one in which the bulk of the population is psychologically as well as objectively secure from the fear of violence, *and moreover* is fundamentally satisfied that the status quo, or some peaceful alteration of it, affords them sufficient opportunity to achieve the things they value. In short, if the status quo is psychologically intolerable for a people, the superficial absence of physical violence is not necessarily the best condition for the achievement of long-term absence of violence. Furthermore, there is a usage of the term violence by which a political and socioeconomic order that is psychologically disruptive and demeaning could be regarded as *violent*. If this usage is accepted, then the case for the necessity of altering the status quo becomes even more compelling.

In many respects this is how African leaders view this dilemma. Their conception of the United Nations, for example, is considerably different from that of the moving forces who created that world organization. The great powers envisioned the UN as an organization devoted to the prevention of the recurrence of German and Japanese militarism and to the general maintenance of peace. African leaders, in contrast, stress those Charter clauses affirming a faith in "fundamental human rights," and the "dignity" and "equality" of all peoples. These may be amorphous goals, but they are no less inspirational than the determination "to save succeeding generations from the scourge of war." [3]

The question then arises, how best to establish a system that provides for an acceptable status quo and for the means of altering it when changes seem warranted. The frightening prospect might be that in a racially and culturally heterogeneous society, perceptions of tolerable life styles may be so internally incompatible that a widely acceptable status quo may be impossible to achieve. Ideally, in that situation the best that could be hoped for would be an approximation of satisfaction on as broad a base as possible. The twin goals of economic welfare and social justice for everyone should be injected into the ideal model here, so that the parochial aspirations of privilege, exclusiveness, and superordination, no matter how keenly desired, would be rejected as values worth fighting for.

Depending on the nature and character of the existing regime, violence then might be a necessary means to the achievement of social ends— including the absence of violence—envisaged as desirable. Despite the apparent paradox, this is how a study of guerrilla warfare fits into the World Order Series. The real, long-range absence of violence demands the establishment of systems founded on the principles of social justice and economic welfare for all peoples. Otherwise the "peaceful" state is tenuous, unless, of course, a major effort at indoctrination is launched by the established regime to regard parochial interests as goals worth defending (even among the underprivileged). Such an orientation has resulted in the Bantu policy presently pursued by the South African government, in which differences, not similarities, are glorified. People, by and large, are not so easily convinced. The success of such a program would be difficult in today's world; more so in tomorrow's.

We mentioned earlier that African leaders appear to have reranked the priorities of the United Nations Charter, favoring human rights over peace. But in one very important respect, deeply shaping the future of

3. A discussion of these issues appears in Ali A. Mazrui, *Towards a Pax Africana: A Study of Ideology and Ambition* (London: Weidenfeld & Nicolson, 1967), pp. 128–146.

guerrilla warfare in Africa, African heads of state and government are clearly more concerned with peace than with the values of dignity and human rights. Where they are willing to take risks to redistribute power and wealth on a global scale, the leaders tend to emphasize the legalistic "equality" of sovereign states at the expense of human equality of individual men. To employ the United Nations, the Organization of African Unity (OAU), or some other international organization in the pursuit of "fundamental human rights" and man's dignity and equality is not the same thing as to disturb the "tranquility" of an indigenously governed state to further ends which they find admirable in the abstract, but disruptive in the concrete. In some respects this is why African states have retreated from the general reliance upon the United Nations for solving African problems. And this also helps explain the ambiguity and apparent inconsistency of some of these leaders regarding the use of force for political purposes, except in the overriding case of white regimes in Southern Africa. It is precisely because the Southern African situations contain, within them, the reality of a universalized struggle and the potentiality of universalized war—possibly triggered by a guerrilla war—that I have dealt so directly with them, particularly in the final chapter.

Chapter Two

THE CAUSES

OF POLITICAL

VIOLENCE

A. *An Abbreviated Model of Political Violence*

Not all violence is politically motivated. Nor is all violence necessarily important to the political system. Likewise, all political violence cannot be termed guerrilla warfare. Guerrilla warfare is a specific form of political violence characterized by a high degree of organization, political involvement, dedication, focus, and fairly explicit goals. Nevertheless, it is a form of political violence and for guerrilla warfare to be perceived as a viable policy alternative by political dissidents, certain conditions associated with the broader generic category of political violence must prevail. It becomes necessary, then, to sketch a simplified and abbreviated model of political violence that will be applicable to our discussion of guerrilla warfare in Africa.

Perhaps the term "model" is a little formalistic here, as it implies a more technical meaning than is intended. "Formulations" might be more in order, since what follows is a loose, suggestive set of conceptualizations. But for my basic purpose—that of outlining a set of interrelated and interacting variables—it is best, probably, to persevere with the term "model," since it conveys with more precision what I am attempting to accomplish. To the specialist this brief model will appear to be inadequate. Certainly there are numerous variables that have some effect on political violence and that have been excluded here, but to include all variables that have some effect on the system would be to create a model so complex as to be useless for our purposes.[1]

Political violence, the dependent variable, is here taken to mean physical attacks upon persons or property associated with the political or civil order.[2] To be sure, it is equally important to recognize that regime violence (i.e., attacks by or sanctioned by the established order on various elements of the population) is a form of political violence, but for our purposes antisystemic violence is the phenomenon we are chiefly concerned with. Regime violence is an important factor affecting the total magnitude of antisystemic political violence and will be treated shortly rather than be included in this particular definition. When men become frustrated in the pursuit of their goals, they experience a state of mind known as anger and manifested as aggressive behavior. Although such aggression may be internalized (i.e., directed against self) or externalized, it is the externalized version that we seek to understand. Naturally, the extent and nature of frustration varies, and with it aggressive behavior varies. What we are concerned with here are the conditions by which aggression may take violent forms aimed at the established political order. Frustration with the established order is the independent variable and will be dealt with in more detail in a subsequent section of this chapter. Suffice to say at this point that such systemic frustration occurs when persons feel that things they value are threatened by the sociopolitical system. The crucial consideration here is the matter of *perception* rather than the actual cause of the frustration itself. By and large, the major form that systemic frustration takes in Africa is that perceived as denying the attainment of values which the frustrated individual does not possess, but which he has been conditioned to desire and believes that he can attain. Occasionally, individuals perceive that the political system is seeking to take away something they value and already possess, but the expression of political violence in this form is usually associated with the coup d'état

1. For the reader who desires a more complete and rigorous product, consult Ted Robert Gurr, *Why Men Rebel* (Princeton, N.J.: Princeton University Press, 1970).
2. I am indebted to my colleague, Professor Don R. Bowen, for conversations relevant to these issues and to his unpublished paper, "A Model of Civil Violence," as a basis for the following discussion.

(military or by some élite group) or with primordial turmoil. Though the latter variety (primordial turmoil) may find expression in some form of guerrilla warfare, the likelihood of its success is limited given the narrow base of its appeal.

But seeking to isolate the conditions that frustrate men is not, in itself, explanatory. We know that men are often frustrated, at least to some degree. We know as well that large numbers of persons may be frustrated and discontented, but may not engage in violent, antisystemic behavior. It becomes necessary to locate additional determinants that serve to increase or decrease the likelihood of violent behavior. Six intervening variables come to mind: (1) the force capabilities of both the regime and the dissidents; (2) the legitimacy of both the regime and those who seek to replace the regime; (3) the norms relating to violence in a system; (4) the factors external to the domestic political system in question; (5) the ideology of the potential dissidents; and (6) the leadership available to the contestants. Each will be dealt with separately.

Severe disparities in the distribution of the means of coercion, particularly if they favor the established order, tend to minimize the likelihood of political violence. If the dissidents possess an overwhelming preponderance of force, it is likely that a single act, usually in the form of a coup, will be adequate to topple the regime. In either case, the total magnitude of political violence will probably be low. More frequently, when systemic frustration is acute, the capability levels of the contending forces are likely to be more symmetrical; in that event, the extent of political violence is likely to be high, and its form will resemble internal war, as opposed to anomic or disorganized turmoil. Such a result precipitates further systemic frustration, and the familiar cycle continues. The Debray thesis of guerrilla warfare is based on the explicit technique of launching military action so that the act of warfare will serve as a catalyst to instigate further frustration and facilitate mobilization of popular discontent.

A legitimate regime is one whose subjects accept its right to rule. When a government enjoys this quality of rightful rule, its goals and policies are generally regarded as proper. The value of legitimacy is that such a regime need not maintain itself primarily by force. Thus, if a regime is perceived to be legitimate, the level of political violence is low, at least among that segment of the population so recognizing legitimacy. It should be clear, however, that two additional features of the quality of legitimacy bear mention. One is that legitimacy is divisible: some segments of society may regard the regime as legitimate at the same time that other segments are convinced of the absence of its right to rule. A fruitful and common avenue for the analysis of political violence is to explore the nature and depth of the divided indicators of legitimacy.[3] A second aspect of legitimacy refers to its temporal quality. The distribution of the perceptions, as well as the intensity of the feelings, can decline or increase with time. Repeated acts (or failures to act) that outrage a society's sense of right may forfeit or bring legitimacy into question. If legitimacy is withheld as an outcome of increasing systemic frustration, political violence grows and the regime must find alternative sources of support. The reaction is often a spread of regime violence and an augmentation of force capabilities on both sides. Both the regime and the potential dissidents at this point are caught up in the problem of establishing their claims to rightful rule. Attempts at coercive social control by the regime (and challengers, on occasion) may occur when it perceives that its support is diminishing. Depending on how the established order employs force, the result may be a widening of feelings of systemic frustration or the establishment of an artificial and ominous calm. Securing the data for assessing the various levels of perceived legitimacy is, at this point, nearly impossible.

A third intervening variable refers to the ways in which the various societies and segments of societies view violence as a political means. Various cultures possess structures of norms governing the use of violence. These may not necessarily be explicit, but they can be studied. A culture may, rather than sanction violent behavior, provide alternate channels to vent anger and frustration—channels which represent no challenge to the established system. Even within a given culture various subgroups may be sanctioned to behave differently with regard to violence. The societal norms affecting violence and the provision of approved, substitute outlets for aggressive feelings deeply affect the magnitude of political violence. These elements must, if at all possible, be explored with regard to various African cultures.

3. See my paper, "Segmented Instability: An Exploration of the Problems of Comparative Analysis," delivered at the Annual Meeting of the Southern Political Science Association, Gatlinburg, Tennessee, November 10–12, 1966 (mimeo.).

External factors can take numerous forms. The initial spark for the political unrest can originate outside the target system. Direct military and economic aid and assistance to either the dissidents or the regime or both can serve to affect the duration and intensity of political violence, and of course, the ultimate outcome of the contest. We have been told countless times of the importance of an accessible sanctuary for guerrilla forces. Unrest abroad likewise has a demonstration effect on both parties. Ideas and examples know no formal political boundaries. These factors will be discussed subsequently in Chapters Five, Six, and Seven.

Ideology is a vital ingredient in any form of revolutionary behavior. Ordinary citizens whose anger and aggression stem from systemic frustration are often perplexed and even fatalistic about their emotions and the future. If they react violently, it is usually without direction or manifest purpose. The result is a series of spontaneous and disorganized acts. So, while systemic frustration is the raw material out of which revolution or internal war is manufactured, other elements must be added to the productive mix. A revolutionary ideology can perform at least four services for the disaffected population. First and most importantly, an ideology contains a set of transcendental objectives with which its adherents can agree and toward which they can labor. Second, it provides a set of images by which the real world can be interpreted. As such a system of knowledge and communication, ideology provides its adherents with an analytical prism through which they see the world and with a set of unified thought patterns that enables them to communicate with one another easily. Particularly useful for revolutionary purposes is the third possible function of ideology as an action strategy and a set of general guidelines for revolutionary behavior. Fourth, ideology serves to condone and justify violent behavior that otherwise would be rejected by traditional belief systems. Thus, ideology is a system of higher rationalization that legitimizes the behavior of its proponents and supplies a symbol of continuity with fallen leaders of the past.[4] An ideology becomes a necessary ingredient to revolutionary behavior since it galvanizes support in the indi-

4. These ideas have been drawn from the excellent discussion of the variegated functions of Marxism-Leninism for Soviet foreign policy found in Vernon V. Aspaturian, "Soviet Foreign Policy," and in Roy C. Macridis (ed.), *Foreign Policy in World Politics,* 3rd ed. (Englewood Cliffs, N.J.: Prentice-Hall, 1967), pp. 65–72. See esp. the map on p. 22.

vidual's mind and among the committed, explains to them the cause of their frustration, focuses grievances on a single target, and convinces the faithful that change is possible, and that fatalism must be abandoned and replaced with positive action of their own making.

For these views to be translated into revolution, leaders are necessary. Not only must such leaders be dedicated and immersed in their revolutionary ideology, but they must be capable of applying it to concrete problems of policy and be imbued with the leadership skills necessary to appraise the political situation accurately and to organize and direct the movement. Without leadership, revolutionary frustrations will probably be dissipated in disoriented, sporadic, and, from the viewpoint of the established order, controlable turmoil.

B. *The Focus of Systemic Frustration*

It now becomes necessary to apply to sections of this model data relevant to the African experience.[5] Let's first look at the independent variable, systemic frustration, to see if we can isolate, at least for analytical purposes, the conditions by which people become frustrated. We said earlier that systemic frustration arises out of feelings that people are being denied or deprived of values they regard as important. Thus we must discuss not only the objective environment, but also the psychological environment that leads to systemic frustration. What we are really concerned with is the relationship between the two environments. Since there is little data available to us regarding the psychological environment among Africans, certain inferences must be drawn on the basis of our knowledge of the objective conditions in which people function. We shall have to concentrate on the objective environment here. To be sure, the correlations between environments are not perfect. Frustration is a perceptual condition that does not always accompany actual relative deprivation. This is why

5. A good, brief, generalized treatment of political conflict in Africa is Aristide R. Zolberg's "The Structure of Political Conflict in the New States of Tropical Africa," *American Political Science Review*, LXII, No. 1 (March 1968), 70–87. Governmental efforts to overcome conflict patterns are treated in Zolberg's *Creating Political Order: The Party-States of West Africa* (Chicago: Rand McNally, 1966).

the presence or absence of the intervening variables discussed above becomes so important.

There are four major sets of conditions that seem to lead directly to systemic frustration in Africa. They are: (1) the generally low level of productivity and the existence of wide inequities in the distribution of the economic values of a society; (2) the inability and unwillingness (in some cases) of the established order to cope with fundamental grievances; (3) the lack or deliberate closure of channels for the legitimate expression of discontent and for the peaceful realization of fundamental societal change; and (4) the set of frustrations related to the heterogeneity of the population. Usually systemic frustration that leads to violent behavior cannot be traced to any single condition described above, but, rather, to an often complex intermix difficult to sort out in any generalizable sense.

RELATIVE ECONOMIC DEPRIVATION. The relatively low level of economic productivity in Africa does not need documentation. The overall material standards of living are low by whatever criteria one wishes to apply. Within Africa there are immense disparities from state to state, as we can clearly see in Table I, which shows the average per capita incomes in African states. But data of this sort is incomplete in regard to our specific interest in political violence.

A more revealing picture can be gleaned by the realization that economic development in Africa usually radiates outward from isolated pockets, or islands, of economic activity[6] (see Map 1). These urban and industrial-mining concentrations that propel economic growth also symptomize the tremendous inequities inherent in the uneven development of retarded and fundamentally capitalistic economies, particularly those based upon external investment or expatriate skills.

Within a given territory there are profound regional differences in the level of economic activity. Actually, it is necessary to develop this argument a step farther to trace the patterns of wealth distribution. These regional stratifications may coincide with known socioeconomic cleavages. The most obvious cleavage is between African and non-Afri-

6. This argument is carefully developed in L. P. Green and T. J. D. Fair, *Development in Africa: A Study in Regional Analysis with Special Reference to Southern Africa* (Johannesburg: Witwatersrand University Press, 1962).

TABLE I

ESTIMATED PER CAPITA GROSS NATIONAL INCOME, 1963–1967
(At market prices, $US)

Rank	Country	Year	GNI/capita
1	Libya	1967	$883
2	Republic of South Africa	1967	618
3	Gabon	1966	392
4	Zambia	1967	298
5	Ivory Coast	1966	256
6	Ghana	1967	252
7	Algeria	1963	245
8	Rhodesia	1967	233
9	Senegal	1966	227
10	Liberia	1966	210
11	Tunisia	1967	208
12	Morocco	1967	191
13	United Arab Republic	1966	189
14	Congo (Brazzaville)	1963	188
15	Swaziland	1966	178
16	Sierra Leone	1963	128
17	Cameroon	1963	120
18	Kenya	1967	117
19	Madagascar	1967	116
20	Central African Republic	1963	113
21	Congo (Kinshasa)	1966	108
22	Mauritania	1963	107
23	Sudan	1963	104
24	Guinea	1963	99
25	Botswana	1966	96
26	Uganda	1967	95
27	Lesotho	1966	88
28	Togo	1963	86
29–30	Gambia	1963	81
29–30	Niger	1963	81
31	Nigeria	1966	77
32–33	Dahomey	1963	75
32–33	Mali	1963	75
34	Portuguese African Territories	1963	71
35–36	Somalia	1963	69
35–36	Tanzania	1967	69
37	Chad	1963	66
38	Ethiopia	1966	64
39	Malawi	1967	51
40	Upper Volta	1966	49
41–42	Burundi	1963	40
41–42	Rwanda	1963	40
	Total, Africa	1963	140
	United States	1967	4,037
	Europe	1967	1,760

Source: United Nations, Statistical Office, Department of Economic and Social Affairs, *Statistical Yearbook, 1968* (New York: United Nations, 1969), Table 191.

can employees in societies with racial heterogeneity. The wage levels that obtain in independent Zambia, for example, are illustrated in Table II.

TABLE II

AVERAGE ANNUAL EARNINGS OF EMPLOYEES,
BY INDUSTRY, ZAMBIA, 1966
(In Pounds)

	African			Others		
	Overall	Gov't	Private	Overall	Gov't	Private
Agriculture	88	134	71	1,548	2,148	1,172
Mining	443	—	443	3,521	—	3,521
Manufacturing	228	254	226	1,756	1,651	1,761
Construction	184	165	192	1,528	1,528	1,925
Electricity, water, and sanitary services	193	179	210	2,557	2,186	2,693
Commerce	241	263	238	1,425	1,546	1,421
Transport and communications	306	271	394	2,262	2,363	1,919
Services (excluding domestic)	223	233	181	1,431	1,605	1,053
All employees	254	214	271	2,194	1,854	2,305

Source: Data abstracted from: Republic of Zambia, Central Statistical Office, *Statistical Year-Book, 1967* (Lusaka: Government Printer, 1967), pp. 40–41.
Note: Estimates are based on earnings in the first quarter, 1966.

This data could be further broken down by age group, region, and ethnic group to lay bare some staggering disparities.[7] In territories where ethnic identities had been eroding, the uneven nature of economic growth has reintroduced stratification based upon primordial considerations.[8] In contrast, there are countries where divisions are growing up across traditional sociocultural lines, creating what amounts to class cleavages, unencumbered by deep ethnic, racial, linguistic, or subethnic concerns. We should not exclude the very real existence of what Mazrui calls the "trans-class

7. For detailed discussions of the resultant patterns of life, see Hortense Powdermaker, *Copper Town: Changing Africa* (New York and Evanston, Ill.: Harper & Row, 1962), esp. pp. 69–147; J. Clyde Mitchell and A. L. Epstein, "Occupational Prestige and Social Status Among Urban Africans in Northern Rhodesia," *Africa*, XXIX, No. 1 (January 1959), 22–40; James R. Scarritt and John L. Hatter, *Racial and Ethnic Conflict in Zambia*, Studies in Race and Nations, II, No. 2 (Denver: Center on International Race Relations, 1970).
8. Professor Ali A. Mazrui has discussed and labelled this problem in "Violent Contiguity and the Politics of Retribalization in Africa," *Journal of International Affairs*, XXIII, No. 1 (1969), 89–105.

man," the person who feels compelled to belong to more than one class in a situation of great structural fluidity.[9] By far the more common pattern in Africa has been ethnic and regional stratification reinforced by uneven economic development and reward. In territories like Rhodesia, Portuguese Africa, and the Republic of South Africa, these sorts of divisions are not simply the fortuitous results of the supply and demand character of the labor market. (See Table III for comparable data on Rhodesia.) Rather, they have been strengthened and maintained by legislation, trade union structure, and immigration patterns, as well as by the social mores of the dominant segment of society.

TABLE III

AVERAGE ANNUAL EARNINGS OF EMPLOYEES,
BY INDUSTRY, RHODESIA, 1969
(in $ Rhodesian)

Industry	Africans	Others*
Agriculture	147	2,857
Mining and quarrying	322	4,224
Manufacturing	476	3,332
Building and construction	371	3,193
Electricity and water	408	3,672
Distribution	436	2,534
Banking, insurance and finance	656	3,110
Transport and communication	638	3,394
Government administration	408	3,082
Education	544	2,700
Health	564	2,314
Private domestic services	244	1,000
Other services	390	2,243
Total	296	2,980

Source: Data abstracted from Rhodesia, Ministry of Finance, *Economic Survey of Rhodesia, 1970* (Salisbury: Government Printer, April 1970), pp. 24–25.
* Includes European, Asian and Colored Persons.

Similar artificial supports for inordinate economic disparities prevail in parts of Black Africa as well.[10] The concept of relative deprivation de-

9. See Ali A. Mazrui, "Political Superannuation and the Trans-class Man," paper presented to the Seventh World Congress of the International Political Science Association, Brussels, September 18–23, 1967 (mimeo.).
10. See esp. René Dumont, *False Start in Africa* (New York: Praeger, 1966), pp.

mands further exploration here. Crawford Young deals in detail with the application of this concept to political unrest in the Congo.[11] He posits that the widespread sense of deprivation that existed in the Congo could be measured along three dimensions: in temporal space, in vertical social space between strata, and in horizontal communal space between ethnic groupings. As he sees it, the temporal dimension has two aspects, "the immediate recollection of a more ordered and materially prosperous life situation, and a utopian vision of future well-being briefly generated by the explosion of terminal colonial nationalism." Thus, the promises of nationalist politicians and the generally optimistic attitudes preceding independence, and also a relative decline in living conditions for large segments of the population, served to accentuate discontent.

The social stratification dimension stems from a rapid growth in income disparities and from the disparities in access to material rewards. Those individuals able to assume occupational roles vacated by expatriates enjoyed tremendous status mobility and rewards therefrom, but only some 10,000 positions were thus available, mostly filled by clerks and military noncommissioned officers. In addition, further concentration of inflated reward positions accrued to certain political appointments and commercial entrepreneurs.

Certain obvious conclusions can be drawn from this presentation. As Young observed:

> The rapid polarization of the socio-economic strata was rendered dramatic in its impact by the frequently conspicuous display of new wealth. The opulent life style of the colonial establishment served as a reference point for the administrative bourgeoisie. . . . A rough estimate of those benefitting materially from independence might total 150,000. Awareness of the new gap between the political-administrative class and laborers, unemployed, and peasantry was general by 1962.[12]

78–97, et passim, who maintains this view with emotional as well as experiential conviction; P. C. Lloyd, Africa in Social Change (Baltimore: Penguin Books, 1967), esp. pp. 304–320; and P. C. Lloyd (ed.), The New Élites of Tropical Africa (London: Oxford University Press, 1966).
11. The following analysis is drawn from Crawford Young, "Rebellion and the Congo," in Robert I. Rotberg and Ali A. Mazrui (eds.), Protest and Power in Black Africa (New York: Oxford University Press, 1970), pp. 969–1011.
12. Ibid., pp. 979–980.

TABLE IV

RISE IN SALARIES BY SOCIAL CATEGORIES, CONGO, 1960–1965

Category	Nominal	Real
Civil Servants		
Auxiliaries (messengers, etc.)	498	102
Clerks	678–1073	139–219
Bureau chiefs	241	49
Permanent secretaries	153	31
Military		
Privates	414	85
Sergeants	571	117
Teachers		
Teachers	333	68
Primary teachers without degree	566	116
Private sector		
Legal minimum (bachelor)	306	63
Legal minimum (married, 3 children)	255	52

Source: Reproduced from Young, "Rebellion in the Congo," p. 979.
Note: Indexes as of December 31, 1965 has as their base June 30, 1960 = 100.

These general conditions were compounded by factors such as a massive rise in unemployment, the growth of female militancy based on obstructed mobility, the development in the provinces of an enormous growth in the lower ranks of the public works system (an illusive form of employment since it was often accompanied by pay arrearages, often up to two years), and the presence of unemployed school leavers in increasing numbers, with their attendant crushed dreams and their determination to do something about their future.

The third dimension of felt relative deprivation—ethnic and regional disparities—cuts horizontally across Congolese society. As Young puts it: ". . . the cognitive map through which groups evaluated the distribution of social and material rewards gave a prominent place to the ethnic landscape." [13] Each group, the beneficiaries of independence and those who suffered by it, maintained linkages based upon ethnicity. At the regional and local levels, as well as at the national level, movements for change and patterns of relative deprivation became identified with particular ethnic groups, or segments thereof, and these designations became increasingly self-reinforcing. Even among groups who shared the same

13. *Ibid.*, p. 983.

socioeconomic grievances, divisions would occur. Economic deprivation, therefore, was not the sole determinant of support for revolutionary change. Although, in the Congolese case, most revolutionaries sprung from economically disadvantaged groups, all deprived groups did not rally to the revolutionary banner. Frequently, local animosities and traditional cleavages were simply reexpressed in socioeconomic terms. In broad terms, there was an overall division between the nodes of intense economic activity (Kinshasa/Lower Congo and Katanga Copperbelt) and the "interior," according to the pattern illustrated by Green and Fair. The tridimensional nature of relative deprivation outlined by Young helps clarify the further questions of who supported the movements and why. In terms of the model outlined in Section A, systemic frustration was widespread throughout the Congo, but the expression it took was differentiated from region to region. This extensive illustration from the Congo experience is used because the Congo has undergone virtually every variety of political violence. It is, in some respects, a microcosm and caricature of Black Africa itself. Such an analysis might be applicable to other territories in Africa where political violence has surfaced or is just beneath the surface—the Sudan, Chad, the Cameroons, Nigeria, and others.

GOVERNMENTAL INEPTITUDE. There are at least three facets of this issue that demand inclusion here: (1) inability on the part of the governments to satisfy expectations that they have encouraged; (2) corruption; and (3) low regime force levels. In one respect, African governments have to withstand the convergence of several forces that seem to have reached their prime in the mid-twentieth century. One is that with independence has come the departure of a fairly substantial segment of the colonial expatriate civil service. Some regimes have been able to make the transition with no really appreciable decline in the quality and efficiency of the services provided. Others, such as the Congo, have suffered tremendously by the precipitous flight of thousands of skilled governmental employees. Unfortunately, however, with the general decline in qualified personnel has come an increasing demand that existing government services not only be improved and expanded, but that the government provide new services as well as move into functions heretofore fulfilled by private groups. In Guinea this led to a virtual standstill in the export-import services and wholesale commercial enterprise when the government decided prematurely to establish government-managed commercial services.[14] Governmental inefficiency is not necessarily a continent-wide phenomenon. It can be isolated, sometimes by service, sometimes by country, sometimes by region or locale. But where it occurs, it contributes to frustration. Occasionally the politicians are themselves responsible for intensifying these frustrations, since they have promised, or appeared to promise, immediate material benefits to those who supported their claims to govern. Not infrequently, the politicians had no intention of attempting to satisfy high expectations. Nevertheless, the government is commonly regarded as responsible for general economic growth. Frustrations that result are often oriented toward the established regime.

The matter of corruption in Africa is a difficult issue to deal with. Most definitions of corruption are culture-bound, particularly as they apply to non-Western countries. By tying corruption to a clear-cut standard, it may be possible to determine a useful definition. Corruption, then, can mean the violation of the letter or spirit of a law by a public official acting for the purpose of private gain. In short, it involves the misuse of authority for considerations of private gain. There is no need to discuss the causes or possible benefits in political or developmental terms. Our primary interest is to sketch the costs of corruption in terms of the growth of systemic frustration. To the ordinary citizen, who neither pockets corrupt money nor can afford to pay it, corruption appears to institutionalize unfairness. His mistrust of government grows as governmental corruption grows, since, ultimately, little is accomplished without a bribe.[15] This in turn leads to a decline in regime legitimacy, as well as to an economic drain as the costs of doing business and administration increase. At the very least, corruption further distorts the already inequitable distribution of national wealth. In societies where resources are scarce, corruption tends to feed upon itself, forcing other public officials, out of self-defense, to indulge. Since there are built-in limitations on the base to which corruption can expand, the final by-product will be widespread growth of disaffection and frustration.

14. S. Amin, *Trois expériences africaines de développement* (Paris: Presses Universitaires de France, 1965).
15. A vibrant portrait of such attitudes is painted in Chinua Achebe's cogent novel, *A Man of the People* (London: Heinemann, 1966).

Not only may the civil service pool of talent be shallow with an accompanying decline in the extent and quality of public service, but the police and military services of a new regime may fail to perform adequate services for either the people or the regime itself. These forces may be unable to provide protection for the citizens or may, even more negatively, be unable to maintain domestic order; indeed, may even contribute to political violence. Military and police forces in Africa have so far been employed primarily for purposes of maintaining internal order. But Black Africa's level of military preparedness is low, in absolute as well as relative terms. The ratio of military to civilian population is about 1:1131 compared to 15:1000 for the United States and 10:1000 for the United Kingdom and the Middle East.[16]

This overall low force level becomes more significant when one considers the additional problems of logistics in underdeveloped countries, and the fact that the indices of instability are high in these states, thereby necessitating a more efficient coercive arm of the regime. What prevails is a modified variation of Boulding's "loss of strength gradient" in which a government's power declines with distance from the capital city.[17] As if these rather straightforward problems were not enough, Africa's militaries must overcome a deep-seated popular fear and distrust of them that dates back many decades.[18] Since independence they have done little to erase this stigma. Attempted coups, mutinies, disorderly attacks upon citizens, the experiences of the Congo and Nigeria, stunning defeats at the hands of small mercenary units, the periodic demands for expanded budgets and privileges, all contribute to reinforcing a negative image. Reputations for ruthlessness are not always associated with a distinction for efficiency. So, a low level of efficiency does not discourage violent expression of systemic frustration.

CHANNELS FOR THE EXPRESSION OF DISCONTENT. It is assumed that in any

---

16. Calculations based on figures for January 1966 drawn from David Wood, *Armed Forces of African States*, Adelphi Papers No. 27 (London: Institute for Strategic Studies, April 1966), p. 28. Comparative data for other regions from I. William Zartman, *International Relations in the New Africa* (Englewood Cliffs, N.J.: Prentice-Hall, 1966), p. 90.
17. Kenneth E. Boulding, *Conflict and Defense: A General Theory* (New York: Harper & Bros., 1960), pp. 227–248, 260–262, and 268–269.
18. For more detail on this point, see Kenneth W. Grundy, *Conflicting Images of the Military in Africa* (Nairobi: East African Publishing House, 1968).

society where resources are scarce, where regime legitimacy is widely questioned, where both economic development or lack of it unleash forces that lead to high levels of discontent, and where socioeconomic transition is destabilizing, systemic frustration is likely to be high. Thus it becomes all the more necessary that the established regime institute procedures and techniques for dealing with expected grievances or, at least, create the appearances of concern and reformist activity. It must, in short, establish and keep open the various channels for the legitimate expression of discontent and the peaceful settlement of societal grievances. It would be naive to expect that grievances will not arise, and blind to think that real complaints can be socialized away by education and indoctrination. Most regimes have created grievance procedures (either by law or in extralegal practice), but usually the range of complaint has certain vaguely defined limits. When the regime feels endangered, it may react by attempting to shut off any kind of expression of discontent. But an unwillingness to resolve legitimate grievances does not result in their disappearance. Frustrated people may, as a consequence, revert to more violent and better organized forms of expression.

HETEROGENEITY OF THE POPULATION. Many aspects of cultural heterogeneity have already been discussed in reference to other aspects of political violence. Actually this is desirable, for it illustrates two points that should be deeply etched in this analysis. First, it indicates the ubiquity of this issue of cultural heterogeneity, not only in spatial and temporal terms, but in its tendency to insinuate itself into virtually all political issues. Hardly a major political event occurs without someone explaining it in terms of the primordial communities that exist in the society in question. Second, it illustrates the constant interaction of variables and, perhaps more importantly for analytical purposes, the difficulty of formulating discrete variables, clearly distinguishable from one another.

The presence of several distinct cultural communities within a single polity in itself poses no insuperable problems for orderly rule. It is the combination of cultural heterogeneity with other issues common in new states that leads to systemic frustration and hence to violent behavior. Thus, when the distribution of economic values, or values relating to political authority, status, and reward are at issue, or when the central government insists on breaking down existing relationships and instituting new, more integrated ones, or simply when frustrations arise when old patterns of life are changed or threatened by socioeconomic change, then the ethnic or subnational focus is often regarded as relevant for the expression of conflicting positions.[19] Despite their ostensible ubiquity and persistence, ethnic factors are not necessarily constant and unassailable.[20] They have, though, an uncanny habit of reappearing, even among population segments frequently and erroneously regarded as having transcended primordial attachments. It becomes necessary to distinguish between ethnicity as a way of life and ethnicity as loyalty to an ethnic group. Thus we should not prematurely regard Africa's nationalist leaders as being "detribalized." They are "detribalized" in the sense that they have abandoned a traditional way of life. But, as Professor Mazrui maintains, "this erosion of traditionality did not necessarily entail the diminution of ethnicity." [21] The sentiments and emotions associated with ethnic identification serve to inflate the importance of cultural distinctions and, when they surface, to make the politico-economic conflict that emerges more profound and bitter. Thus, ethnic issues are often, though not the fundamental cause of conflict, the structural lines on which the struggle is organized and expressed. Income distinctions can be superimposed upon ethnic labels and thereby obfuscate the initial cause of the conflict.[22] It is not always easy, therefore, to discern the root cause of violent behavior by the context in which it is expressed and the form it takes.

Table V attempts to depict in graphic form the model outlined thus far.

19. See Clifford Geertz, "The Integrative Revolution: Primordial Sentiment and Civil Politics in the New States," in Geertz (ed.), Old Societies and New States (New York: Free Press, 1963), pp. 105–157; Lloyd, Africa in Social Change, pp. 288–303.
20. See the excellent paper by Nelson Kasfir, "The Decline of Cultural Subnationalism in Uganda," in V. A. Olorunsola (ed.), Cultural Nationalism in Africa (forthcoming); and also Robert H. Bates, "Approaches to the Study of Ethnicity," (unpublished paper, mimeo., 30 pp.), which tests various explanations of ethnicity with data from a copper town in Zambia.
21. See Mazrui, "Violent Contiguity," 93. Professor Mazrui prefers the term tribalism to ethnicity. See also Robert Melson and Howard Wolpe, "Modernization and the Politics of Communalism: A Theoretical Perspective," American Political Science Review, LXIV, No. 4 (December 1970), 1112–1130.
22. See, for example, Richard L. Sklar, "Political Science and National Integration— A Radical Approach," Journal of Modern African Studies, V, No. 1 (May 1967), 1–11.

TABLE V

AN ABBREVIATED MODEL OF POLITICAL VIOLENCE—VARIABLES

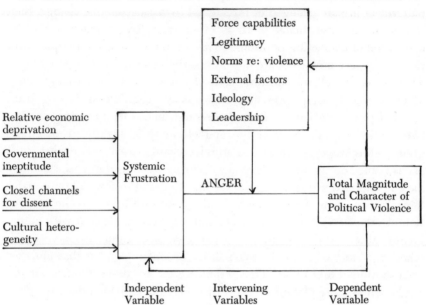

c. *Political Violence in Africa*

Before moving into a discussion of guerrilla warfare in Africa, a few general words about political violence in Africa are in order. By this point it should be evident that political violence can be categorized in a number of ways, depending on the criteria employed.[23] We are interested primarily in intrastate (domestic) violence of political importance which is antiregime in purpose. By and large, the violence guerrilla warfare exemplifies would fall within this concern. Although it obviously has interstate ramifications and it is likely that external events contribute to sustaining guerrilla efforts (and to sustaining the regime as well), guerrilla

23. Two useful examinations of approaches to typologies can be found in Victor T. LeVine, "The Course of Political Violence," in William H. Lewis (ed.), *French-Speaking Africa: The Search for Identity* (New York: Walker & Co., 1965), pp. 58–79; and Harry Eckstein, "Toward the Theoretical Study of Internal War," in Eckstein (ed.), *Internal War: Problems and Approaches* (New York: Free Press, 1964), pp. 1–32.

warfare is primarily a form of internal, or civil, war. Any typology of political violence, then, that would cover adequately the sorts of phenomena discussed in the first two sections of this chapter must include, at least, dimensions based on spatial, effectual, structural, and goal considerations. Along the various continua that might be constructed, these varieties of political violence may be found: demonstration, riot, strike, turmoil, partisan conflict, communal warfare, mutiny, assassination, and coup. Stated briefly the problem is this: there is a tremendous variety of classificatory schemes and a diversity of approaches. These analytical and conceptual challenges grow out of the scope and universality of political violence.

Moreover, the magnitude of political violence in Africa is relatively high, as demonstrated by the large number of refugees fleeing unrest or the threat of violence in its various forms, and the magnitude of acts of political violence quantifiable despite the data limitations noted earlier. Although many of the causes of guerrilla warfare are the same as for political violence in general, it becomes necessary to delimit the phenomenon—guerrilla warfare—so that our analysis can proceed unencumbered by extraneous data.

From one perspective, guerrilla warfare is a form of *political* and *military* warfare in which relatively small units try to isolate even smaller units of the enemy and, in a quick engagement, defeat or inflict losses upon them and then disperse before larger units with superior fire power and superior technology can be brought to bear against the guerrillas. The guerrilla forces attempt to maintain the initiative and to engage the enemy only when the guerrillas are prepared for the confrontation. In such operations a premium is placed on speed, mobility, organization, planning, initiative, surprise, and intelligence. As Samuel Huntington says, "Guerrilla warfare is a form of warfare by which the strategically weaker side assumes the tactical offensive in selected forms, times and places." [24] But this definition is only a part of a definition. It is inadequate for it omits at least two additional crucial dimensions of guerrilla warfare. First of all, it places too much emphasis on tactical military considerations. To be sure, in all types of war, tactics of this sort can be employed, but

24. Samuel P. Huntington, "Guerrilla Warfare in Theory and Policy," in Franklin Mark Osanka (ed.), *Modern Guerrilla Warfare: Fighting Communist Movements, 1941–1961* (New York: Free Press, 1962), p. xvi.

the philosophy of guerrilla warfare sees in this sort of encounter not simply tactical advantage, but strategical advantages as well. Thus, the whole rationale of those who utilize guerrilla warfare (as opposed to guerrilla operations) is the steady physical and psychological deterioration of a numerically and materially superior enemy by a series of numerous small encounters, until such time that the guerrilla forces decide to escalate or raise the level of warfare to more conventional proportions. Second, by being overly concerned with military considerations, there is a temptation to overlook the fundamentally political component of a guerrilla strategy. Not only does the choice of a guerrilla strategy enable an ostensibly inferior military force to defeat an ostensibly superior enemy, but, just as importantly, there are political ramifications of this strategy. The successful employment of guerrilla warfare is ideally accompanied by a high level of political as well as military organization, involving large numbers of people, concerned with political mobilization, participation, and indoctrination. Not only does guerrilla warfare provide a materially weaker movement the chance for military success, but it also contains the organizational wherewithal to structure a governmental apparatus once victory in the field is assured. Indeed, under the ideal theoretical model, the two components—military and political organization—function simultaneously and in concert and frequently involve the same persons. These considerations shall be dealt with in some detail later. Thus, though it is perhaps neat to categorize *forms* of warfare on the basis of military criteria, as does Huntington, it is rather misleading in the case of guerrilla warfare.[25]

25. *Ibid.*, pp. xv–xxii.

Chapter Three

AFRICAN CONCEPTIONS
OF VIOLENCE

As a rule, the more short-term the effort at forecasting in international politics, the more necessary it becomes to identify and view the subject matter from the perspective of the relevant actors. The more distant, temporally, the concern, the more important become the systemic factors in relation to individual, voluntaristic factors.[1] Thus it seems essential to be able to see the situation through the eyes of the actors, to identify their aims (ultimate as well as strategic), and the motives and intentions underlying their behavior. Although this study is not solely concerned with international politics and is by no means an exercise in short-term forecasting, it strikes me that these principles are applicable to previewing all complex political phenomena. To a large extent, motives, ideologies, and attitudes are themselves a part of the system, perhaps less mercurial than we might presume, and they deserve a fuller explication than is often afforded them. A good deal might be gained, for purposes of this study, by attempting to reconstruct the images and goals of the actors, not in an individualistic or idiosyncratic context, but in a generic sense.

1. See, for example, Saul Friedländer, "Forecasting in International Relations," in de Jouvenel, *Futuribles*, II, pp. 28–86.

A. A Variety of Formats for Political Utopia

All African guerrilla movements can be grouped into five basic categories, depending on the purposes for which they are fighting. Obviously other criteria could be employed to categorize such movements and we will attempt to construct a more complete typology of African guerrilla movements in Chapter Five. Meanwhile we can say that guerrilla movements could arise, and in some cases have arisen, to achieve: (1) independence from colonial rule; (2) majority rule in territories dominated by white settlers; (3) economic independence and revolution by unseating indigenous, neo-colonialist governments; (4) national self-determination (secession) from independent, indigenous governments; and (5) transnational unity leading eventually to Pan-African unity. For each of these political utopias there is a counterutopia—a conservative utopia (Mannheim would call it an ideology) designed to preserve the established system, and frequently to justify and rationalize position, privilege, or status, or what has been internalized as "right," "just," or "inevitable." Actually, revolutionary forces likewise attribute qualities of righteousness, justice, and inevitability to their own utopias. The result of such a fundamental attitudinal alignment is to make accommodation and peaceful settlement of differences unlikely. Implicit, if not explicit, in most of the arguments of both belligerents is the view that the only way to secure a long-lasting absence of violence is to eliminate the phenomenon that is opposed. In the words of ZAPU's (Appendix I contains a complete list of abbreviations used in this book) National Treasurer, Jason Moyo, to the World Assembly for Peace (East Berlin):

> The question can never be HOW to deal with this class of reckless international criminals, because the answer is clear. Force must be met by force. We do not subscribe to the theory that peace is the balance of opposing forces. Peace must be the result of crushing all the reactionary force. They must be defeated to realize peace.[2]

Thus, in his view the causes of war—capitalist or expatriate imperialist control—can only be eliminated by violently exorcising that element from the body politic. But once the situation is altered, it is felt that warfare

2. *Zimbabwe Review* (Lusaka), I, No. 3 (August 1969), 6. His emphasis.

can be and will be eliminated as a means of settling disputes. In short, a "new order," a genuine utopia will be created representing a revolutionary approach to social affairs.

It is not unusual for a single movement to regard itself as struggling to achieve at once several of the utopias mentioned above, or to designate its opponents as the incarnation of more than one of the evils to be combatted. The revolutionary nationalists battling the Portuguese can at once talk about national self-determination, independence, socialism, and majority rule. Those who oppose the government of Chief Jonathan Leabua in Lesotho profess to be opposing racialism, minority rule, and neo-colonialism, and to favor national self-determination. These categories are not mutually exclusive in the eyes of the guerrilla leaders.

The ultimate ends invariably center around the desire for self-expression as a "people" (however constituted), dignity and justice, economic development and the material well-being of the people, and ultimate peace. Even where short-run economic growth might appear to favor the status quo, and where revolutionaries admit that material sacrifices must be made, they continue to see long-range economic viability as a function of revolutionary change.

The five categories represent to some extent a logical progression in the historical pattern of African political change. Movements to achieve independence from colonial rule have, with the exception of Portuguese Africa and a few enclaves of France and Spain, run their course. At present the second category—majority rule in independent white-settler territories (Rhodesia and South and South West Africa)—seems, along with the movements in Portuguese Africa, to be the likely arena for the near future. However, movements aimed at indigenous governments present tremendous possibilities for revolutionary and secessionist leaders (categories 3 and 4). Indigenous governments, after all, seem less prepared to cope, militarily and politically, with well-organized guerrilla movements. The fifth category, leading to Pan-African unity, seems, at least at the present, to be an unlikely guerrilla utopia for the next few years. Pan-Africanism is a principle to which most African leaders regularly pay lip-service. But commitment to Pan-Africanism would have to be intently and widely accepted in African value structures before the risks of a guerrilla-type movement could be broadly assumed.

B. *The Role of Violence*

The selective utility of violence has come to be widely recognized by Africa's leaders. This represents a steady evolution over the past twenty years or more in thought patterns regarding violence, drifting away from Gandhian precepts and toward Fanonesque ones. The general temper of African nationalist and Pan-African independence movements and the views of individual officials and leaders have displayed these tendencies. Even when the circumstances of particular issues lead such persons to eschew violence in the specific, a willingness to admit the theoretical efficacy of violent means for other cases is more broadly held than earlier in African history. It would be helpful to trace briefly this progression of thought.

Throughout the forties and fifties and into the sixties there seemed to be a commitment among most nationalist and independence movements to achieve their goals by nonviolent means. The influence of M. K. Gandhi was profound. Reflecting on his formative years in the United States and England, Kwame Nkrumah wrote in his autobiography:

> At first I could not understand how Gandhi's philosophy of non-violence could possibly be effective. . . . The solution of the colonial problem, as I saw it at the time, lay in armed rebellion. . . . After months of studying Gandhi's policy and watching the effect it had, I began to see that, when backed by a strong political organization it could be the solution to the colonial problem.[3]

Out of this "conversion" Nkrumah developed his theory of "positive action—a combination of non-violent methods with effective and disciplined political action." [4] This was to be the strategic guideline for Ghana's independence movement. Even a Patrice Lumumba could declare unambiguously: "We condemn violence. Our weapon is non-violence because we believe that one can achieve anything through peaceful means." [5]

3. Kwame Nkrumah, *Ghana: The Autobiography of Kwame Nkrumah* (New York: Thomas Nelson & Sons, 1957), p. xiv.
4. *Ibid.*, p. xv.
5. From Jean Van Lierde, *La Pensée Politique de Lumumba* (Paris: Presence Africaine, 1963), p. 23, quoted in René Lemarchand, "Patrice Lumumba," W. A. E. Skurnik (ed.), *African Political Thought: Lumumba, Nkrumah, Touré,* Monograph Series in World Affairs, V, Nos. 3 and 4 (Denver: Social Science Foundation and Graduate School of International Studies, University of Denver, 1968), p. 56.

Others, such as Nyerere, Kaunda, various South African nationalists, Mboya, Senghor, the Nigerians, and most of the French-speaking Africans, added their voices to this general attitude. Even the *União das Populações de Angola* (UPA) was, as late as March 1961, an avowedly "peaceful" organization. Less than a few days later, the revolution in Angola had erupted with UPA leadership at the helm.[6]

This attitude was at first reflected in the pronouncements and resolutions at various Pan-African meetings. For example, at the first All-African Peoples' Conference in Accra, Ghana, in 1958, the issue of violence as a means for independence struggle was hotly debated.[7] The Algerians, deeply involved in a guerrilla war against France, tried to persuade their brothers to stand behind them on their employment of violence. A large majority of the delegates felt that "violence as a policy could not work." They took the position that no nationalist party would choose a policy of violence unless driven to it, and thereby grudgingly resolved to support "all those who resort to peaceful means of non-violence and civil disobedience as well as to all those who are compelled to retaliate against violence to attain national independence and freedom for the people."[8] Nevertheless, the Conference did reject violence as a considered means of struggle.[9]

Later that year an even more positive stand was taken by the Pan-African Freedom Movement of East and Central Africa (PAFMECA). In its original 1958 constitution, one of the five aims of the organization was "To champion non-violence in the African nationalist struggles for freedom and prosperity."[10] The nonviolent persuasion continued to prevail at the Accra Conference on Positive Action and Security in April 1960, largely a product of Nkrumah's Gandhian penchant and his status at that time in the Pan-African movement.

But this view was being undermined by changing conditions. At the

6. John Marcum, *The Angolan Revolution,* Vol. I, *The Anatomy of an Explosion, 1950–1962* (Cambridge, Mass.: M.I.T. Press, 1969), pp. 139–140.
7. Tom Mboya, *Freedom and After* (London: Andre Deutsch, 1963), p. 50. Mboya had been Chairman of the Conference.
8. Colin Legum, *Pan-Africanism: A Short Political Guide* (New York: Frederick A. Praeger, 1962), p. 229.
9. *Ibid.,* p. 43.
10. See Appendix B in Richard Cox, *Pan-Africanism in Practice: PAFMECSA, 1958–1964* (London: Oxford University Press, 1964), p. 83.

March 1961 Cairo All-African Peoples' Conference the delegates endorsed "the necessity in some respects to resort to force in order to liquidate colonialism." The temper of this conference was altogether different from that of the Accra conference three years earlier. Two conferences at Addis Ababa, one in 1962 and the second in 1963, marked most clearly the growing acceptance of violent means. The first was a conference at which PAFMECA was expanded to include the Southern African liberation movements and at which a new organization, PAFMECSA, was born. Influenced by the new participants and their more militant dedication, delegates reacted enthusiastically to a call to arms by Nelson Mandela of the African National Congress (ANC) of South Africa. Urging his colleagues to recognize the need for sabotage and the bankruptcy of nonviolence, he carried the day.[11] J. D. Msonthi of the Malawi Congress Party continued in this vein by stating that "force is bound to be used because it is the only language that imperialists can hear. No country ever became free without some sort of violence. . . ." [12] The only delegate who reportedly did not applaud this point was Kenneth Kaunda of Zambia.

At the second Addis Ababa meeting in May 1963 the OAU was established. Embodied in the First Resolutions of the OAU (Resolutions 10–15) are provisions for the creation and operation of a committee to coordinate and finance liberation activities among the various movements. By this point, Professor Mazrui comments, "African Gandhism was now nearly dead." [13]

This shift from African Gandhism was general, but not always eagerly accepted. Julius Nyerere was speaking for many leaders when he said:

> Our preference, and that of every true African patriot, has always been for peaceful methods of struggle. We abhor the sufferings and the terror, and the sheer waste, which is involved in violent upheavals, and believe that peaceful progress is worth some sacrifice in terms of time.

11. This account of the delegate response is drawn from Cox, *Panafricanism,* pp. 51–58. The Mandela address appears in *Pan-African Freedom Movement for East, Central and Southern Africa, Addis Ababa Conference, February 2–10, 1962* (Addis Ababa: Africa Department of the Foreign Office, 1962), pp. 29–35.
12. *PAFMECSA, Addis Ababa Conference,* p. 78.
13. Ali A. Mazrui, *Violence and Thought: Essays on Social Tensions in Africa* (New York: Humanities Press, 1969), p. 36.

> But when the door of peaceful progress is slammed shut and bolted
> then the struggle must take other forms; we cannot surrender.[14]

Nevertheless, driven to this alternative, they didn't hesitate to make the
difficult decision. The resolutions of international conferences were a re-
flection of the views of a number of the more influential and vocal leaders
of the continent. They had become increasingly a function of the circumstances of the struggle for independence and of their growing disillusionment with nonviolent approaches as they came to face more
intractable white regimes in Central and Southern Africa. Perhaps the
most significant about-face is attributable to President Kaunda. No
stronger proponent of nonviolence had risen to such a governmental level
in Africa.[15] His conception of "humanism" had been founded on a respect
for the dignity and individual worth of every man. By his own interpretation, he sought to combine Gandhi's policy of nonviolence with
Nkrumah's "positive action." [16] But with the discouraging experience of
Rhodesian UDI gnawing at his mind, Kaunda made the reluctant transition. The intransigence of the opposition, in his view, drove him to it.

Curiously, though African Gandhism might have been dead, at least
one revolutionary body, the ANC of South Africa, felt the need to recon-
cile its violent stance with Gandhi's doctrine. In an unsigned article
entitled "From Gandhi to Mandela," in its official organ, a spokesman
noted that Gandhi never resolved, "except abstrusely," the problem of
disarming the people in the face of an enemy determined to rule by force.
On the contrary, Gandhi is quoted favorably and at length, to the effect
that:

> Where the choice is set between cowardice and violence I would ad-
> vise violence. . . . This is because he who runs away commits mental
> violence; he has not the courage of facing death by killing. I would a

14. Julius K. Nyerere, *Tanzania Policy on Foreign Affairs: Address by the President,
Mwalimu Julius K. Nyerere, at the Tanganyika African National Union National Conference—16th October, 1967* (Dar es Salaam: Ministry of Information and Tourism,
Information Services Division, n.d.), p. 9.
15. Kaunda's commitment to absolute nonviolence, which appears to date from the
late 1950's, culminated in his restriction and imprisonment in 1959. See Richard Hall,
The High Price of Principles: Kaunda and the White South (London: Hodder &
Stoughton, 1969), pp. 43–51.
16. Kenneth D. Kaunda, *Zambia Shall Be Free: An Autobiography* (London: Heinemann, 1962), pp. 88–91, 140, 152. See also Kaunda, *A Humanist in Africa: Letters
to Colin Morris* (London: Longmans, 1966).

thousand times prefer violence than the emasculation of a whole race. I prefer to use arms in defence of honour rather than remain the vile witness of dishonour.[17]

Thus, despite the distortion of the spirit and total thrust of Gandhian teaching, ANC contends that by taking up arms it is not acting in contradiction of Gandhi.[18]

The ANC and others as well see violence as a natural "extension" of the forms of political action attempted in the past. According to one PAC official:

> Force is an extension of all the possible nonviolent avenues that have been tried and have failed; thus, force is a logical sequence in the progression of trying to obtain objectives. Force and nonviolence are interdependent.[19]

This surprisingly Klausewitzian doctrine of violence views the independence struggle as a form of escalatory politics by which revolutionary forces employ at each successive stage the political means they deem adequate to carry the people with them and maintain their revolutionary fervor and base. At each stage, however, they are foiled and therefore raise the stakes and the level of political conflict. Apparently, when these ideas are applied, there is no qualitative transition from nonviolent to violent means.

Actually, this sort of view is not common among African thinkers and leaders. More frequently they tend to be more pragmatic and practical, and to recognize the qualitative distinction between the two varieties of behavior. In their eyes, nonviolence succeeds or fails depending upon the nature of the opposition and the political environment within which it operates.[20] And that environment has two contexts, internal and international. Nonviolence is an appeal to moral conscience. If the regime in power has no sensitivity to moral suasion, nonviolence is left without any impact, in a localized sense. But leaders still might fruitfully employ nonviolent techniques if they thought these tactics might attract atten-

---

17. "From Gandhi to Mandela," *Sechaba* (London), III, No. 5 (May 1969), 10.
18. *Ibid.*, 12.
19. Morley Nkosi, in John A. Davis and James K. Baker (eds.), *Southern Africa in Transition* (New York: Praeger, 1966), p. 280. See also Oliver Tambo (ANC), *ibid.*, p. 223.
20. See, for example, Arthur N. L. Wina and Ndabaningi Sithole, *ibid.*, p. 240.

tion and support externally. To be sure, "no outside person, however sympathetic, can make a people free"; to borrow the words of President Nyerere, "this they have to do for themselves, with their own hands and brains, and their own sufferings." [21] But the direct support outsiders could render a liberation movement and the pressure they might bring to bear on the target regime are not inconsiderable. Herein lies the tragedy of Africa's first nonviolent steps toward independence in Southern Africa. The insensitivity of the outside world has not gone unnoticed by Africa's leaders. The late Tom Mboya remarked, for example, that the world rewards violent behavior. Violence, because it is newsworthy, helps create the conditions in which the world takes notice of the sufferings of those under colonial rule. Experience shows, he writes, that the world only helps African nationalists who have become active, and never before.[22] The demonstration effect of violent behavior has many dimensions, not the least of which is the impact it makes on opinion and policy abroad.

There are other reasons for the adoption of violent means. Most African leaders would contend that violence is not of their own instigation. Rather, violence is an integral part of the established order in white-dominated (one could go further and say minority-dominated) states. The late FRELIMO leader, Eduardo Mondlane, once bitterly told an American audience: "People here in the United States ask: Are there any chances of violence in South Africa? What do they mean? There is already violence in South Africa. . . . To understand the Portuguese machinery for suppressing Africans' political rights is to appreciate the inevitability of violence." [23] Drawing upon the examples of Algeria, Kenya, and Angola, Tom Mboya once framed a rule that "in any colony where there has been considerable white settlement, violence has become inevitable, although it was not the original policy of the nationalist party." [24] White settlers invariably place obstacles in the way to independent, majority rule. In short, in the view of most African leaders, violence does not originate with the Africans. Violence by Africans is frequently a reaction to forceful provocation by the regime in power. On the other hand, this

21. Nyerere, *Tanzania Policy*, p. 10.
22. Mboya, *Freedom and After*, pp. 50–52.
23. Mondlane in Davis and Baker (eds.), *Southern Africa in Transition*, p. 278.
24. Mboya, *Freedom and After*, p. 50; see also Nkosi in Davis and Baker, *Southern Africa in Transition*, p. 280.

simplistic rationale, though accurate in many instances, ignores much of sociological theory regarding violent behavior. Violence may indeed feed on itself. And repeated acts of violent repression do invite retaliation and serve as catalysts for counterviolence. But the sort of violence that leads to guerrilla warfare is at heart a result of a genuine conflict of interests—often irreconcilable interests. No matter how "fair," "legalistic," and noncoercive the regime may be, there arrives a point beyond which interests cannot be compromised or accommodated. It is academic at this point who strikes the first blow.

Still, it is wise to bear in mind that the privileged order may, in order to protect its privileges, engage in preemptive violence, sensing that to fail to do so might lead to an unfavorable redistribution of power. To have a vested interest in the status quo is not always to be committed to the absence of violence. Such a view assumes that the underprivileged instinctively are more violent than the privileged. Yet we know that, at the individual level, the protective instinct leads to violent behavior more readily than the acquisitive one. Group conceptions of protection and conservation are probably not much different. The insecure regime is a far more dangerous animal than the ambitious poor.[25] Despite the tendency of the established regimes to urge nonviolence and order, in practice coercion has been a frequent and ready ally of the insecure status quo.

C. *Conclusions*

What does this evolution in general attitudes toward violence mean for the future of political violence in Africa? We have seen a growing disillusionment with nonviolence and a growing willingness to approve and employ violent means to foster commonly accepted goals. However, it appears that almost without exception the views discussed above were offered in reference to colonialism and white rule. Concepts like freedom and majority rule are bandied about with conviction, but clearly the context intended is the struggle against non-African control of the lives of Africans. There is an unspoken pigmentational component to expressed attitudes about violence. To a large extent this is a negative image of a pigmentational set of attitudes on the part of the white world.

25. See the excellent discussion of these points in Mazrui, *Pax Africana*, pp. 144–145.

This is not to say that Africa's leaders are racist. On the contrary, though there are some who see violence as a just form of retribution against racist policies of white governments, the overwhelming majority of Africa's leaders are nonracists, committed to the eradication of racism, despite an acute sensitivity to racial issues. The pigmentational component is born of experience and historical priority. A white man suppressing a black man is in their view something more abhorrent than a black man suppressing another black man, despite the fact that the one who is suppressed is, in actual terms, no better for it. The former represents a form of insult to all blacks; the latter is regarded as an unfortunate concomitant of the less palatable features of politics. It is also a function of experience, in that white regimes still prevail in a portion of Africa and stand as a symbol of the impotence of African states to control their own destinies. Pronouncements in the abstract are thus without meaning given the complexities and realities of white domination in Southern Africa.

There is, moreover, a natural resistance to violence when confronting matters of dealing with an indigenous government. Kwame Nkrumah has been one of the few heads of state or government who has also been an outspoken proponent of popular, organized violence to unseat indigenous governments.[26] Even when leaders admit the efficacy of the use of violence for self-defense, they are unwilling to sanction a broadened doctrine of violence. Four African states recognized the government of Biafra, largely for "humanitarian" reasons. But there is an understandable hesitancy to make ex cathedra declarations that might be interpreted against their own governments. The public outcry among heads of state and government when Chou En-lai uttered his famous challenge, "Revolutionary prospects are excellent throughout the African continent," illustrates this point.[27] Even when many African governments came to the

26. See Ghana, Ministry of Information, *Nkrumah's Subversion of Africa* (Accra-Tema: State Publishing Corp., 1966); Ghana Information Service, *Nkrumah's Deception of Africa* (Accra: State Publishing Corp., 1967); and Nkrumah, *Revolutionary Warfare*.
27. Speech of February 3, 1964 in Somalia. *Afro-Asian Solidarity Against Imperialism: A Collection of Documents, Speeches and Press Interviews From the Visits of Chinese Leaders to Thirteen African and Asian Countries* (Peking: Foreign Language Press, 1964), p. 274. For a subsequent clarification of this statement at a press conference, see *ibid.*, pp. 285–286.

assistance of the Gbenye-Soumialot regime in the eastern Congo during the civil war of 1964–1965, the pigmentational component was just beneath the surface. Not only did some approve of the use of violence against the Tshombe government, but they materially assisted the rebel forces. In the eyes of his continental peers, Moise Tshombe was the embodiment of neo-colonialism and European exploitation of Africa, his race notwithstanding. His presence, the way he maintained himself in power (with white mercenaries and European military assistance), his ideological conservatism, his personal record of duplicity—all prompted the radical African leaders to insist that Africans alone must solve African problems. But the more common pattern, then as now, was one of reticence to open a Pandora's box of issues closer to home.

Although governmental leaders may be reluctant to transfer a doctrine of the legitimacy of violence from the question of European rule to one of unjust or unpopular African governments, the lesson has not been lost on some African politicians, and on those people who are sufficiently dissatisfied with the established order to risk participation in movements seeking its violent removal. Just as African intellectuals in preindependence times could not be denied the teachings of Jefferson, Lincoln, Marx, Lenin, and Rousseau, so African revolutionaries cannot be shielded from relevant ideas and doctrines to justify and strengthen their cause.

We have spoken so far largely about leadership attitudes. They are, however, the sounding boards which not only shape popular attitudes, but which reflect them as well. Many of the objective and subjective conditions for violent upheaval are present in parts of Africa, and they are likely to be so for many more years. Periodic assassinations and coups may hold out a hope for improved government, but there may be a point at which, like in Latin American politics, the people will come to see this institutionalized instability as contributing little to changing their lives. This can lead to cynicism or to a determination to change things. To expect the conditions contributing to widespread violence to disappear with a superficial coup at the top is perhaps as naive as to have expected rapid fundamental change to have resulted from the coming of independence in the first instance. Likewise, to deny independence is no answer, for no long-range improvement of these conditions can be expected until self-government is achieved and a truly popular government, operating in the people's interests, is a reality. What is necessary is to focus and harness discontent, and then to provoke a catalyst to set it all in motion. Provided some elements of leadership have come to accept the need for violent change—and this has been the direction in which thought has moved over the past decades, particularly in the groups associated with the southern quadrant of Africa—it is likely that this will contribute significantly to the incidence of violence in the continent.

Chapter Four

WHY CHOOSE GUERRILLA STRUGGLE?

Reasons for the adoption of guerrilla strategies for the conduct of revolutionary struggle in Africa are bound up in the sociopolitical conditions of Africa's discontented populations and in their conceptions of the doctrine and reality of guerrilla warfare. Bearing in mind that guerrilla warfare is a form of *political* and *military* warfare involving tactical and strategic dimensions, we shall describe how various African elements (status quo as well as revolutionary) regard guerrilla warfare. An attempt will also be made to see how African thought and practice have drawn upon non-African theories and experiences of guerrilla warfare. One object is to see if ideas and methods developed elsewhere have been creatively adapted to African conditions, and to assess the extent to which African guerrilla fighters and leaders are aware of the crucial role of theory in successful guerrilla movements abroad.

Even if it can be demonstrated that African guerrillas are aware of "classical" thought about guerrilla warfare, it would be virtually impossible to posit a causal relationship between, let us say, familiarity with the ideas of Mao and the field behavior and performance of a given guerrilla movement. More than likely, numerous, more researchable objective conditions shape actual strategy and tactics. A knowledge of the ideas and experiences of other groups similarly situated could be a vital factor in the ultimate outcome of a given revolutionary war. Such a knowledge could well serve as a catalyst to precipitate a movement, or might provide its leaders with encouragement and suggestive guidelines that might supply the ingredient which turns a marginal effort into a victorious one.

A. *Communist Theories of Guerrilla Warfare*

It is generally assumed that Mao Tse-tung contributed more to a general theory of guerrilla warfare than any single individual and that the impact of his thought upon guerrillas and counterguerrillas is widespread. By and large this is a correct appraisal. But it is far too easy to ignore the contributions of pre-Maoists on this subject.

What we now call guerrilla warfare is an old technique. But it was not until the twentieth century that the element of systematic strategic planning was added. T. E. Lawrence first reduced guerrilla warfare to a set of principles. Guerrillas before Lawrence had employed guerrilla tactics because they were obvious alternatives given their circumstances. But Lawrence, the first guerrilla leader to see that the ultimate objective of guerrilla warfare is not necessarily fighting, adopted guerrilla strategy after careful thought.[1]

Clearly, guerrilla warfare is not an exclusively Communist weapon. But Communist practitioners and theoreticians have done more than others to perfect and systematize the instruments of what they have variously labelled "guerrilla warfare," "irregular warfare," and "partisan warfare." Virtually every important Communist thinker, from Marx on, has addressed himself to the subject. Nevertheless, despite the success of the Russian partisans in World War II, no single doctrine of guerrilla warfare was formulated by European Communists.[2]

1. See T. E. Lawrence, *Seven Pillars of Wisdom: A Triumph* (New York: Doubleday, Doran & Co., 1939), pp. 188–196.
2. Pre-Maoist Communist thinking about guerrilla warfare is discussed in C. Aubrey Dixon and Otto Heilbrunn, *Communist Guerrilla Warfare* (New York: Praeger, 1955), pp. 19–33; Otto Heilbrunn, *Partisan Warfare* (New York: Praeger, 1962); John S. Pustay, *Counterinsurgency Warfare* (New York: Free Press, 1965), pp. 22–28; and Walter D. Jacobs, "Irregular Warfare and the Soviets," in Osanka, *Modern Guerrilla Warfare*, pp. 57–64.

Mao Tse-tung, by refining and systematizing thinking about guerrilla warfare, made guerrilla warfare both militarily and politically comprehensible and set it in the context of the class struggle. It is basic to Marxist thought that no one relinquishes power voluntarily. Revolution cannot be born without violence. And such struggle inevitably develops from a confrontation of inherently hostile socioeconomic classes. To Mao, war (like revolution) must follow a "scientifically ascertainable" course. Mao's skill was in his ability to pull together into a single operational theory a disparate body of ideas and data previously available and to abstract a set of principles with broader application than many at first realized.

What exactly does the "Glorious Military Thought of Chairman Mao" have to say about guerrilla warfare? What new ideas or new interpretations of old ideas does he offer? In its barest essentials, Mao gives us two new ideas and a set of categories regarding the phases through which a guerrilla war ought to progress.[3]

The relationship between political and military forms of class struggle has long been perplexing. On the one hand, Mao puts more emphasis on the need for military power than had earlier Marxists; on the other hand, he displays an acute awareness of the dependence of military force on political dynamism. By a classic example of Hegel's Unity of Opposites, Mao could show how indispensable military power is to secure and implement political objectives and, yet, still proclaim the primacy of political purpose to supply the military arm with the basis and guidance needed to compensate for technical and mechanical military inferiority. By its nature, China's bitter, complicated, and drawn-out guerrilla war forced Mao to realize that sheer survival, if nothing else, rested on the possession of military power. He expressed the relationship these ways:

having guns, we can create Party organizations . . . . We can also

---

3. This discussion is heavily dependent upon the following analyses of Mao's military thought: Samuel B. Griffith, II, "The Glorious Military Thought of Comrade Mao Tse-tung," *Foreign Affairs,* XLII, No. 4 (July 1964), 669–674; Edward L. Katzenbach, Jr. and Gene Z. Hanrahan, "The Revolutionary Strategy of Mao Tse-tung," in Osanka, *Modern Guerrilla Warfare,* pp. 131–146; Pustay, *Counterinsurgency Warfare,* pp. 28–41; Tang Tsou and Morton H. Halperin, "Mao Tse-tung's Revolutionary Strategy and Peking's International Behavior," *American Political Science Review,* LIX, No. 1 (March 1965), 80–99.

create cadres, create schools, create culture, create mass movements. Everything in Yenan has been created by having guns.[4]

＊ ＊ ＊

When the Red Army fights, it fights not merely for the sake of fighting, but to agitate the masses, to organize them, to arm them, and to help them establish revolutionary political power; apart from such objectives, fighting loses its meaning and the Red Army the reason for its existence.[5]

The interacting message is one of a constant process of renewal of political dynamism by military victory, and military strength by political support of the people, particularly the peasants.

The grand strategy which broke so conspicuously with previous Communist thought was Mao's concept of surrounding the cities from the countryside and thereby isolating the enemy from the peasantry and from one another. Like most of Mao's ideas, this particular strategy had direct relevance for the objective conditions he faced. Given his inferior forces and the enemy's concentration in urban areas, it was to be expected that the location of a base area, the choice of targets, and the form of military operations were all based upon his desire to exploit the weaknesses of the enemy. The countryside strategy reversed the sequence of the Bolshevik seizure of power in 1917 and enabled Mao to claim that he was creatively applying Marxism-Leninism to China.

For a long time the Reds were in a weakened condition. Mao soon learned that military planning demanded a revised sense of "time." According to traditional Western approaches to war, victory or defeat is usually attributed to the factor of the concentration of forces. If state A has more and better equipment and trained men to bring to bear in a battle against state B, all other things being equal, A will win. War is viewed simply as a function of technology and superior force. If Western military men introduce time into the equation, it is figured in terms of hours, days, weeks, months, maybe years. Mao figured in terms of decades. To Mao, a long war is not to be avoided. On the contrary, the longer the war, the better the chances for victory. Time, to Mao, is an ally,

4. Mao Tse-tung, *Selected Military Writings* (Peking: Foreign Languages Press, 1963), pp. 272–273.
5. Mao Tse-tung, "On the Rectification of Incorrect Ideas in the Party," in *Selected Works*, Vol. I (London: Lawrence & Wishart, 1954), p. 106.

and time can be made to neutralize and ultimately triumph over technology.

Time is, in turn, closely related to space. As Katzenbach and Hanrahan expressed it, "unlimited time depends primarily on unlimited space." [6] But space in military terms is more complicated than simple square mileage. In the context of guerrilla warfare, military space could be expressed in symbolic form as:

$$MS = Mi^2 + Ob + San - CT$$

where MS = Military space; Mi^2 = Square mileage; Ob = Obstacles; San = Access to a sanctuary in a neighboring state; CT = Effective and defensible communications and transport networks. In this way a few square miles of mountainous jungle may be as strategically invulnerable as, let us say, a hundred square miles of prairie or, perhaps, a thousand square miles of flat plain crisscrossed by roads and telephone wires and dotted with airstrips and radio transmitters.[7] Military space is an asset of no mean proportion and can be made to yield time, which in turn might yield revolutionary organization, popular power, and finally victory. Herein lies Mao's preoccupation with a countryside strategy.

In this very brief review one can see how Mao's theory of guerrilla warfare is, in fact, a product of his perception of the objective conditions in which the Chinese Communist leaders found themselves. It amounts to a theory of substitution in which a revolutionary movement, recognizing the paucity of its material assets, has to rerank the elements of war, or else give up in utter frustration against impossible odds. In this sort of situation the Marxist materialist and determinist is forced to admit the virtues of voluntarism. Man's will can be made to supersede the material realities. Statements like, "Weapons are an important factor in war but not the decisive one; it is man and not material that counts," are indicative.[8] The minds of men then become as important as the weapons they possess. A view of warfare germinated in the daily practice of battle becomes, on contemplation, a systematic theory of war in which men are

6. Katzenbach and Hanrahan, "Revolutionary Strategy of Mao," p. 135.
7. *Ibid.*
8. Mao, "On the Protracted War," in *Selected Works*, Vol. II (London: Lawrence & Wishart, 1954), p. 192.

substituted for machines, space for technology, political mobilization for control of industry, and propaganda for ammunition.

Mao's doctrine of protracted war follows a three-stage progression. From the point of view of the guerrillas, the first stage is one of "strategic defensive" in which the guerrilla forces must retreat, attempting to slow the enemy's advance, harass him, destroy his vitality, and at the same time conserve their own energy. This slips into the second stage of stalemate in which the guerrillas prepare to assume the offensive. The war is now in a prolonged state of equilibrium, but by this stage revolutionary morale is rising and the enemy, having failed in its original purpose of a quick victory, is beginning to weary. Guerrilla warfare is now the principal form of warfare, supplemented by mobile and positional warfare. During the third stage, "strategic offensive," larger and larger units participate on the revolutionary side. Guerrilla warfare is no longer the principal technique, being replaced by positional and regular warfare.

All this could be succinctly summed up in Mao's dictum, "The enemy advances, we retreat; the enemy halts, we harass; the enemy tires, we attack; the enemy retreats, we pursue." In other words, in order to preserve your own forces, you must learn the lesson that you fight when you can win and run away when you cannot.[9] It is a first-class military and political mind that can correctly appraise when to move from one stage to the next or, if necessary, when to revert to the tactics of an earlier stage in order to assure survival.

B. *Is Mao's Doctrine Universal?*

To what extent are these principles applicable to other revolutionary situations? Peking itself seems to be ambiguous on this question. On the one hand are the numerous statements that revolution is not for export. On the other, Mao's writings and those of other Chinese revolutionaries indicate that Mao's thoughts contain universally valid principles that can be "creatively adapted" to concrete situations elsewhere. Creative adaptation in this context implies flexibility in strategy and tactics, but the message comes through often and clearly that various colonial and semicolonial countries should follow the path taken by the Chinese people.

9. Mao, *Selected Works*, I, pp. 124, 222.

Revolutionaries abroad were quick to seize upon the ideas developed by Mao. Ho Chi-minh, Truong Chinh, and General Vo Nguyen Giap of Vietnam practically internalized Mao's military thoughts, despite the considerably different objective conditions prevailing in Indochina.[10] After all, the Vietnamese revolutionaries were fighting a colonial war, not a civil war.[11] For the most part, however, Vietnamese leaders merely restated and simplified Mao, maybe altered a bit of the terminology (e.g., Giap relabels the stages—contention, equilibrium, and counteroffensive), but by and large they added or altered little. Giap's one chief extension to the theory of guerrilla warfare sought to render Mao's doctrines more useful in dealing with revolutions against colonial powers that in the metropole were essentially democratic, rather than against invading armies (the Japanese), or an indigenous force or government (the Kuomintang or the Nationalists). Giap sensed some crucial political-psychological shortcomings that weaken a democratic system involved in a protracted, inconclusive military operation. In all likelihood, Giap contended, public opinion in the democratic state will not easily accept "useless bloodshed" or escalating military budgets without clear-cut purpose or the prospect of genuine victory. The result is foolish promises of quick victory by its leaders or optimistic or inaccurate reports to obscure bad news. In the end however, Giap concludes, democratic politicians are forced to compromise rather than take the unpopular course of sustaining a semipermanent anti-guerrilla war.

In like measure, Che Guevara modified slightly Mao's theory of guerrilla warfare.[12] His book is essentially a manual of military techniques and tactics with little attention to strategic problems. Mao had not been especially concerned with the initiation of hostilities. Chinese conditions had already triggered revolutionary violence. In contrast, the Cuban revolutionary cadres were obliged to create the events that would precipitate

10. See Vo Nguyen Giap, *People's War, People's Army* (Hanoi: Foreign Languages Publishing House, 1961); Pustay, *Counterinsurgency Warfare*, pp. 41–44; and Robert B. Rigg, "Red Parallel: The Tactics of Ho and Mao," in Osanka, *Modern Guerrilla Warfare*, pp. 268–273.
11. A fine discussion of distinctions between the Chinese and the Vietnamese wars appears in Chalmers Johnson, "The Third Generation of Guerrilla Warfare," *Asian Survey*, VIII, No. 6 (June 1968), 440–447.
12. Che Guevara, *Guerrilla Warfare* (New York: Vintage Books, 1961, 1968). Cf. Pustay, *Counterinsurgency Warfare*, pp. 44–49.

a popular uprising under their supervision. Guevara was intent on demonstrating that rather than concentrating first on political education and organization, the first order of business is to create a military focus for struggle. In Guevara's words, "It is not necessary to wait until all conditions for making revolution exist; the insurrection can create them." [13] Around this core of fighters a political movement will be born in the fires of battle. It is significant, however, that Guevara was, to a large extent, applying Mao's dicta to social conditions radically different from China's.

Mao's ideas are not, by themselves, an invincible tool. Malayan and Filippino Communists were to learn this. But a general theory was created, and it remained for others to adapt it and to build upon it for their own purposes. Given propitious conditions and a dynamic, creative leader, the substance of Mao's message is persuasive and tempting.

It could be argued that the entire foreign policy of the Chinese People's Republic is an extension and glorification of Mao's revolutionary strategy of which guerrilla warfare is so vital a part. Chinese leaders apparently believe that their own future is tied up with the success of revolutionary struggle in the underdeveloped world. The Chinese seek to lead an aroused underdeveloped world that encircles the developed world. This is a global version of Mao's conception of the Chinese civil war of countryside against city. In the words of China's influential Minister of Defense, Lin Piao:

> It must be emphasized that Comrade Mao Tse-tung's theory of the establishment of rural revolutionary base areas and the encirclement of the cities from the countryside is of outstanding and universal practical importance for the present revolutionary struggles of all the oppressed nations and peoples in Asia, Africa, and Latin America against imperialism and its lackeys. . . . The basic political and economic conditions in many of these countries have many similarities to those that prevailed in old China . . . . The peasants constitute the main force of the national-democratic revolution against the imperialists and their lackeys. . . . The countryside, and the countryside alone, can provide the broad areas in which the revolutionaries can go forward to final victory. . . . Taking the entire globe, if North America and West-

13. Guevara, *Guerrilla Warfare*, p. 1.

ern Europe can be called "the cities of the world," then Asia, Africa, and Latin America constitute "the rural areas of the world." [14]

In the early 1960's the Chinese strategists looked to Africa as the pivot of the anticolonial struggle. "When the time is ripe," one authoritative Chinese military journal put it, "a revolutionary upsurge will engulf the African continent." [15] Even more specifically, in 1964 *Jenmin Jih Pao,* the Communist party daily, expressed the hope that the revolutionaries in the Congo would follow the pattern of guerrilla struggle in South Vietnam.[16]

It is really the successful example of China and her followers, rather than Mao's ideas themselves, that appeal to Africa's revolutionaries. A recent ZANU editorial, for example, stated that its vote for the most significant event of the 1960's goes to "brother guerrillas" in South Vietnam, who have helped demonstrate the "invincibility of Peoples' Wars." [17] It is the reality and prospect of battlefield success that furnishes the appeal of Mao's thoughts and not an inherent applicability as such.

c. Guerrilla Training for Africans

We know that the Chinese and the Cubans have been anxious to impress African revolutionaries with the efficacy of their systematic applications of Mao's and Guevara's general principles of guerrilla warfare.[18] But what sort of evidence is there that Communist guerrilla ideas and practices have made an impact upon Africa? There are at least three different ways by which such political-military ideas and techniques can be transmitted from one movement to another with some degree of permanency: first,

14. Samuel B. Griffith, II, *Peking and People's War: An Analysis of Statements by Official Spokesmen of the Chinese Communist Party on the Subject of Revolutionary Strategy* (New York: Praeger, 1966), pp. 94–95.
15. As quoted in Tsou and Halperin, "Mao's Revolutionary Strategy," 82–83.
16. *New York Times,* June 25, 1964.
17. *Zimbabwe News* (Lusaka), IV, No. 16 (December 31, 1969), 1. For a similar laudatory message see Fanon, *Wretched of the Earth,* p. 55. An ANC tribute appears in *Mayibuya* (Lusaka), No. 10 (May 1969), Resolution 11 of the ANC Conference at Morogoro. Two MPLA interviews published separately by the Liberation Support Movement (Seattle: 1970) deal with this: see *Daniel Chipenda,* p. 19; and *Spartacus Monimambu,* p. 13.
18. Indication of this can be found in Fritz Schatten, *Communism in Africa* (New York: Praeger, 1966), esp. pp. 187–223; John K. Cooley, *East Wind over Africa: Red China's African Offensive* (New York: Walker & Co., 1965); and others.

through direct participation in someone else's guerrilla struggle; second, via formal instruction; third, by means of exposure to guerrilla thinking in printed and vocal form.

As yet, ideological adherence to the concept of the essential unity of all Africans has not led to the realization by many Africans that another man's revolutionary war is one's own vital struggle as well. Few Africans, for truly fraternal reasons, have volunteered to join fellow Africans of another territory in a guerrilla war.

The most prominent case to date involves the joint ZAPU-ANC operations in Rhodesia in the summer of 1967. In a sense they were really two separate fighting units who happened to be travelling together when they were intercepted by the common enemy. There was little tactical coordination between the two units, and the operation could not be construed as an effort by South African revolutionaries to fight for Zimbabwe's independence in Zimbabwe military units commanded by Zimbabwe nationalists.[19] They simply fought together out of necessity with no coherent plan of combat. Since then, however, this relationship has been improved and formalized with the creation of a joint military committee, but this "united front" has yet to prove its effectiveness on a massive scale.

The most anomalous fact is that some African nationalists actually have participated in other guerrilla wars, but on the side of the colonial powers. Numerous Black Africans have fought against the ALN in Algeria, and before them, many of the Algerians who later joined the ALN had themselves gained their first guerrilla experience in Indochina against the Viet Minh. Likewise, a number of the guerrilla officers and fighters in the Portuguese African colonies earlier fought on the Portuguese side and some of the guerrillas in Kwilu and the eastern Congo had been in the ANC before joining the revolutionaries. It is ironic that practical field knowledge of guerrilla strategy and tactics for most African guerrilla revolutionaries with prewar experience came in battle against guerrilla fighters rather than alongside them. It seems, however, that no African guerrillas have had direct field experience fighting in China, Vietnam, or Cuba on the side of successful guerrilla movements.

19. For a critical appraisal of this operation from an ANC revolutionary, see Matthew Nkoana, "The Struggle for the Liberation of Southern Africa," Part II, *Africa and the World*, IV, No. 39 (January 1968), 17. For further details see Alan Rake, "Black Guerrillas in Rhodesia," *Africa Report*, XIII, No. 9 (December 1968), 23–25.

Formal instruction in guerrilla strategy and tactics has been the most fruitful media for transmittal of Communist doctrine of guerrilla warfare. Virtually every major guerrilla movement in Africa in the 1960's has sent a few select recruits to China, Cuba, the Soviet Union, North Korea, and/or elsewhere for intensive instruction. The courses in China have been of varying duration and content. By and large, however, curriculum has not concentrated so much on theory, but rather on tactical and technical matters. Invariably, the men trained in China have returned to Africa to serve primarily as instructors themselves, giving such training a multiplier effect. We have no way of knowing exactly how many Africans have gone to China for guerrilla training, but a fair guess might put the number between 400 and 600. The Cubans as well have actively sought to spread their doctrine of peasant revolution in Africa. At the Cuban Academies of Marxism-Leninism, Agitation, and Guerrilla Warfare, instruction is offered, it is claimed, to over 700 "scholarship" students from all over Black Africa.[20]

Regarding Africa, however, one gets the impression that the Cubans and the Chinese, despite their convictions that their respective brands of guerrilla warfare could have wider appeal, are more inclined to invest their efforts in training selected revolutionaries to subvert governments and movements at the top and to agitate from the bottom to gain short-term advantage.

By far, more potential guerrillas are reached by Chinese and Cuban instructors functioning directly in Africa. Chinese guerrilla instructors have worked in at least three countries—Congo (Brazzaville), Ghana, and Tanzania—and Cubans have been in possibly as many.[21] Russian instructors were also present in the early 1960's. Students came from practically every country in Black Africa in many of which there was no open warfare and with which the host governments had ostensibly correct relations.

The pedagogical emphasis in these courses is on military technique and tactical planning. One captured document from a Ghanian camp

20. "Pablo Ribalta, el agente de Castro en Tanganyika," *Bohemia Libre* (Miami), June 23, 1964.
21. *Times* (London), March 12 and 24, 1968; *Africa Research Bulletin*, [Hereinafter cited as *ARB*], V, No. 10 (November 15, 1968), 1211C-1212A; *New York Times*, November 21, 1966; and *Nkrumah's Subversion*, pp. 6–27, 56–59, 67–69.

manned by Chinese noted two fundamental teaching aims of the courses: (1) "to learn the basic techniques of explosion and the uses of mines and how to organize and direct explosions," and (2) "to learn some preliminary knowledge of the basic guiding thinking of armed struggle and the basic ways of waging guerrilla war." To this end, of the twenty days of instruction, thirteen were to be devoted to "explosion techniques," three to tactics, two to review of material, and only two days to "basic guiding thinking on armed struggle." [22] One former ZANU guerrilla, who had infiltrated into Rhodesia and later escaped, had publicly written about his six-months training in Ghana. He, too, had observed a similar orientation. "The main emphasis was on teaching us sabotage; . . ." he said. "Very little time was spent on teaching us to use rifles and sub-machine guns, on the grounds that we were not to engage in positional warfare." He went on:

> In lectures, we were taught the principles of war and guerrilla tactics according to Mao Tse-tung, given lectures on the People's Army of China and shown films on how they fought the Japanese. We also had lessons on how and from where to begin the Zimbabwe revolution. . . . We thoroughly enjoyed the course, but the Chinese instructors did not satisfy me. They refused to discuss politics or Communism, about which I was curious, saying one day that they had not come to teach us their ideology but how to liberate ourselves.[23]

Thus, although Chinese instructors, using literature printed in China, were in charge, the primary concern was to prepare technically competent fighters, not guerrilla thinkers and strategists. The doctrinal message was never deep below the surface. President Kaunda of Zambia advances a most engaging viewpoint that others likewise have felt, when he says:

> The only [sic] people who will teach young Africans to handle dangerous weapons are in the Eastern camp. How can we expect that they will learn to use these weapons without learning the ideology as well? When they come back we can expect not only a racial war in Africa, but an ideological one too.[24]

An even greater proportion of Africa's guerrillas have been trained in

22. *Nkrumah's Subversion*, pp. 67–69.
23. Hassan Chimutengwende, "My guerrilla fight against Smith," *Sunday Times* (London), March 24, 1968, p. 5.
24. *Times* (London), March 12, 1968.

Africa by Africans, usually by their fellow nationals and usually in the target country. FRELIMO claims that 80 percent of its fighters are trained within Mozambique. Internal training was the pattern in the Congo uprisings of 1963–1965, the "Mau Mau" movement, and guerrilla movements currently being fought in the southern Sudan, and Guinea (Bissau). The same claim is made by Zimbabwe revolutionaries. Nevertheless, during the initial stages of a guerrilla war, the availability of a contiguous sanctuary, or at least a noncontiguous host country that can supply training facilities and assistance, seems crucial.[25] At least ten African states have willingly collaborated by supplying training sites for contiguous and sometimes distant revolutionary movements. Probably more men have been trained in Algeria, the two Congos, and Tanzania than in the other countries. Ghana (during Nkrumah's rule), Congo (Brazzaville), and Somali seemed most inclined to cooperate with movements from already nominally independent states.

It is significant that, given their choice, African guerrilla leaders apparently prefer to call upon Algeria to assist them in training their recruits. The reasons are fairly clear and practical. Algeria is, of course, the only African nation to win independence from a determined colonial power in a protracted guerrilla war.[26] There is little stigma attached to association with another revolutionary African country, and such association would not jeopardize potential or actual assistance and support from either the East or the West, or from any country within the Communist camp. This can be said of few other sources of instruction, including some other African states. Algerians themselves are eager to cooperate with other anticolonial movements, particularly those from the Portuguese colonies as well as with various guerrilla elements from the Congo.

The Western world gets particularly alarmed by the material assistance that China offers to African guerrilla movements, as if Chinese money or hardware could somehow be transformed into a devotion to the doctrines of Mao. For some reason it is believed that Communist

25. A more comprehensive treatment of these issues appears in my article, "Host Countries and the Southern African Liberation Struggle," *Africa Quarterly* (New Delhi), X, No. 1 (April–June 1970), 15–24.
26. See Helen Kitchen, "Conversation with Eduardo Mondlane," *Africa Report*, XII, No. 8 (November 1967), 32. The Chinese themselves have attested to the appeal of Algeria to other African revolutionaries: see *Afro-Asian Solidarity*, pp. 65, 69–70, 71.

ideology is difficult if not impossible to resist for Africans exposed to Communists, in any capacity. In its most extreme form this view has been expressed by Justice Ludorf of the Supreme Court of South Africa. His decision in the case of thirty-seven accused insurgents from South West Africa contained a rather ludicrous rationale for not sentencing the accused to death penalties. In part his decision read: "In my view it has been proved that the Accused, *because of the level of their civilisation,* became the easy misguided dupes of Communist indoctrination. Had it not been for the active financial and practical assistance which the Accused received from the Governments of Moscow and Peking and other countries, they would never have found themselves in their present predicament." [27] The element of indebtedness to those who render concrete assistance in time of need is hard to assess. It is not likely, however, that it alone can provide the recipient with a comprehension of the importance of ideology, nor an understanding of any particular ideology, least of all a commitment to one. If similarities between patterns of thought prevail, the reasons are not necessarily because of inherent weaknesses on the part of the recipients, or because of a vigorous proselytizing effort on the part of the donor. More than likely, one could find a more persuasive explanation in an examination of the conditions facing the various movements and a genuine desire to duplicate the field successes of the emulated.

One form of material exposure is directly related to the acceptance of the doctrine of guerrilla warfare: the distribution of Communist literature among guerrilla fighters. From virtually every guerrilla movement since the Algerian War we have heard reports that Maoist literature has been found among the belongings of captured guerrillas or in overrun guerrilla camps.[28] There is no question but that Mao's *Selected Military Writings,* his *Problems of War and Strategy,* and Guevara's *Guerrilla Warfare* have been widely distributed among African guerrillas and more than likely have been read by many leaders and revolutionary politicians. The

27. My italics. As quoted in Republic of South Africa, Department of Foreign Affairs, *South West Africa: Measures Taken to Combat Terrorism* (Pretoria: Government Printer, February 1968), p. 7. The case is The State vs. Eliaser Tuhadelini and others.
28. For a few examples, consult Cooley, *East Wind over Africa,* pp. 101–102; *New York Times,* August 2, 1964; and *In the Supreme Court of South Africa. Transvaal Provisional Division. State versus Eliaser Tuhadelini and 36 Others* [undated mimeographed judgment of January 26, 1968], p. 35.

extent to which they have influenced African thinking can be discerned in the following sections.

D. *African Theories: Reliance upon the Peasantry*

African thinking about guerrilla warfare can be divided into three identifiable major themes. These might be designated: (1) reliance upon the peasantry; (2) political-military interaction; (3) the protracted war. These categories do not include a discussion of choices of tactics and techniques, most of which differ little from the practice among guerrillas elsewhere in the world.

It would seem almost axiomatic that a guerrilla movement that functions in a continent where probably 90 percent of the population is rural and that seeks to achieve durable political power should seek to establish sound roots among the peasantry. Moreover, there are practical reasons for this preference. Generally speaking, relative deprivation in the African countryside has been greater than in urban centers.[29] People in small towns and villages are not unaware of economic conditions elsewhere in the state. Their hopes and aspirations are acute and high. But just as the central government has been unable to introduce adequate levels of economic progress in rural sectors, so it has been incapable of convincingly establishing the reliability of its coercive authority in the countryside. Central government power is usually greatest in the capital. Consequently, those who seek to organize a revolutionary movement seem inclined to concentrate in areas where relative deprivation is high and the effectiveness of the instruments of deterrence is low: in short, where the government is most vulnerable. The countryside is the logical arena.

There are at least two other reasons that prompt such strategic considerations. One has been the repressive effectiveness of counterrevolutionary operations in population centers during the initial, usually organizational, stages of the movement. The lesson is not lost on those who have

29. See Gil Carl AlRoy, "Insurgency in the Countryside of Underdeveloped Societies," *Antioch Review*, XXVI, No. 2 (Summer 1966), 149–157; Renée C. Fox, "Traditionality and Modernity in the 1964 Congo Rebellion," presented at the Lecture Series of the Comparative Program on Religion and Society, Institute of International Studies, University of California, Berkeley, February 17, 1969 (mimeo.); and Young, "Rebellion and the Congo."

survived and fled into exile.[30] To be sure, the vast cities of South Africa afford some measure of anonymity and secrecy, but networks of informants invariably render revolutionary activity dangerous. The second reason is particularly apparent in the cases of the movements aimed at Angola and Mozambique. There, so much depends upon an adequate and continuous supply of refugees for recruitment, information, and support. In Angola the Bakongo, and in Mozambique the Makonde—each with significant population segments across the borders in the Congo and Tanzania—quite naturally served as the core groups for UPA/GRAE and FRELIMO, respectively. Neither was an especially urbanized people in the Portuguese territories it fled. Reliance upon them practically precluded an urban-based movement. Even bearing in mind these points, it would be possible to argue that guerrilla movements in Southern Africa, particularly in Rhodesia and South Africa, show greater urban proclivities than elsewhere in the continent.

Further consideration of the potential for urban-based uprisings in South Africa is in order. Despite governmental intentions to implement "separate development" by restricting the entry of Africans into designated "white" urban areas, the continued movement of large numbers of Africans into these areas has been undeniable. The tremendous shortage of white labor has necessitated such a growth pattern. The 1970 census figures are not yet available, but preliminary estimates indicate an increase of 1,400,000 urban Africans over the 1960 census figures. This would mean roughly a 25 percent increase in the last ten years added to the 17 percent increase in the decade of the 1950's.[31]

A high proportion of the almost two million Coloreds (approximately 70 percent) and of the about 614,000 Asians (over 80 percent) are also urban dwellers. So, despite government insistence that "separate development" is working and that the Bantu homelands are increasingly attractive to South Africa's Africans, the fact remains that nonwhites in urban

30. For a discussion of these organizational issues see Edward Feit, "Urban Revolt in South Africa: A Case Study," *Journal of Modern African Studies*, VIII, No. 1 (April 1970), 55–72.
31. *Star* (Johannesburg), Weekly Air Edition, September 19, 1970, p. 12. Recent ANC literature, though, concentrates on the need to trigger guerrilla warfare in the countryside. See the broadside, "These Men Are Our Brothers; Our Sons," distributed illegally in Cape Town, Port Elizabeth, East London, and Johannesburg in November 1969.

areas are growing in numbers, and posing greater problems for regime control.

It is also clear that urban nonwhites are more politically attentive and subject to daily exposure to the insults of petty apartheid and the insecurities of an indecisive implementation of "separate development" and "group areas" controls. It is here, then, that seething discontent is most acute and felt relative deprivation greatest. And it is here, one might expect, that the catalysts and the sparks for ultimate mass struggle will first appear.

TABLE VI

AFRICANS IN SOUTH AFRICAN URBAN AREAS

Year	Number	Percent of Total African Population
1946	1,902,000	24%
1951	2,391,000	28%
1961	3,471,000	32%
1970 (est.)	4,860,000	33%

For a long time it has been assumed by African politicians and reliable analysts of African affairs that the cockpit of African politics elsewhere on the continent was the city. Power was most evident there. Therefore, in order to gain power or to study politics meaningfully, one had to concentrate on power relationships at the center. The coup d'état seemed quicker, neater, and easier than the sustained guerrilla war. We are learning now, however, that power in the capital is ethereal and ephemeral. Although African politicians and thinkers have talked about the fundamental importance of the peasant masses, few behave toward the peasantry as though it were really crucial. Grievances among the peasants are real and too frequently ignored. Thus, Africa's most promising revolutionary movements in the future might be founded upon a peasant base. But, just how much have African revolutionary thinkers dealt with the revolutionary possibilities of the rural masses?

If one could construct a composite ideology based on the thinking of revolutionaries in territories where guerrilla war has erupted, one would find a *professed* dependence upon the rural population. For example, Pierre Mulele gave a strange twist to Mao's aphorism about guerrillas being fish and the people the water. Mulele said: "Village people are like water and all the others [?] are like fish in the water." [32] But the intent was clear. The Kwilu rebellion would be based on "village people." Likewise, the ideology of the "Mau Mau" was built in part upon the Kikuyu claims to alienated rural lands, and on their deep attachment to the soil.[33] Somali guerrilla claims upon Ethiopia and Kenya territory had been rooted in the desires of rural nomadic herders. Additional illustrations could be mentioned throughout Africa.

A celebrated ideologist who glorified the revolutionary character of the peasantry in Africa was Frantz Fanon. *Wretched of the Earth* in one regard is a romantic paean to the peasant warrior. The revolution must be with and of the people: ". . . in the colonial countries the peasants *alone* are revolutionary." [34] Expressing an almost Jeffersonian sense of values, Fanon and other guerrilla leaders reject the cities. It is for the leaders to transform the peasant revolt into a revolutionary war and this comes through education and indoctrination. Large-scale peasant risings need to be controlled and directed along certain channels. Unorganized efforts can only be a "temporary dynamic." "Success" presupposes clear objectives, a definite methodology, and a consciousness of the role of the masses. The political education of the masses is "a historic necessity." This testimony has been borne out in numerous spent and unsuccessful African guerrilla uprisings. Perhaps it can best be seen in the meteoric history of the 1964 Congo rebellions. Young identifies three kinds of leadership elements, each trying to appeal for support: the exiled plotters who focused on seizing power in Leopoldville; the local conspirators who were preoccupied with exterminating local rivals; and the rural organizers who, basing their appeal on local grievances and calling for radical social transformation, tried to structure and to channel discontent along military

---

32. As quoted in Renée C. Fox, Willy De Craemer, and Jean-Marie Ribeaucourt, " 'The Second Independence': A Case Study of the Kwilu Rebellion in the Congo," *Comparative Studies in Society and History,* VIII, No. 1 (October 1965), 96.
33. Donald L. Barnett and Karari Njama, *Mau Mau from Within: Autobiography and Analysis of Kenya's Peasant Revolt* (New York: Monthly Review Press, 1966), pp. 198–203.
34. Fanon, *Wretched of the Earth,* p. 48; and also pp. 87–117. Italics added.

lines.[35] Rural organizers were by far the most successful of the three. Still, they failed to supply long-range purpose and administrative skill to the movement. Without direction and institutional expression, grievance alone is an inadequate base for revolutionary longevity. The movement died as rapidly as it was born.

To be sure, the "rural" and "urban" designations badly distort the social realities of Africa. Significant portions of guerrilla aspirations are what could be regarded as "modern," generally identified with those who have drifted to the cities. Still, the cities in Africa are what might be called first-generation cities, that is, the dominant portion of their African populations migrated to the cities. Moreover, the city populations are in constant flux, as earlier migrants return to the countryside and new migrants take their places. Often life styles and thought patterns change little with physical relocation. So a case can be made that the dichotomy erected by analytical scholars is a misleading one in its African setting.[36] Still, on the basis of the locational genesis, organizational concentration, derivation of supporters, scene of conflict, and ideological appeal, it may be defensible to regard the more successful African guerrilla movements of the future as manifestly peasant-rural movements. This may well be the case even though the dominant leadership element may be drawn initially from intellectual-urbanized groups.[37]

Certain traditional characteristics of African society pose distinctive and knotty problems that guerrilla leaders elsewhere did not have to face. Their expression among African guerrillas complicates the application of alien techniques to struggle there. Guerrilla leaders in Algeria, for example, despite their peasant appeal, did not have to face precisely the kinds of problems that those in the Cameroons, Congo, Kenya, Sudan, or Southern Africa do. First is a plethora of difficulties growing out of ethnic heterogeneity. One factor contributing to the success of most guerrilla movements in the world is a widespread sense of national identity. The presence of identifiable outsiders focuses discontent against a common enemy. In Africa, although antiforeign motivations are a significant source of guerrilla strength, the designation "foreigner" often has a more par-

35. M. Crawford Young, "The Congo Rebellion," *Africa Report*, X, No. 4 (April 1965), 6–11.
36. Fox, "Traditionality and Modernity," pp. 60–63, *et passim*.
37. See Fanon, *Wretched of the Earth*, esp. pp. 85–117.

ticularistic association. Loyalties and horizons are narrower. The guerrilla leaders can attempt to widen them, and in some instances have succeeded. In other cases the leadership itself has narrow vision. In order to find a catalyst capable of causing the initial eruption, however, local grievances may be exploited and traditional local animosities sharpened.

Even when the enemy is clearly identifiable (e.g., an alien, racially distinct colonizer or permament minority), political commitment to high-risk involvement demands a heightened sense of loyalty and purpose diffi-cult to find in territory-wide movements in Africa. If the enemy is internal, as in the Congo, loyalties become even more fragmented as local ethnic juxtapositions dictate who is for and who is against the movement. Lo-calized symbols may increase the intensity of loyalties, but they automati-cally compress the territorial extent of the appeal. When a movement based on local symbols extends beyond its ethnic territorial base, the guer-rilla fighters take on the complexion of hostile occupiers rather than that of a liberating force.[38] Even if symbols are widened and a coalition of ethnic forces can be constructed, charges of ethnic favoritism often lead to the alienation of elements otherwise inclined to support the movement.

The administration of "liberated" territory aggravates the problem. The demands of governing rural areas are minimal compared to the tasks of administering urban centers. Most rurally-based movements do not exhibit the qualities or depth of leadership needed. If the guerrilla war is still in progress and leadership is limited, maladministration is likely. This was the case in the Congo. In short, as the guerrilla conflict succeeds militarily, it may sow the seeds of its possible defeat politically. Once re-moved from their original base, the guerrillas are no longer of the people, as local inhabitants perceive it. Rapid military success, then, might well contribute to eventual weakness. The challenge is not so much a dearth of administrative talent (which is real), but a profound ethnic diversity.

Another issue, related to the previous one and almost as pervasive, which movements founded upon the support of the disadvantaged peas-antry have to face, is that elements of traditional thought deeply shape individual and group performance.[39] According to Fox, the worldview of

---

38. Charles W. Anderson, Fred R. von der Mehden, and Crawford Young, *Issues of Political Development* (Englewood Cliffs, N.J.: Prentice-Hall, 1967), pp. 136–137.
39. For discussions of Congolese rebel thought see Fox, "Traditionality and Moder-

the Congo rebels was fundamentally "traditional and Bantu." The political ideology of the movement may have been "modern," but the roots of guerrilla support and sometimes of guerrilla behavior, even in battle, could be described as "magico-religious." [40] Implicit in any viable modern theory of guerrilla warfare is a high measure of cognitive accuracy, rationalism, and calculation. To be victorious in battle one must study the enemy and one's own forces, understand their weaknesses and strengths, and commit one's own forces only when victory is assured. There is little room for inaccuracy, irrationalism, and superstition. Yet, we are familiar with stories of war charms and rites of guerrillas in the Congo, the oathing ceremonies among the Kikuyu, the magico-religious specialists attached to various fighting units dispensing *dawa* (powers of invulnerability and strength), the pre- and postbattle ritual, and the mystical qualities attributed to certain leaders, living and dead. Each of these practices was more or less institutionalized in various movements. It is likely that as experience grows, so will skills of cognition, interpretation, and leadership. Traditional patterns of thought and behavior will be discouraged and discarded as they prove faulty in practice.

In the short run, though, these patterns might serve well the purposes of the guerrilla struggle. Not only were the Congolese *simbas* convinced of their supernatural qualities, but the local populations and, more importantly, the armed forces of the government of the Congo also tended to believe that the rebels were invulnerable. Fox suggests an additional way that magico-religious thought patterns contributed to rebel success.

> Paradoxically, one of the most innovative features of the war magic was the fact that by encompassing many different tribal traditions, it made manifest and helped to systematize beliefs and rituals common to them all. In so doing it not only acted as an internal cement for the rebellion. It also may have furthered the development of a neo-traditional basis for cultural unity that has significance for the national integration of Congolese society.[41]

nity," *passim;* Young, "Rebellion and the Congo," *passim;* for "Mau Mau" ideology see Barnett and Njama, *Mau Mau from Within,* pp. 189–203; for PAIGC thought see Ronald A. Chilcote, "The Political Thought of Amilcar Cabral," *Journal of Modern African Studies,* VI, No. 3 (October 1968), 373–388.
40. Fox, "Traditionality and Modernity," pp. 23ff. and 37–44.
41. *Ibid.,* p. 44.

By and large, however, this facet of rebel ideology serves to diminish the long-range military effectiveness of the guerrilla movement and to narrow its popular appeal, particularly insofar as the war rites employed are ethnically distinct. Fanon assumed that when the peasant who had been raised in the "magical superstructure which permeates native society" gets a gun and indulges in a sort of cathartic violence, he becomes miraculously free of irrationality. "After centuries of unreality," he wrote, "after having wallowed in the most outlandish phantoms, at long last the native, gun in hand, stands face to face with the only forces which contend for his life—the forces of colonialism." [42] This fanciful version of the sudden transformation of deeply ingrained social thought and behavior patterns is shattered by evidence emerging from the Congo and elsewhere.

These are just some of the ramifications of revolutionary movements intimately dependent on peasant support. A reliance on rural populations will grow out of the exigencies of the situation rather than out of an intellectualized dedication to theoretical constructs. What is clear, however, is that Africa's guerrillas are becoming increasingly aware of the revolutionary potential of what had once been regarded as a politically retarded and quiescent countryside. The real conflict of attitudes comes over the political-military relationships that inevitably arise in any such movement.

E. African Theories: Patterns of Political-Military Interaction

The goals of guerrilla struggle, whether it be a "war of liberation" against a colonial power or a revolutionary conflict to destroy an indigenous, nominally independent government involve both the necessity to win battles in the field and the need to establish and maintain political order in those areas torn from the control of the central government. A viable theory of guerrilla warfare, therefore, should include both political and military components.

The most fundamental divisions that arise over the issue of political-military interaction revolve around the matter of priorities and the initiation of the struggle. One group of leaders argue that emphasis must be placed on establishing a sound popular base in order to facilitate success-

---

42. Fanon, *Wretched of the Earth*, p. 46; see esp. pp. 43–46.

ful military operations. The other persuasion contends that a vanguard of dedicated guerrilla fighters can, with a few well-planned military attacks, actually precipitate a revolutionary response from the people despite their initial lack of political involvement. In reality, seldom are positions so polarized. Regardless of general preferences, both sides are aware that political support and military success are both essential ingredients of a dynamic movement. Even within a single movement, thinking on both sides of the issue is evident. Indeed, individual leaders vacillate on this question. So what we are dealing with here is a somewhat artificial distinction. It is purely for analysis that it is drawn.

Emphasis on the political arm is the traditional Marxist-Leninist position, although acceptance of this view does not necessarily make one a Communist. It has long been a tenet of Communist revolutionary thought that revolution is impossible without a "revolutionary situation." The people must be aware of their deprivation, conscious of their class status, convinced that violent revolution is the only possible remedy, and that revolution can succeed if supplied with the proper leadership and organization. A good example of this view is expressed by ANC leader Joe Matthews: ". . . there does not exist a revolutionary situation in South Africa at the moment, a revolutionary situation [which is the] *essential precondition for an insurrection.* . . . [But] there is the case in which conditions exist for the organisation of an armed revolutionary struggle, extending over a period of years." [43] However, Matthews and the ANC leadership are coming around to the view that South Africa is becoming ripe for revolution and certainly will be within a few years.[44]

In such a position a premium is placed on preinsurrection political education and organization. Revolutionary leaders must make the masses conscious of their relative condition and, more importantly, make them cognizant that guerrilla warfare can improve their lives. There is some evidence that African guerrilla leaders have taken pains to carry the

43. Italics added. Joe Matthews, "Forward to a People's Democratic Republic of South Africa," *Sechaba* (London), I, No. 9 (September 1967), as quoted in Martin Legassick, "The Consequences of African Guerrilla Activity for South Africa's Relations with her Neighbors," paper presented at the Annual Meeting of the African Studies Association, November 3, 1967 (dittoed), p. 4.
44. Joe Matthews, "The Development of the South African Revolution," *Sechaba* (London), III, No. 12 (December 1969), 5–8.

message to the peasantry before the outbreak of fighting. In the Kwilu rebellion, for example, Mulele—perhaps the most ideologically attentive Congolese revolutionary—concentrated on the ideological indoctrination of guerrillas and the populace. In secret training camps, recruits were given systematic training constantly relating to the village. Trainees periodically returned to local villages to proselytize and to learn from the people.[45] Some analysts maintain that the primary reason why the PAIGC is successful against the Portuguese in Guinea (Bissau) has been its careful preparation of the peasantry before the war.[46] Reverend Uria Simango— one of the triumvirate that had assumed FRELIMO leadership after the assassination of Eduardo Mondlane (he was later suspended from the movement)—once had been asked what had been FRELIMO's most important victories so far. He replied that there were three: first, the formation of a liberation movement; second, "the unity of our educated and uneducated people"; and third, "the emergence of nationalism." "With these three victories *the real fight began.*" [47] According to Mondlane, every area of Mozambique has a FRELIMO team working clandestinely to train leaders and provide civic education to enable the people to understand how they relate to the overall revolutionary strategy.[48]

In contrast, a relatively new innovation in guerrilla thought has emerged, taking its cue from the Military Mao (as opposed to the Political Mao) by way of Regis Debray, the interpreter of Guevara.[49] Based upon his Latin American experience, Debray argues that guerrilla contact with the civil population must be kept to a minimum. Rather than swimming like fish in the water of the peasantry, the guerrilla must be self-sufficient. The movement must be structured so that the people are not aware of guerrilla activities. Political propaganda is unnecessary to win over a quiescent populace. The war itself, the very reality of fighting on behalf

45. Fox, De Craemer, and Ribeaucourt, " 'The Second Independence,' " 103–105.
46. John A. Marcum, "Three Revolutions," *Africa Report*, XII, No. 8 (November 1967), 17–18; Gérard Chaliand, *Armed Struggle in Africa: With the Guerrillas in "Portuguese" Guinea* (New York: Monthly Review Press, 1969); and Basil Davidson, *The Liberation of Guiné: Aspects of an African Revolution* (Baltimore: Penguin Books, 1969).
47. Italics added. Quoted in Nkoana, "Struggle for Liberation," Part II, 16.
48. Interview with Mondlane in Kitchen, "Conversation with Mondlane," 49.
49. Regis Debray, *Revolution in the Revolution? Armed Struggle and Political Struggle in Latin America* (New York: Monthly Review Press, 1967).

of the people's interests, serves political purposes. First of all, it is visible, tangible evidence that the regime is not invulnerable. The longer the fighting continues, whether or not real "victories" are registered, the better the chances of convincing the peasantry that guerrilla warfare *can* succeed. Secondly, fighting is catalytic. It sets in motion a set of actions and reactions that increase political consciousness, grievance, economic dislocation, and governmental repression—just what the guerrillas desire. Unwittingly, the government in a sense takes over the responsibility of radicalizing the masses. Thirdly, successful guerrilla operations can perhaps liberate enough territory to create an internal base area. This has the important propaganda effect of denying the government forces access to a segment of the population, as well as providing the guerrillas with free access to them. If a liberated area is organized well, it represents an object lesson to other peasants of what life might be like in a "free" country. But this course involves a high measure of risk because, if the war is begun too soon and is squelched, a negative object lesson has been registered, making future efforts that much more difficult. Fanon, although by no means naive with regard to the need for political education, shares this perspective. In his estimation the war must be started first. Violence is "a cleansing force." Violence alone "makes it possible for the masses to understand social truths and gives the key to them." It frees the native from an "inferiority complex and from his despair and inaction; it makes him fearless and restores his self-respect." [50] Once the armed struggle is launched the leadership must, through political education, transform the peasant revolt into a revolutionary war. The armed uprising is the detonator, the spark.[51]

By and large, African guerrilla movements would prefer to begin with political organization first, although some behave as though they preferred the second position. Each leader, as well, seems aware of the political ramifications of successful military performance. The mix is complicated, often implicit, and generally pragmatic, depending on the necessities of the day.

Organizationally, African revolutionary movements reflect this dual-

50. Fanon, *Wretched of the Earth*, pp. 73 and 117.
51. Nkoana, "Struggle for Liberation," Part I, *Africa and the World*, IV, No. 38 (December 1967), 11.

ism. Problems of coordinating political and military endeavors are immense. Generally what exists is a central political organization (either a central committee or a government in exile) that operates outside the target territory and that purportedly directs both political activities and the guerrilla war. The military arm takes control of the day-to-day struggle in the target areas, often including political education and organization in occupied and contested areas. This dual military-political role of the guerrilla forces epitomizes the problems of coordination. Not only is there the difficulty of the political arm maintaining supervision and asserting ultimate control over potentially autonomous sources of power, but even within the military arm divisions arise between various instrumentalities. Algerian FLN-ALN functionaries, despite a surprising degree of unity, occasionally competed openly for popular support and, later, political power. The internal battles among exiled southern Sudanese politicians, and between the politicians and the military wing, the *Anya' nya,* are commonplace. Once territorial bases are established, these clashes are aggravated.

What is invariably necessary is a strong party that can assert its dominance over the guerrilla army. This, eventually, is how the FLN guided Algeria to independence, although individual military leaders, even after independence, obstructed the centralization process. Rather than being a strictly political against military dispute, it appeared to grow out of regional cleavages which were further reflected in the regional structure of the ALN, as reorganized in 1956. The six *wilaya* geographical commanders were practically autonomous leaders, directing both military and political affairs in their own territories. At independence, the FLN had to bring together coalitions of *wilayas* to outmaneuver individual military leaders. Moreover, being in the field and having already established the machinery of battle and administration, *wilaya* commanders had a certain advantage not easy to overcome. Eventually, however, the centralization process was completed. Other African movements can expect problems of this sort in the future.[52]

52. On the structural format of African guerrilla movements, see C.R.I.S.P., *Congo, 1965: Political Documents of a Developing Nation* (Princeton: Princeton University Press, 1967), pp. 89–125, 146–183; Barnett & Njama, *Mau Mau from Within,* pp. 149–192; Chaliand, *Armed Struggle in Africa, passim;* Joan Gillespie, *Algeria: Rebellion and Revolution* (London: Ernest Benn, 1960), pp. 91–111; and Amilcar Cabral,

Crucial to what a guerrilla movement accomplishes is how it manages the territory it occupies. Almost all African guerrilla leaders have dealt publicly with this question, some (among them Cabral, Mondlane, and the FLN leaders) more fully than others. A lack of planning and management of this facet of the struggle proved disastrous in the Congo. There the acquisition of territory was a Pyrrhic victory. For lack of adequate supervision, power gravitated into the hands of men whose behavior defeated the purposes of the rebellion.[53] Indications are that FRELIMO and PAIGC are best prepared for eventual political concerns. In their "liberated areas" effective programs of formal and political education are being established. A rudimentary economic system and a formalized legal structure are being instituted. In the cases of these two movements, leaders have been skillful in responding to the needs of the movement. Rather than following a preconceived doctrine created while out of power, they have evolved a series of pragmatic responses based on experience.

F. *African Theories: The Protracted War*

The Chinese and Algerian wars have made an indelible imprint on guerrilla thinking in other ways too. Increasingly, African leaders are beginning to realize that victory will not be easy, that wars will be protracted —indeed, that guerrilla forces can use time to their own advantage. The level of comprehension and dedication to the time variable does not appear to be as advanced in Africa as it had been in China, but it is becoming more and more crucial to guerrilla planning there. One regional guerrilla commander in Angola has said: "This is a war of the will. It took the Algerians seven years before the French gave in. We are just as determined." Another stated: "We will never be able to match the Portuguese man for man. But we can make a lot of trouble until the politicians find a settlement. And we can wait. Time is our best friend."[54] Expressions

---

"Le développement de la lutte de libération nationale en Guinée 'Portugaise' et aux Iles du Cap Vert en 1964," (PAIGC, mimeo., Conakry, 1965), p. 3.
53. Anderson, von der Mehden, and Young, *Political Development,* pp. 128–138.
54. *New York Times* (West Coast edition), December 16, 1963, and August 25, 1962. See also, for example, Matthews, "South African Revolution," 6; and *Zimbabwe*

of this view can be located with increasing frequency.

An awareness of military time also presumes a knowledge of certain tactical as well as strategic realities. First of all there must be the realization that guerrilla warfare is only a preliminary stage, albeit an important one, on the road to the use of other military techniques. Second, leaders must understand the virtues of extending the struggle while keeping the level of military confrontation low, in order to exhaust the enemy psychologically as well as physically. Third, they must have a comprehension of the value of fighting experience, both in planning each attack, and in assessing when it is time to move into larger scale warfare. Finally, of course, comes the hard lesson of self-reliance: that one cannot depend upon outsiders to sustain the war, despite the obvious importance of help from abroad. To build up the reserves and skills necessary to do it yourself is a long-term process. Additionally, political considerations relating to forging a common national consciousness in the shared experiences of extended military struggle are not ignored. Mondlane put it clearly: ". . . the fact that the war will be drawn out in this way may in the long run be an advantage to our ultimate development. For war is an extreme political action, which tends to bring about social change more rapidly than any other instrument. . . . This is why we can view the long war ahead of us with reasonable calm." [55] At heart, Mondlane was stating the crux of the utility of guerrilla warfare as a political strategy, as distinguished from a military strategy or tactic. Increasingly, after some initially sobering experiences, African guerrillas have come to understand the possibilities and problems of protracted war.

G. *Counterguerrilla Thinking in Africa*

Military men and governmental officials assigned the task of combatting guerrilla uprisings in Africa have read and thought as much about this form of warfare as have the revolutionary leaders themselves. The Portuguese and French colonial forces and soldiers of Rhodesia and South

News (Lusaka), IV, No. 16 (December 31, 1969), 2. For a contrary view see SWAPO President Sam Nujoma's speech in *Namibia News* (London), III, Nos. 1–3 (January–March 1970), 3–5.

55. Eduardo Mondlane, *The Struggle for Mozambique* (Harmondsworth: Penguin Books, 1969), pp. 219–220.

Africa get at least as much training in antiguerrilla tactics and operations as do African revolutionaries in guerrilla practices.

Whereas the principal thrust of revolutionary ideology is nationalism, self-determination, and independence,[56] leaders in white Southern Africa fancy themselves as "bulwarks" against the domination of the African continent by "alien" powers. They talk repeatedly about defending Western civilization and Christianity against the incursions of Communist Russian and Chinese influence, not only in their conceptualization of guerrilla warfare in Southern Africa, but in their view of world politics in general. As they see it, without Southern Africa the West would be strangled to death by Communist control of critical resources and the sea lanes to Asia. To a large extent this is a geopolitical attitude in fairly simplistic terms. A domino theory of Southern African international politics is popular, particularly among the Rhodesians, who have an inflated impression of the importance of their position. The Rhodesian Secretary for External Affairs put it this way: "If we go, Mozambique can't hold out for six months; the others would fall in order." [57] But this perspective has an almost mirror image among African revolutionaries. Discussing the geopolitical future of Southern Africa, Emile Apollus of the United Nations Council for Namibia, has stated: "If there is any validity to the domino theory anywhere, it is in Southern Africa. And here the weak link is the Smith regime in Zimbabwe. If it falls, Angola and Mozambique cannot be held. That leaves only South Africa. She will be the last bastion." [58] Thus Southeast Asian thought patterns are accepted in Southern Africa, among both antagonists.

The Portuguese have had far more practical experience fighting revo-

56. The ANC of South Africa tends to see itself in global rather than territorial terms, but this is largely a function of its identification with Marxism-Leninism and the Soviet Union. See *Sechaba* (London), III, No. 7 (July 1969). This global perspective is also evident among the various combinations of revolutionary movements from different territories (e.g. ZAPU-ANC and CONCP). See, for example, the final resolution of the Mobilization Committee of the International Conference in Support of the Peoples of Portuguese Colonies and Southern Africa, Khartoum, January 18–20, 1969. Reprinted in *Namibia News* (London) II, Nos. 4–6 (April–June 1969), 6–10.
57. Personal interview, August 25, 1969; see also the propaganda pamphlets published by the Ministry of Information, Immigration and Tourism, Salisbury: *Rhodesia in the Context of Africa* (1966); *Red for Danger* (November 1967); and *Zambezi—Red Frontier* (October 1968).
58. As quoted in *News/Check* (Johannesburg), IX, No. 7 (October 2, 1970), 12.

lutionary nationalists than the other Southern African regimes. Special counterinsurgency training was instituted in 1961, accompanied by an increased reliance upon officer training in counterinsurgency techniques in United States military schools. A growing sophistication in strategy is evident too. The present Portuguese military Commander-in-Chief in Mozambique is reported to be the author of a volume on the strategy and tactics of guerrilla warfare.[59] Psychological campaigns designed to win over the peasantry have been attempted. As one district governor in Angola put it: "This is a war for population, not for territory." [60] At least that much the revolutionaries and the Portuguese agree upon—guerrilla struggle is as much a political contest as a military one.

South African interest in the domestic dangers of a popular uprising or of externally based incursions has been heightened by hostilities in surrounding territories. South Africa has come to see herself in the context of black Africa—not in isolation. One book dealing with the war in Angola begins this way: "Only a few hours flying time from Johannesburg a savage war is being fought between the Portuguese army and black guerrilla terrorists. The war is creeping slowly, inexorably, closer to the borders of the Republic." [61] Reaction to the struggle in Mozambique has been equally intense, and the decision to assist the Rhodesians with men and materials is obvious testimony to South Africa's sense of concern and her inclination to look at guerrilla warfare in Southern Africa regionally rather than territorially.

The view seems widespread that not only must South Africa develop a superior intelligence system, but officials are hinting at the possibility of preemptive strikes against countries harboring guerrilla fighters. Both Prime Minister J. B. Vorster and Minister of Defence P. W. Botha have stated that African countries that continue support for revolutionaries against South Africa might themselves be the targets for raids aimed at destroying guerrilla bases in the same fashion that Israel did in the face

59. In a biographical sketch of General Kaulza de Arriaga, in *Rhodesia Herald* (Salisbury), August 29, 1969, p. 13.
60. *New York Times*, August 6, 1969. See also Douglas L. Wheeler, "The Portuguese Army in Angola," *Journal of Modern African Studies*, VII, No. 3 (October 1969), esp. 431–437.
61. Al J. Venter, *The Terror Fighters: A Profile of Guerrilla Warfare in Southern Africa* (Cape Town: Purnell, 1969), p. 5.

of guerrilla attacks launched from Jordanian territory.[62] Perhaps South Africa may not be seriously considering such a course at present, but the statements stand as a warning to Zambia that she too may be a target of violence.

A nation-wide survey indicates that the chief fear for the future among the whites of South Africa is the threat of black "terrorists" from neighboring states. The question posed and the responses given were:[63]

Here is a list of factors that people have mentioned to us. Which one of these factors or problems do you personally think is the greatest threat to South Africa's future?

Population explosion	6%
Soil erosion	10
An uprising of the Bantu population	12
Drought	27
Black terrorists from neighbouring states	40
None of these	6
Total	101% [sic]

In this case over one-half of the white population interviewed was alarmed about the possibility of some form of violent revolutionary activity by blacks. The South African government seeks to manipulate this widespread popular interest by turning it from an element of fear to a potential source of strength and white unity.

A knowledge of guerrilla theory and behavior can serve counterguerrilla purposes too. The status quo military forces are reading Mao and trying to devise counterinsurgency techniques accordingly, with some success. Perhaps the most vulnerable status quo forces are the indigenous African governments. Few have actually attempted to prepare their military men for guerrilla warfare.[64] This overall lack of preparation and forethought about guerrilla uprisings is one strong argument in favor of launching guerrilla hostilities first and then attempting to mobilize the peasantry. Otherwise, prior political organization and indoctrination might serve to tip off the regime of potential sources of conflict. The tre-

62. Vorster's Rustenburg speech, *ARB*, IV, No. 10 (November 15, 1967), 891B; and Botha to the House of Assembly, April 5, 1968, reported in *ARB*, V, No. 4 (May 15, 1968), 1047C–1048A.
63. *Rand Daily Mail* (Johannesburg), August 18, 1969.
64. One notable exception was the 1968 Gabonese military maneuvers against a hypothetical paramilitary subversive force. See *West Africa* (London), No. 2683 (November 2, 1968), 1300.

mendous military success of Congolese rebel forces against the ANC is solid testimony to the appalling weakness of that army against guerrillas. In less than ten months, relatively inexperienced, untrained and poorly armed, disorganized, and uncoordinated guerrillas managed to "take over" approximately one-third of the territory of the Congo state. This lesson cannot be lost on potential dissidents inclined to revolutionary solutions.

H. *Conclusions*

In conclusion, African theories of guerrilla warfare are truncated, disjointed, unrefined, eclectic, nebulous, and situationally specific. These observations are not offered by way of criticism. On the contrary, the reasons for these qualities are understandable given the nature and spread of guerrilla warfare in Africa. The struggle is still in progress, and it is natural that leaders have not spent the time systematizing their ideas. Moreover, their ideas are in flux, based on an expanding and kaleidoscopic body of experiences. There is no reason to doubt that, once victory is registered, some African revolutionary will refine and reduce his thought into an identifiably African theory of guerrilla warfare. It will probably be heavily laced with Maoist conceptions. Mao simply cannot be ignored. Granted, his ideas are not a secret weapon that guarantees victory. The concept of class struggle, although a crucial component of Mao's ideas, is not absolutely imperative with regard to his theory of guerrilla war. Divorced from its class context, his military thinking still makes a good deal of sense to revolutionaries the world over. Consequently, his ultimate contribution to African guerrilla thought will be more than residual. Africans are capable of and in need of a great measure of creative modification of external ideologies, if they are to be adaptable at all. The end product will more than likely be a curious, but dynamic mix.

A more significant observation in terms of the future for guerrilla warfare in Africa is that both revolutionaries and the forces of status quo, particularly in white-dominated Africa, are becoming increasingly attuned to the uses of guerrilla struggle and are preparing themselves, militarily, organizationally, and ideologically, for a protracted conflict. By viewing potential conflict in "just war" and "zero-sum" terms, they are precipitating the bloody confrontation both claim they seek to avoid.

When conflicting positions are no longer negotiable, as they appear at present, manifestly hostile and uncompromising elements prevail. This may not entirely be the case in portions of Africa where black governments exist. There, alternative avenues for accommodation and settlement —bargaining, partial secession, and coup—may be invoked. But the likelihood of these outcomes are diminished and, indeed, are extremely low in white-dominated Africa, at least as long as present-day values and perspectives are perpetuated. The same ZANU editorial quoted above, predicted confidently: ". . . if the last decade belonged to the Asian guerrilla, the next will sure as hell belong to the armed blacks of Zimbabwe, Mozambique, Angola, Namibia, Guinea Bissau and South Africa." [65]

65. *Zimbabwe News* (Lusaka), IV, No. 16 (December 31, 1969), 1.

Chapter Five

THE MOVEMENTS
AND THE WARS

A. *A Typology of African Guerrilla Movements*

Before we can plunge into a description and preview of the various guerrilla movements that have operated, are operating, or are likely to be operating in Africa in the future, it is first necessary to attempt to introduce a crude typology of guerrilla movements that can enable us to make comparisons between movements. This exercise also serves to remind us of the tremendous variety of movements possible and, it will be seen shortly, the difficulties of discrete and unmistakable categorization. Numerous criteria for categorizing such movements could be employed, and it would be virtually impossible to include all but a few into any manageable scheme. The typology to be outlined here seeks to discuss guerrilla movements along two dimensions, each consisting of two closely related criteria. In this way we can limit ourselves to sixteen types in a 4 × 4 matrix.

One can categorize a guerrilla movement on the basis of: (1) the kind of target regime it seeks to displace; (2) the sort of political system (in general terms) it seeks to establish; (3) the character of the groups within the territory to which it makes its primary appeal and from which it gains recruits and followers; and (4) the techniques it employs in the conduct of political-military activities. The first criterion is a fairly clean and applicable classificatory tool. It is easy to identify *target regimes*. For our purposes we shall use three such targets—white colonial, white independent, and indigenous black governments. On the basis of the type of established order, there is little difficulty recognizing the *goals* for which movements struggle. We are content here to utilize declared, general, and uncompromisable structural political goals. There seems to be a natural match-up between targets and goals in all but the indigenous black category. In this last category two general types of systems are sought, depending upon whether it is perceived that the target indigenous government is class-based (neo-colonialist), or tribally based. Thus, along the vertical axis we have four categories: white colonial (independence), independent white (majority rule), indigenous black (secession; autonomy from the central authority), and indigenous black (revolution; overthrow of the central regime).

The horizontal dimension is made up of two other criteria, combined into four classes. The criterion of *appeal* is divided into two crude bases, ethnic and national. The problems of discrete categorization are numerous, since no single movement appeals to only one sort of people. There may be distinctions between the character or ideology of the appeal (which may be national and modern) and the locus of recruitment (which may be primordial). There may even be understandable factual disagreements over the composition of followers or the motives for joining, even though the majority of members may appear to be drawn from a single, identifiable, ethnic group. Since we might assume that no single movement would purposely narrow the base of potential support by making a patent appeal to primordial loyalties, we would prefer to look, if possible, at the actual composition of the leadership and rank and file of the movements. If, in a heterogeneous state, attachments to and membership in the guerrilla movement are fundamentally ethnic, tribal, clan, or religiously based, then we refer to the appeal of the movement as ethnic. In this categorization we will attempt, where possible, to assume modernity of appeal. Because a movement must begin somewhere and must have initiators and leaders, ethnic appeal may seem to be descriptively accurate when, in fact, it is a premature designation. Or, indeed, it may be accurate even though motive is not fundamentally ethnic. Despite its ostensibly arbitrary quality, this criterion is, nonetheless, useful analytically. The designation national refers to attachments that transcend primordial loyalties and appeal to transitional men, men who function essentially outside the primordial milieu or who see their interests bound up in the establishment of modern, national economic, social and political structures.

The second component of the horizontal dimension refers to the organization and operational style, code, or *technique* of the movement. Again, one can refer to two basic styles, traditional or modern. The latter applies to post-World War II techniques of guerrilla organization and operation developed in Asia and later in Algeria, and the former (traditional) relies fundamentally upon less systematic and more superstitious techniques (e.g., the widespread use of *dawa*, "magic," or precolonial rites of warfare). In some situations traditional techniques may well be the more effective and the more rational, even for a movement with modern goals. More likely, however, is the combination of the two styles, and herein lies the challenge of sometimes arbitrary designations. For this reason, some of the movements included in Table VII are tentatively labelled and may deserve inclusion in more than one cell. Their style, or technique, is not altogether clear because it is many-faceted. We may construct a typology of movements as follows:

We shall return to this typology later. First, it is necessary to describe more specifically several of the guerrilla movements in Africa, past and present, grouping the data according to the vertical dimension in Table VII. Although the coverage will be brief, it is hoped that relevant generalizations can be drawn, that similarities can be pointed up, and the important distinctive features noted. (Appendix II contains brief factual summaries of the major guerrilla organizations currently operating in Africa.)

B. *Wars against Domestically Democratic Colonial Powers: Kenya and Algeria*

THE MAU MAU MOVEMENT, 1952–1956.[1] "Mau Mau" is a term associ-

1. The material in this section was drawn chiefly from Carl G. Rosberg, Jr. and John Nottingham, *The Myth of "Mau Mau": Nationalism in Kenya* (Nairobi: East African Publishing House, 1966); and Barnett and Njama, *Mau Mau from Within*. The Kenya (colonial) government position is detailed in F. D. Corfield, *Historical Survey of the Origins and Growth of Mau Mau* (London: HMSO, 1960), Cmnd. 1030; and J. C.

TABLE VII

A TYPOLOGY OF AFRICAN GUERRILLA MOVEMENTS

		THE APPEAL AND TECHNIQUES OF THE MOVEMENT			
		Ethnic-Traditional A	*Ethnic-Modern* B	*National-Traditional* C	*National-Modern* D
TARGET AND POLITICAL GOAL	I. White Colonial (Independence)	I.A Malagasy Mau Mau	I.B	I.C UPC Mau Mau	I.D FRELIMO, PAIGG, MPLA, FLN, SWAPO, GRAE/UPA
	II. White Independent (Majority Rule)	II.A Pondoland	II.B	II.C Poqo	II.D ZAPU, ZANU, ANC
	III. Indigenous Black (Secession or Refusal to Recognize Authority of Central Government)	III.A Mpeve (Kwilu) (Mar. 1962) Baluba (Nord Katanga) vs Katanga Government (Aug. 1960–62)	III.B Anya'nya Shifta (Som.) Eritrea Lib.	III.C	III.D
	IV. Indigenous Black (Revolution)	IV.A Mulelists	IV.B Chad	IV.C UPC	IV.D CNL

ated with a political movement which grew up around 1950 among the Kikuyu in the Central Province of Kenya. Among those who participated in the movement, Mau Mau was not commonly used. Rather, although the derivation of the name is unclear, it was more generally employed by the Europeans, their governments, and their press. Members of the

Carothers, *The Psychology of Mau Mau* (Nairobi: GPO, 1954). There are a dozen or more book-length accounts by various participants and observers, both European and African, but there is little serious scholarship on the subject, except for the first two books mentioned above; principally the first, since only the commentaries by Barnett in the second purport to be scholarly.

movement preferred other names, among them the Kikuyu Central Association (KCA), a radical group active within the Kenya African Union (KAU); *Gikuyu na Mumbi,* referring to the "founders" of the Kikuyu tribe; and *Uiguana wa Muingi* or simply *Muingi,* meaning literally "The Unity of the Community," or "The Community," or "The Movement." [2]

Just as the origins of the term Mau Mau are questionable, the organizational outlines of the movement itself are hazy. Through the haze, however, can be seen the KCA. That organization was formed in 1924 and declared illegal in 1940, even though it continued to be active within the KAU, the trade union movement, and the independent church and school movement. It was a select and, of necessity, a secret association with membership limited to individuals of proven dedication and reliability. In mid-1950, however, KCA leaders decided to broaden their membership by establishing an underground mass movement. Conditions among the Kikuyu made them ripe for recruitment and militancy. Despite the postwar economic boom in Kenya, "trickle down" was marginal. The long-standing grievances growing out of the alienation of historically Kikuyu land had not been improved. The settler minority had been growing in size, as had been the Kikuyu population cramped into the Reserves, into Nairobi and the towns, and as "squatters" and laborers on European farms. Increasingly, settler politics had asserted itself over the interests of Africans. Despite token representation on advisory bodies, little had been done to improve African political rights and economic conditions, and no relief was in sight. Indeed, worsening conditions for the Africans seemed to be an explosive ready to be detonated by the inclination of the settlers to demand greater independence from the British government—the pattern later fulfilled by Rhodesia UDI in 1965.

KCA recruiters found little resistance to their appeals for tribal unity, as they administered an "oath of unity" based upon Kikuyu solidarity and demanding strict secrecy and total commitment. The importance of oaths in Kikuyu ritual has been well documented. The first oathing, despite features repulsive to the Europeans and the strong element of coercion employed, was widely popular. It has been estimated that up to 90 percent of Kikuyu adults took the first oath. In an elaborate initiation ceremony, the initiate not only joined the movement but became, in a

2. See Barnett and Njama, *Mau Mau from Within,* pp. 51–55.

sense, a "reborn" member of the tribe. As frustrations and repression grew, the oathing was transformed into more bestial ritual, increasingly proclaiming the need for violence against not just Europeans, but against anyone who remotely assisted the Europeans or who failed to assist the movement. This second oath, the *batuni* or "warrior oath," was introduced around mid-1952. Oathing practices became even more repulsive to non-Kikuyu after the Emergency was declared and the fighters moved into the forest.

The exact dates for the commencement of the movement or the opening of hostilities are hard to determine. In 1952, a number of violent acts were committed against government "loyalists" and their property. In October, the assassination of Senior Chief Waruhiu of Kiambu triggered government reaction. Although these incidents were most likely initiated by local leaders, they were not unrelated to the new *batuni* ceremonies. These acts of violence set off a series of severe countermeasures characterized by the declaration of a State of Emergency on October 20, 1952. But the movement was unprepared for open warfare at this time, having no master plan or organization geared for revolutionary struggle or modern guerrilla warfare, and no regular and reliable supply of arms, ammunition, or other materials. Just as significant for the ultimate military failure of the movement is that non-Kikuyu people of Kenya (except for the related Embu and Meru) had not joined the movement in substantial numbers. The movement was simply not prepared for the revolutionary situation to which it had contributed.

Within a few days of the declaration of Emergency, almost 200 prominent African leaders were arrested, including Jomo Kenyatta, and the movement found itself without informed leadership or counsel. This practically wiped out its key leadership committees and severed the coordinating linkages between central institutions and the rank and file in the Reserves. Quickly deploying its military and police forces, the government temporarily immobilized the decapitated movement. Within weeks, however, thousands of young Kikuyu, Embu, and Meru militants drifted into the forests and mountains to join in the "Land Freedom Army" to achieve their political and economic ends by the use of force. On the farms, in the cities, and in the Reserves, the difficult task of organization for supply commenced.

On the night of March 26, 1953, two well-organized Mau Mau raids were staged. At Naivasha about 80 fighters surprised a police post, released prisoners and, more importantly for the movement, broke into the armory and drove off with a truckload of ammunition, rifles, and automatic weapons. Since a shortage of weapons and ammunition contributed to the military defeat of the movement, it is significant that this was the first and last major arms seizure of this sort. The second raid that night, against government "loyalists" at Lari, alienated potential outside support and possibly Kikuyu support as well. In this massive operation involving some 3,000 Mau Mau, at least 97 "loyalists" and their dependents were hacked to death, their property and livestock destroyed. But in the battle and ensuing pursuit and investigation, the government forces killed many more times that many Kikuyu. The Lari raid was the largest single "Mau Mau" military operation of the Emergency. It served, however, to galvanize the Security Forces to take seriously their responsibilities.

The uprising never reached the stage of genuine guerrilla warfare. The young militants who grouped themselves in the forests of the Aberdare mountains and Mount Kenya, and elsewhere, were as badly organized throughout the struggle as the government was in the opening phases. Despite their growing numbers which reached a peak of about 15,000 by mid-1953, the fighters lacked the training and leadership required for sustained and effective guerrilla warfare. There had been some ex-servicemen who had fought with the British in Burma, but problems of organization were too great for their limited experience. By March 1955, their force strength had dwindled to 5,000 and by December 1955, to 1,500.[3] Long before that, from about mid-1954, the primary concern of the forest fighters was simply survival. Virtually all of their raids henceforth concentrated on securing food and supplies. The capture of Aberdare leader Dedan Kimathi in October 1956 signalled the practical end of the military hostilities.

The appeal of the Mau Mau movement was based on a combination of factors. First, the Kikuyu possessed a deep tribal identity and, though unity is too strong a word given traditional sociopolitical organizational patterns, a group solidarity that was extremely high in the postwar years

3. *Ibid.*, pp. 439, 489.

and was only diminished by the terrorism of both the fighters and their sympathizers on one hand, and the repression and counterviolence of the government forces and the "loyalists" on the other. A militant political organization promising to struggle for land and freedom had a receptive constituency. Secondly, oathing—while it forged unity and made converts of the fence sitters—tended to narrow the basis of appeal to the Kikuyu, Embu, and Meru and, among those peoples, to the more superstitious and illiterate. The first few months of the Emergency itself and counterinsurgency policies of the Kenya government actually forced a number of otherwise passive supporters into the forests to join guerrilla bands. Clearly, though the ideological liturgy of the movement called for independence for all Kenya and freedom and land for all Africans in Kenya, and though efforts were made to mobilize the other tribes, the base of appeal was nevertheless limited to the 1,500,000 Kikuyu and related peoples. And the Kikuyu tribes constituted only 30 percent of the Kenyan Africans. As unity and solidarity were strengthened, so appeal was narrowed; Mau Mau faced a universal organizational problem.

Likewise, the strategy, techniques, and organization of the movement gravitated between those of the modern guerrilla and those associated with primordial resistance movements. Obsessed with the need for group solidarity, the movement concentrated on punishing "loyalists" rather than on striking against government targets, and thereby securing the material for conducting a full-scale guerrilla struggle. The virtual uniqueness (in its success) of the Naivasha raid is indicative of the strategic and tactical bankruptcy of the movement. And because of their lack of weapons and ammunition the fighters seemed preoccupied with simple survival—in effect, defensive almost from the start. Moreover, the central ideological and operational roles of superstition and the *mundo mugo* (a war magician who blessed and cleansed warriors and who, in some units, as the struggle progressed, came to determine the time and place for raids) tended to render field operations less effective and coordinated planning practically useless.

Throughout the struggle the movement lacked centralized organization and leadership. With the decapitation of the central organs of KCA and KAU in October 1952, the inexperienced and uneducated men and women who fled to the forests were incapable of achieving the level of

coordination and discipline necessary for sustaining a guerrilla movement. Superficial unity was established in August 1953 with the formation of the Kenya Defense Council. While the council had the authority
to formulate overall strategy and policy, enact rules and regulations, and
sit as the highest judicial body, it lacked the power to implement and
enforce its policies and rulings. Rather, individual leaders of decentralized camps and sections held effective power, and only on voluntary
grounds recognized and became members in the council. Strong leader-
follower-locality ties and loyalties predominated in the movement. Cooperation rather than coordination was the best that could be hoped for.
Virtually no central lines of communication and coordination existed between the regional movements—Aberdares, Mt. Kenya, Nairobi, Kiambu,
and the isolated units in the Rift Valley and the Reserves. Even within
the regions, for example the Aberdares, locational breakaway groups, the
establishment of independent *komerera,* and divisions among leaders
based on educational levels and personality differences made decentrali-
zation a most debilitating internal problem.

In military terms the Mau Mau movement frittered away practically
all of the assets it initially possessed. It alienated the intense popular
support it enjoyed in Kikuyuland. It failed to exploit the control it had
gained over the forests by enticing and then ambushing government units.
Its lack of offensive strategy dissipated the high motivation and discipline
that characterized the men who entered the forests. Despite its impressive
mobility in difficult terrain, it allowed the enemy to carry the war to it,
rather than seizing and holding the initiative. By the end of 1953, some
10,000 British and African soldiers, 15,000 full-time police plus 6,000
part-time auxiliaries, and the Kikuyu Home Guard of about 20,000 were
thus able to isolate and thereby destroy the forest units, mostly psychologically, by forcing surrender and "rehabilitation."

This ostensible military failure is somewhat misleading for, in the
long run, it prompted the colonial power to assert its own interests over
those of the parochial settler minority, and to prepare for a speeded-up
transition to independence under an African government. In the end the
nationalistic demands of the KCA, the KAU, and the Mau Mau, whatever
their organic linkage, were met. Despite its categorization as an I.A-type
movement, Mau Mau paved the way for more modern and national ends.

ALGERIA, 1954–1962. Militant nationalism has a long history in Algeria. But the guerrilla struggle which led directly to Algerian independence can be traced, structurally, to the proletarian nationalism of Hajj ben Ahmed Messali. After a number of his organizations were outlawed in the 1920's and 1930's, Hajj Messali formed the *Parti Populaire Algérien* (PPA) in 1937 which, after being driven underground in 1939, developed a *Mouvement pour le Triomphe des Libertés Démocratiques* (MTLD) within which was formed a secret terrorist society, the *Organisation Spéciale* (OS). By 1949 the latter had 1,900 members. French authorities responded by arresting OS leaders and driving the rest into exile. Many of the founding members of OS then formed a *Comité Révolutionnaire d'Unité et d'Action* (CRUA) and it was this group that planned the coordinated attacks of October 31–November 1, 1954, marking the opening of the war. Messali, however, ended his association with the movement in January 1955 and set up a rival group that functioned more in France than in Algeria. By the end of the war it had been destroyed.

The Algerian war exploded with about thirty ambush and arson attacks on French military and police targets. A few hundred poorly armed insurgents struck widely scattered targets, although most were in eastern Algeria, in the area of the Aurès mountains. Then the groups withdrew to set up bases for continuing operations from fairly secure mountain hideouts. The Aurès mountains had for years been a region of resistance to central authority. Occupied by Berber speakers with a sociopolitical organization of segmental tribes made up of fractional families, the region is composed of settlements that fragmented internally but united if threatened by a third party. The rebels exploited this traditional form of fractional competition, finding allies among various factions.

By April 1956, French sources estimated that there were 8,500 rebel fighters with an additional 21,000 auxiliaries. That figure was to grow to about 120,000 fighters in 1957–1959 and dip to around 40,000 at the ceasefire. At first, the government was incapable of preventing the westward spread of the rebel following along the mountain ridges of the Atlas. But by April 1956, French force levels were expanded to about 450,000 (through conscription and a redeployment of European and African-based units). French tactics were altered to include the *quadrillage*, a grid system that called for the occupation of the centers in force, and the use of mobile units (paratroopers and Foreign Legionnaires) to search out the enemy in the back country. This enabled the French to limit the activities of the *Armée de Libération Nationale* (ALN) in the hinterland and forced the Algerians to counter with an offensive strategy of terrorist attacks in the urban centers. The psychological and political effects of urban terrorism benefitted the independence movement, but militarily it proved ineffective.

Once contained within Algeria, the ALN was forced to find greater support abroad, and their newly independent (1956) neighbors, Tunisia and Morocco, permitted the operation of training centers for Algerian recruits. By late 1957, there were over 60,000 Algerian refugees in Tunisia and 40,000 in Morocco, and the "external" army of 25,000 troops was larger than the "internal" army of 15,000. In response, the French constructed elaborate barriers of electrified barbed wire, alarm systems, mine fields, and observation posts along the frontiers with Morocco and Tunisia. By sealing off the internal fighting zones from the external armies, the French concentrated on internal military operation. They were able to break down communication between ALN military districts and to prevent the ALN from mounting large, battalion-size countermeasures. The French also attempted to separate the insurgents from their popular base by relocating some 1.8 million civilians between 1955 and 1961. Psychological warfare, utilizing mass propaganda and social services as well as torture and indoctrination, sought to come to grips with the vital rebel-population relationship, but the nationalist spirit remained unbroken.[4]

Unfortunately for the French, military containment within Algeria proved inadequate for the problems at hand. Although they were able to drive wedges between nationalist leaders and units, and to isolate rebel groups from one another and from their popular base, the French were thoroughly unable to deal with growing "external" armies, the trump card for the nationalist bargaining teams. Efforts to immobilize the external forces, for example the bombing of the Tunisian border village of Sakiet Sidi Yussef, tripped off international criticism that contributed to

4. See Joseph Kraft, *The Struggle for Algeria* (Garden City, N.Y.: Doubleday & Company, 1961), esp. Chap. 4; Jean-Jacques Servan-Schreiber, *Lieutenant in Algeria* (New York: Knopf, 1957).

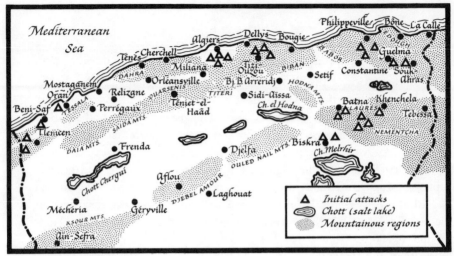

NOVEMBER 1954

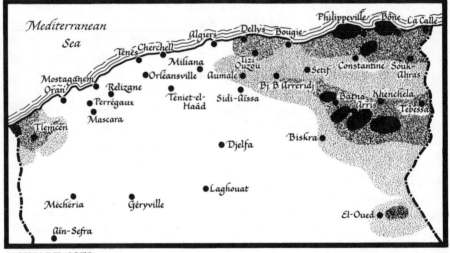

JANUARY 1956

MAP 1

NATIONALIST MILITARY ACTIVITY
November 1954–November 1958

Source: Joan Gillespie, *Algeria: Rebellion and Revolution* (London: Ernest Benn, 1960), pp. 200–201.

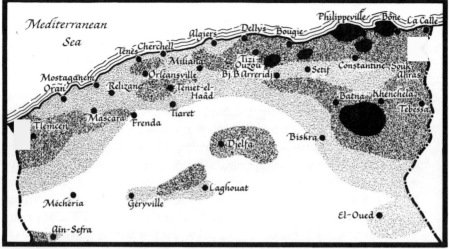

AUGUST 1957

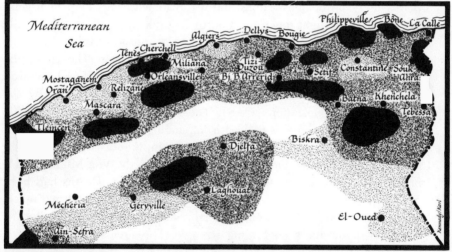

NOVEMBER 1958

From January 1956 on, black sectors indicate zones secured by nationalist forces. In the dark grey areas, nationalist forces are able to introduce a
considerable degree of insecurity. The light grey areas indicate the general
range of operations by nationalist forces.

French governmental instability. Indeed, though the thrust of the internal insurgent forces had been blunted by the end of the war, the external army loomed ominously in the wings, a force in the negotiations as well as in future Algerian politics. The French separated the population from the rebel fighters, but the nationalist cause did not flag. The same cannot be said of the French citizenry, which became badly divided. The most dissident elements were the French *colons* in Algeria. They could admit of no compromise in their superordinate position in relation to the Muslim majority. Throughout the struggle they were a constant irritant and threat to the French government and its bargaining flexibility. To a large extent they shared attitudes with units of the professional French army. These animosities between metropolitan France and her overseas territories and their defenders had been longstanding, but during the Algerian conflict they reached violent proportions. The first confrontation, propelled by *colon* demonstrations and a threatened army coup in Algeria in May 1958, brought down the Fourth Republic and ushered de Gaulle to power. The second, in May 1960, was an unsuccessful settler-army leader insurrection against the de Gaulle government. The third, the April 1961 abortive "putsch of the generals," was triggered and followed by a campaign of terrorism against Muslims. It had been led by the Secret Army Organization (OAS). The revolt was put down and the terrorism fizzled as *colons* fled with impending independence.

Within France, war weariness was setting in. France had been humiliated in World War II and had been defeated by the Viet Minh in Vietnam. The war in Algeria was to drag on for 7½ years. Deaths had been conservatively estimated at over 19,000 in Algeria and 4,900 in France. Costs were set at $5–10 billion. Internal political and economic strife was too deep to survive a continuing struggle. The French people insisted ultimately on a negotiated settlement.[5] The fact that the Algerian nationalists had not won militarily was not too important: they had not lost either, and this represented the essence of political victory. As one spokesman put it in 1959: "We know that we cannot defeat the French Army in battle, but we can fight a guerrilla war for ten years, if necessary, and the French will some day weary of the struggle." [6]

5. See William G. Andrews, *French Politics and Algeria: The Process of Policy Formation, 1954–1962* (New York: Appleton-Century-Crofts, 1962).
6. *Ibid.*, p. 189.

At the eve of the rebellion, CRUA was transformed into the *Front de Libération Nationale* (FLN) and the *Armée de Libération Nationale* (ALN).[7] The former was to be the political center of the movement. Leadership consisted of young military men possessing a great deal of localized power, and a few nationalists making up a Cairo-based external delegation. The military men were organized into six military districts, or *wilayas*, and a seventh *wilaya* comprising metropolitan France. The external delegation sought to obtain arms, supplies, and external political support for the internal army. The unity of the movement was shaky and in August 1956 some 200 leaders from the interior met in the Soummam River valley to reorganize their efforts. This Congress created a *Conseil National de la Révolution Algérienne* (CNRA), a protoparliament, and two high-level committees representing the military-civilian dichotomy in the movement. A provisional government was announced in September 1958. The principle of "priority for the interior over the exteriors" was established, a principle more difficult to sustain when French military pressure mounted. The rifts within the movement—external–internal, military–civilian, Berber speakers–Arabic speakers, *wilaya–wilaya*, local–central—seemed to be aggravated by French military successes. Though divisions were glossed over during the struggle, the postwar period saw them provide the bases for domestic Algerian political conflict.

In every sense the FLN-ALN independence fighters can be regarded as an I.D-type guerrilla movement. The goal was clearly independence on a national scale. The appeal was consistently national in scope. Although the first base of the revolt was the Aurès mountains, and the key *wilayas* throughout the war were the Aurès and Kabylie—both drawing their strength from Berber speakers—the movement aspired to transcend sectional, linguistic, and tribal interests. Moreover, the movement succeeded in these goals. The guerrilla strategy and techniques employed by the FLN-ALN movement were modern in every sense. They never lost sight of their ultimate political end, and of the obvious linkage between popular support, external aid and assistance, and long-range strategic planning. In the planning and conduct of the war, Algerian

7. An early and somewhat structural discussion of the organizational features of the movement appears in Gillespie, *Algeria*, pp. 91–111. Especially useful is William B. Quandt, *Revolution and Political Leadership: Algeria, 1954–1968* (Cambridge, Mass.: M.I.T. Press, 1969).

military leaders had been inspired by the classic texts on guerrilla warfare. They borrowed ideas and techniques from Mao, the Yugoslav partisans, and the Viet Minh, and then creatively applied them to significantly altered Algerian conditions. It is for these reasons—flexibility, creativity, and success—that later African guerrilla movements anxiously turned to the Algerians for inspiration, advice, and assistance.

Despite the numerous and significant distinctive characteristics of the two movements struggling to achieve independence from domestically responsible colonial governments, the Mau Mau and the Algerian movement share a great deal in common. Both were involved in a brutally violent war. The violence was direct and personal. Torture was a common feature of governmental policy and ritual assassination frequent for suspected collaborators. In terms of actual military confrontation, Mau Mau was brief and geographically limited, but it was no less bloody than the 7½ years of Algerian warfare; indeed, it was a good deal more so, proportionately. In Algeria approximately 0.26 percent of the Muslim population had been killed; in Kikuyuland the figure was 0.76 percent. It was the settler minorities in each instance that probably led to open warfare by their prewar uncompromising policies and resistance to reform. The same minorities were most repressive during the war in dealing with the indigenous peoples. In Algeria the OAS was feared and in Kenya the Kenya Regiment, made up of settlers, had a reputation for brutality. In both cases, settlers often regarded the wartime as one of open season on Muslims and Kikuyu.

Clearly, internal fissures and lack of coordination could be found in both movements, but for Mau Mau they proved crucial in their military defeat. The Algerians managed to minimize the effects of their internal divisions, or they at least prevented them from weakening profoundly the conduct of their war. Rather, the pattern was of guerrillas being unable to "win" militarily and yet able to "win" politically. The Algerian payoff from the war was more direct; the costs to the French were more intolerable. Since the guerrilla movement was notably more successful in Algeria, and the political negotiation process was directly linked to their field successes and later to stalemate, one cannot attribute Algerian independence to any measure of French foresight. In the Kenya case, the British had earlier recognized the problems of dealing with the settler minority. The Mau Mau Emergency precipitated a willingness by the British government to consider an African-governed independent state sooner than settler pressure would have tolerated, but the linkage between Kenya's 1963 independence and the Mau Mau was more tenuous and circuitous. Nevertheless, the linkage is real and must not be ignored.

c. An Unbending Colonial Power: Portugal in Africa

The independence movements in the three Portuguese African territories owe their genesis to similar underlying conditions.[8] Socioeconomically and structurally, Portuguese colonial rule in Africa did not differ markedly from territory to territory. And these conditions, in turn, grow out of the curious role of the overseas territories in shaping Portugal's self-image and her place among the world's powers. Since the establishment of Dr. António Salazar's *Estado Novo* in the 1930's, Portugal's African territories have played a central role in Portuguese politics and her plans for economic development. Portugal attempted to sell her self-appointed, five-century-old concept of "civilizing mission" by emphasizing her commitment to an official policy of assimilation. By policy pronouncement she insisted that any inhabitant of her overseas possessions could become the legal equal of any metropolitan Portuguese, if he was willing and able to abandon his African culture and become Portuguese in every cultural respect. Even if this had not represented racial arrogance, it would have revealed an unbecoming cultural arrogance. But it was, in addition, racially discriminatory, for the standards set for acquiring *assimilado* status were so stringent that a high proportion of metropolitan Portuguese could not have qualified if they had to gain citizenship in this fashion.

8. This account must be supplemented by consulting the following: James Duffy, *Portuguese Africa* (Cambridge, Mass.: Harvard University Press, 1959) or, by the same author, *Portugal in Africa* (Cambridge, Mass.: Harvard University Press, 1962); David M. Abshire and Michael A. Samuels (eds.), *Portuguese Africa: A Handbook* (New York: Praeger, 1969) or Ronald H. Chilcote, *Portuguese Africa* (Englewood Cliffs, N.J.: Prentice-Hall, 1967); plus materials cited herein pertaining to individual territories. Two extensive papers prepared for delivery at the Annual Meeting of the African Studies Association, Montreal, October 15–18, 1969, relate specifically to independence struggles in Portuguese Africa: Ronald H. Chilcote, "Conflicting Nationalist Ideologies in Portuguese Africa: The Emergence of Political and Social Movements, 1945–1965," (86 pp.); and Paul M. Whitaker, "The Liberation of Portugese-held Africa: Assistance to the Nationalists from Africa and Abroad," (34 pp.).

Moreover, opportunities for securing the minimum standards for approval were not equally available. The result was that by 1961, when the status of *assimilado* was abolished and a general assimilation of all Africans in Portuguese territories was legally proclaimed, fewer than one-half of one percent of the African populations had become "assimilated." In 1951 Portugal, in an effort to avoid international pressures regarding her colonies, officially incorporated her overseas possessions into the Portuguese state. By making them an "integral part of the Portuguese State" she could better fulfill her "historic mission of colonization" in order "to diffuse among the populations inhabiting [the overseas territories] the benefits of [Portuguese] civilization." [9] Thus Portugal stated firmly and without equivocation that she intended to remain in Africa indefinitely. Not once has she hinted at future decolonization, or even admitted the possible efficacy of the principle. A sort of self-fulfilling prophesy is hoped for by the Portuguese. One Portuguese officer put it this way: "The Americans can never win in Vietnam, because everybody knows that sooner or later they will be leaving. Here we shall win because everybody knows we are staying." [10] Here then is one of the primary reasons for political militancy among African nationalists—avenues for peaceful and meaningful reform or an ultimate transition to independence are dogmatically closed.

Ambitious schemes and theories for "civilizing" Africa have emanated from Lisbon. But Portugal's material means to accomplish these ends are meager and the government's conviction to change the status quo in sociopolitical terms is absent. Rather, they seek superficial change to exploit and reinforce the status quo. African territories are too important to Portugal's economy to contemplate a revolutionary withdrawal. Not until war in Angola erupted in 1961 was major change in educational and other social welfare areas seriously contemplated and initiated.[11] The "too little, too late" aphorism was again pertinent.

The root causes of African nationalism in Portuguese Africa can be

9. From the [Constitutional] Amendment Law No. 2048, June 11, 1951, as quoted in Marcum, *Angolan Revolution*, p. 5.
10. As quoted in George Martelli, "Conflict in Portuguese Africa," in Abshire and Samuels, *Portuguese Africa*, p. 420.
11. See Michael A. Samuels and Norman A. Bailey, "Education, Health, and Social Welfare," in Abshire and Samuels, *Portuguese Africa*, pp. 178–201.

seen in the actual conduct of the native and labor policies of these territories and in the basic living conditions these policies spawned. Despite
the rationalizing and engaging philosophy of "Lusotropicology," [12] and
a far more relaxed legal and social attitude toward racial integration
compared to the other regimes in white Southern Africa, the actual effects
of governmental policy have been to create a society with marked socioeconomic discrepancies based upon color. To be African in Portuguese
Africa is to be exploited and subjected to numerous indignities Europeans
need not confront. Although these indignities are not necessarily racial
in character (though color is a convenient identification), the overall
pattern is undeniable. Seldom is a European challenged for an identity
card—his appearance is sufficient privilege. The African has not been
accepted—as a man of color or as an African. Without either political
power or organized economic power, Africans have been the objects of
exploitation. Low wages, various forms of contract labor, and Labor
Codes for skilled, semiskilled, and rural workers are designed not so
much to protect the laborer, but to provide a steady flow of labor
for the economic enterprises of the territories. In Mozambique, for
example, wages reflect this discriminatory pattern (see Table VIII).

TABLE VIII

AVERAGE ANNUAL GROSS WAGES BY RACE

	Escudos	U.S. Dollars	Percent of Industrial Work Force
Industrial Sector—1962			
Non-Africans	47,541	1653.60	10%
Africans	4,104	142.74	90%
Agricultural Sector—1961			
Europeans	5,837	203.03	
Africans	2,151	74.82	

Source: Allison Butler Herrick et al., Area Handbook for Mozambique (Washington:
G.P.O., 1969., p. 267.

12. Most elegantly exposited by Gilberto Freyre and published by the Portuguese
Government's Agência Geral do Ultramar in Portuguese Integration in the Tropics
(Lisbon: 1961) and The Portuguese and the Tropics (Lisbon: 1961).

These figures vary radically by district, with lower African wages being paid in the areas of greatest unrest—Tete, Zambézia, Cabo Delgado, and Niassa. Likewise, distinctions in every facet of living standards and public services reflect this basic exploitative policy and admit of few opportunities for fundamental change. It is in this sort of milieu that the political unrest of the 1960's first broke the surface. The superficial calm belied the simmering discontent of the postwar years.

ANGOLA: ENTERING THE SECOND DECADE.[13] "By the beginning of 1961," wrote John Marcum, "Angola was a black powder keg with a ready fuse." An economic recession led to wage cuts, growing unemployment, and a fall in commodity prices and increasing discontent. The spark was supplied in the Kasanje region of the north, where cotton growers went on a rampage against the Portuguese and their property. The movement, essentially spontaneous and without structure, was quickly suppressed and Maria's War, as it had been called, ended. But many of the activists and victims of Portuguese retaliation fled from Kasanje to the Congo. There they came into contact with the *União das Populações de Angola* (UPA). Under the leadership of Holden Roberto, the UPA had set up its headquarters in the Congo in 1958 and had attempted to organize a political underground to function inside Angola.

A second set of explosions occurred in Luanda in February 1961. These events coincided with rumors that the hijacked Portuguese liner *Santa Maria* might be landing at Luanda, so foreign journalists were on the scene. While Maria's War went unreported, the Luanda uprising, better organized and less spontaneous, provided the world with unquestionable evidence that nationalism was not nonexistent in Portuguese Africa. The attack on the main political prison and the resulting European and African mob activity have generally been attributed to the *Movimento Popular de Libertaçaõ de Angola* (MPLA), which was later to become active in eastern and south-central Angola.

13. The definitive treatment of this war is Marcum, *Angolan Revolution.* A relatively recent, pro MPLA, account is Basil Davidson, "Angola in the Tenth Year: A Report and an Analysis, May–July 1970," *African Affairs* LXX, No. 278 (January 1971), pp. 37–49. Additional materials in English are: George M. Houser, "Nationalist Organizations in Angola: Status of the Revolt," in Davis and Baker, *Southern Africa in Transition,* pp. 157–179; and, Anonymous, "Realities of Angolan Struggle," *The New African,* VI, No. 2 (October 1967), 10–14. From the perspective of a South African correspondent, see Venter, *Terror Fighters.*

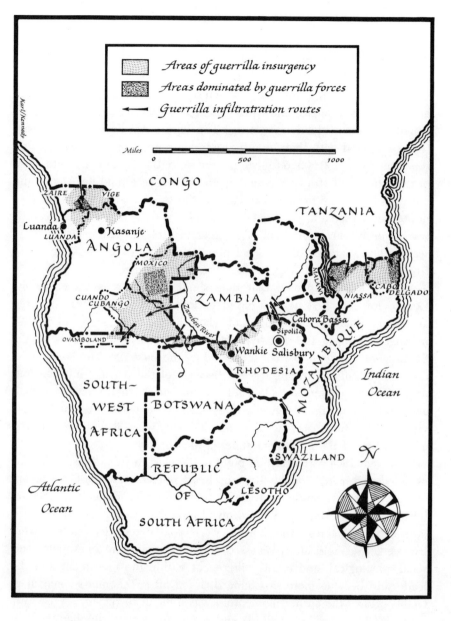

Legend:
- Areas of guerrilla insurgency
- Areas dominated by guerrilla forces
- → Guerrilla infiltratration routes

Miles
0   500   1000

Karl J Kennedy

CONGO

ZAIRE VIGE

Luanda
LUANDA

Kasanje

ANGOLA

MOXICO

CUANDO
CUBANGO

OVAMBOLAND

Zambezi River

ZAMBIA

TANZANIA

MALAWI

NIASSA

CABO
DELGADO

Cabora Bassa

Sipolila

Wankie Salisbury

RHODESIA

MOZAMBIQUE

Indian
Ocean

SOUTH~
WEST
AFRICA

BOTSWANA

REPUBLIC
OF
SOUTH AFRICA

Atlantic
Ocean

SWAZILAND

LESOTHO

N

MAP 2

GUERRILLA WARFARE IN SOUTHERN AFRICA, 1970

A third set of coordinated operations, on March 15, 1961, marked the opening of full-fledged insurrection. This uprising was organized by young UPA militants, and was characterized by general and widespread attacks on Europeans and their isolated farms throughout northern Angola. It was a bloody first strike. The Portuguese authorities and settlers responded with their own indiscriminate reign of terror and within the year some 150,000 refugees poured into the Congo. Despite UPA organization and strategic planning, the Portuguese hold on Angola did not crumble. They managed to confine the theater of battle to an area in northern Angola approximately 150 miles wide and 200 miles deep. It was to be a war of attrition. The chief task of the nationalists was to secure the assistance of the local population, but they sought to do so from bases outside of Angola. Results were marginal.

It was to be expected that they should turn for assistance to the Congo. Angola's first peasant-based nationalist movement was initiated among the Bakongo, one million of whom live in the Congo and 500,000 in Angola. During the first five years of the rebellion the bulk of the fighting was confined to areas inhabited by the Bakongo. The Portuguese, unable to eliminate the insurgency because of the passage into and out of the Congo, were nevertheless able to concentrate their forces in a small area and to neutralize UPA guerrillas. Congolese assistance thus became vital to the nationalists—perhaps too vital—for when it was reduced, the effectiveness of the movement suffered measurably.

The year 1964 was a turning point in the war. In July, Moise Tshombe assumed power in Leopoldville and almost immediately the Government of the Angolan Republic in Exile (GRAE) found it difficult to conduct business in the Congo. GRAE received less official cooperation, its military activities across the border were constricted, its leaders were harassed. And field effectiveness declined. With failure in Angola, personal, ideological, and ethnic differences within the movement and the leadership became more pronounced. Even after Tshombe's removal in October 1965, the earlier momentum was difficult to regain.

In 1966 and 1967 new efforts and a new front were supplied. MPLA, operating out of the Congo (Brazzaville), attacked the Portuguese enclave of Cabinda (this front has since been pacified). More significantly, MPLA and UNITA (*União Nacional para a Independência Total de*

Angola) struck across the Zambian and Katangese frontiers to breathe new life into the nationalist struggle. Moreover, the MPLA fronts in the Moxico and Cuando Cubango districts have become far more active than the GRAE struggle in the northwest.

In effect, however, when we discuss the guerrilla war in Angola, we are really talking about three distinct movements. Though each is modern in technique and aspires to national appeal, in reality their leadership and rank-and-file membership is characteristically regional and ethnic. UNITA, founded in 1966, is a southern-oriented, predominantly Ovimbundu group. GRAE, because of its inability and unwillingness to move outside its northwest–Kinshasa axis, has become increasingly a Bakongo movement. MPLA, more broadly based than the others, tends to be led by a mulatto and Mbundu intelligentsia from the Luanda-Catete region and to gain its greatest support from the urbanized sectors of the 1.1 million Kimbundu-speaking peoples of north-central Angola. All movements, given their goals, nationalist appeals, strategic and tactical styles, tend to fall into the Type-I.D category. Where ethnic predominance is evident, it is more fortuitous than intended.

No progress has been made to resolve the long-standing conflict among the Angolan nationalists and little prospect for immediate change seems likely. The war, or the three wars, have suffered from a lack of coordination; indeed, from actual violent conflict among the movements. Today, the only active guerrilla offensive is MPLA-directed and takes place in Moxico and Cuando Cubango, west of the Zambian border, with extensions into the central provinces of Malange and Bie. The GRAE/UPA triangle has shrunken under Portuguese pressure and a lack of external support. It is little more than a defensive operation of symbolic significance for the government in exile. Much like the war in Algeria, a military stalemate exists, though both sides insist that they are making political progress. But unlike the Algerian experience, the level of military activity is low, the nationalists are not unified, and the colonial power is not responsible to a domestically alert and critical citizenry.

GUINEA (BISSAU).[14] The most effective nationalist guerrilla movement

14. Accounts in English of this war for independence are just beginning to become available. Among them are Chaliand, *Armed Struggle in Africa*, originally published in Paris in 1967; and Davidson, *The Liberation of Guiné*. These are well-written

in Africa today is the *Partido Africano da Independência da Guiné e Cabo Verde* (PAIGC). Organized in 1956 by Amilcar Cabral, a Cape Verdean agronomist, the movement at first sought to persuade the Portuguese to introduce political and economic reforms in Guinea. Failing at this, and responding to the violent repression of a strike by Bissau dock workers at Pijiguiti in August 1959, PAIGC vowed to resist the Portuguese "by all possible means, including war." But the movement at that time was small (about fifty active workers) and concentrated in Bissau. They began their task by sending young militants to Conakry and elsewhere for training and then into the countryside to politicize the peasantry. Cabral was exceptionally skillful at reading the peasant mind and understanding popular grievances. In a few years time, they were prepared to open the revolutionary war for independence. The townsmen and mulattos had decided to mobilize the villagers and, having won a narrow base of peasant support, in early 1963 launched their war. The base widened rapidly and by 1964 a shift from localized guerrilla warfare to coordinated mobile warfare was launched with the establishment of a regular army, *Forces Armées Révolutionnaires du Peuple* (FARP). With these developments and the subsequent expansion of the war, geographically and in intensity, the force levels have grown accordingly. Considering

TABLE IX

MILITARY FORCE LEVELS IN GUINEA (BISSAU)

	1962	1964	1965	1967	1968	1969	1970
Portuguese forces	1,000	8,000	16,000	20,000	30,000	35,000	37,000
PAIGC forces		3–4,000	8,000	9,000	9,000	9,000	10,000

that Guinea (Bissau) has an estimated population of 800,000, the magnitude of military preparedness is high. The expansion of the war beyond those areas of initial fighting in the south front has yielded PAIGC "control" of approximately one-half of the mainland territory. An additional one-quarter is contested. The Portuguese "control" the other quarter

---

journalistic analyses strongly sympathetic to the revolutionary movement. Earlier accounts include I. William Zartman, "Guinea: The Quiet War Goes On," *Africa Report*, XII, No. 8 (November 1967), 67–72; and Chilcote, "Political Thought of Cabral," 373–388. Cabral's ideas appear more fully in Amilcar Cabral, *Revolution in Guinea: An African People's Struggle* (London: Stage 1, 1969).

plus about twenty of the main towns and their immediate environs. "Control," however, is a dubious word in this context. The Portuguese maintain fortified towns and "strategic hamlets" in the style of Vietnam, Burma, and Kenya. Moreover, they can still move in force throughout the countryside to supply their towns, though in some regions only air supply is possible. The areas "controlled" by PAIGC, on the other hand, are constantly vulnerable to air strikes. Nevertheless, the party seeks to organize and administer its liberated areas, providing governmental, health, and educational services, and a modicum of economic infrastructure to revolutionize the country.

The Portuguese attempted a variety of strategies and tactics to suppress the revolt, but to little avail. Despite the relative worthlessness of Guinea to Portugal, and the enormous expense of maintaining their tenuous presence in this swampy and forested territory, the Portuguese insist that they cannot and will not negotiate a settlement or effect a withdrawal. PAIGC stands ready to negotiate a peaceful withdrawal of the Portuguese, but to the latter the war in Guinea is symbolically momentous for the continuation of their rule elsewhere in Africa. So Portugal is unable to recover control of Guinea, at any price, and she will not relinquish it. PAIGC is not in a position as yet to administer a *coup de grâce*. So the war drags on. Had the regime been a colonial power recognizing the efficacy of ultimate decolonization, PAIGC might well be ruling in Bissau today.

PAIGC, as an African guerrilla movement, is rather unique in many critical respects. It has managed convincingly to build a united and disciplined movement out of traditionally fragmented, disparate, and even in some cases hostile peoples. But although tribalism is minimized, PAIGC fervently preaches the need for attention to local issues and specific grievances. In this way rhetoric is related to the people's experiences and needs. Thus ideology is made relevant. The principle of talking out policy decisions at various levels is perhaps closer to reality in the PAIGC than anywhere else in the continent. Even military tactical decisions are discussed until each participant understands his assignment.

In the administration of the liberated areas, PAIGC has sought to revolutionize the structure and practice of government. Cabral insists that the most difficult battle facing his people is "this battle against our-

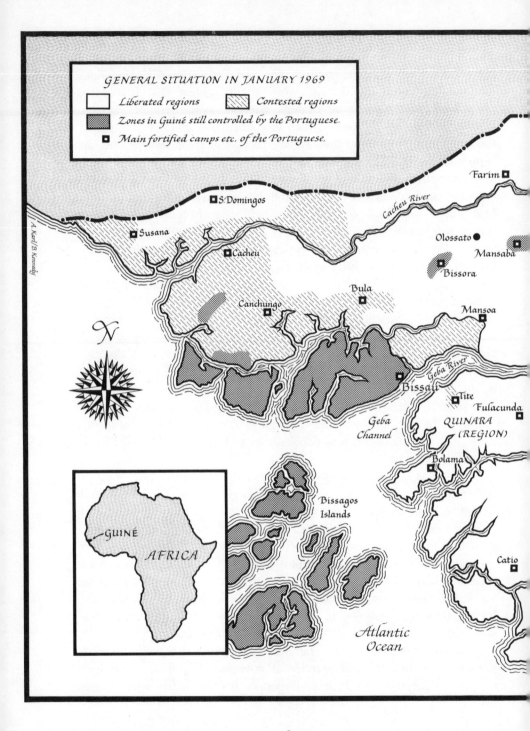

GENERAL SITUATION IN JANUARY 1969

☐ Liberated regions   ▨ Contested regions

▩ Zones in Guiné still controlled by the Portuguese.

▪ Main fortified camps etc. of the Portuguese.

Farim

S. Domingos

Cacheu River

Susana

Olossato

Mansaba

Cacheu

Bissora

Bula

Mansoa

Canchungo

Geba River

N

Bissau

Tite

Fulacunda

Geba
Channel

QUINARA
(REGION)

Bolama

GUINÉ

AFRICA

Bissagos
Islands

Catio

Atlantic
Ocean

MAP 3

LIBERATION OF GUINEA (BISSAU)—GENERAL SITUATION, 1969

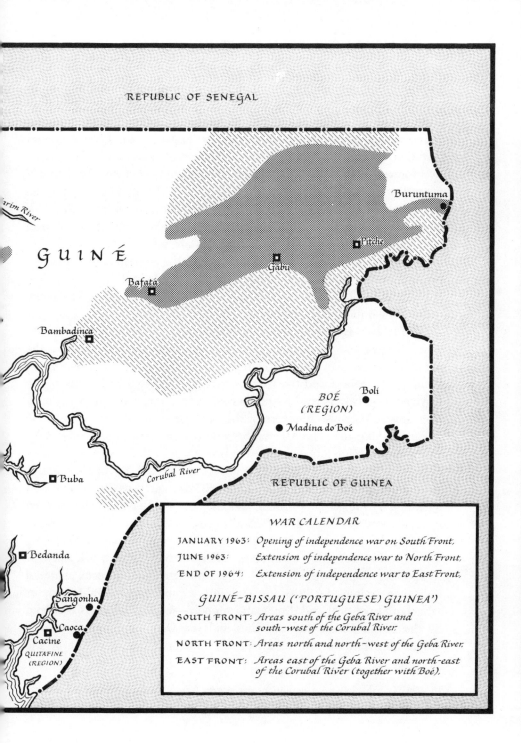

REPUBLIC OF SENEGAL

rim River

GUINÉ

Buruntuma

Pitche

Gabú

Bafata

Bambadinca

BOÉ
(REGION)

Boli

● Madina do Boé

☐ Buba

Corubal River

REPUBLIC OF GUINEA

☐ Bedanda

Sangonha

Caoca

Cacine

QUITAFINE
(REGION)

WAR CALENDAR

JANUARY 1963: *Opening of independence war on South Front.*

JUNE 1963: *Extension of independence war to North Front.*

END OF 1964: *Extension of independence war to East Front.*

GUINÉ-BISSAU ('PORTUGUESE) GUINEA')

SOUTH FRONT: *Areas south of the Geba River and
south-west of the Corubal River.*

NORTH FRONT: *Areas north and north-west of the Geba River.*

EAST FRONT: *Areas east of the Geba River and north-east
of the Corubal River (together with Boé).*

Source: Basil Davidson, *The Liberation of Guiné: Aspects of an African Revolution*
(Harmonsworth: Penguin Books, 1969), pp. 168–169.

selves." [15] The problem of overcoming "internal contradictions in the economic, social and cultural reality" is paramount. National liberation is not so much the right of a people to rule itself, but the right of a people to recover its interrupted history. This, he argues, "calls for a profound mutation in the condition of those [colonized or neo-colonized] productive forces, [and therefore] we see that the phenomenon of *national liberation* is necessarily one of revolution . . . ." Revolution, in turn, demands not just "national independence" but indigenous "liberation." A new society must be built along socialist lines. The content of Guinean socialism seems to be far more complete than other African socialisms. Whether this dedication can be transferred to the government of an independent state remains conjectural. Temptations to selfishness are then inflated. But Cabral believes that the unity forged in battle will promote national liberation and revolution.

The PAIGC is equally intent on maintaining the indigenous character of its struggle and revolution. Though it would be the first to admit the initial importance of the hospitality and assistance of the neighboring Republic of Guinea and the later assistance of Senegal to the north, the movement quickly moved its nerve centers into the liberated areas once that became possible. The core of the movement has always been inside of Guinea (Bissau). The Algerian situation of an external army and delegation representing interests different from those of the center never arose in Guinea, nor did the "mountain-topism" of GRAE/UPA in Kinshasa or the various groups attached to Dar es Salaam and Lusaka, unable and unwilling to break the Gordian knot. To be too heavily dependent on external assistance would, in Cabral's eyes, destroy the very purpose of the struggle. It would "rob my people of their one chance of achieving a historical meaning for themselves: of reasserting their own history, or recapturing their own identity." Thus, though PAIGC seeks material assistance, training facilities for nonmilitary (and, earlier, military) personnel, and political and diplomatic support—most of which is tendered by the Soviet Union and its allies and the OAU—the movement has sought to avoid the use of foreign "volunteers" in any aspect of the struggle.

15. This and the following quotations are drawn from Cabral's speeches and reports, as quoted in Davidson, *The Liberation of Guiné*, pp. 72–90.

MOZAMBIQUE.[16] The Mozambican rebellion officially commenced on September 24, 1964, when guerrilla units that had crossed the Ruvuma River between Tanzania and Mozambique attacked Portuguese military installations. However, actual military operations were preceded by years of planning and organization by the *Frente de Libertação de Moçambique* (FRELIMO), a coalition of nationalist parties in exile, put together in 1962. Dr. Eduardo Mondlane, its first leader, had worked hard to secure unity in the movement (which has somewhat disintegrated since his assassination) and was able to gain the support of the OAU at its Addis Ababa meeting in May 1963. Then began the difficult task of political and military organization inside Mozambique, as well as training and financing operations from outside. Careful preparation paid dividends. Although the Portuguese had since 1961 expected an assault from Mozambican nationalists in Tanzania, they were unable to uncover FRELIMO's military cadres in the Cabo Delgado, Niassa, and Tete provinces. Unaware of the details of FRELIMO's military plans, the Portuguese decided to defend the 500-mile Ruvuma River frontier, a physically demanding assignment. They concentrated on training volunteers, constructing landing strips and new roads, and modernizing their armed forces in the region. But, still, the initiation of hostilities caught them off guard.

After more than seven years of fighting, the war is not going especially well for the rebels (see Map 2). In 1966 the guerrilla general staff moved part of its headquarters from Tanzania to Mozambique. Its field operations had been widened although it had been forced to retreat only in the Tete and Cabo Delgado Provinces which border on Rhodesia and Malawi. Even in Tete, however, COREMO (a rival nationalist body) made its presence felt by periodic probing operations. An estimated 8,000 guerrillas managed to engage and harass at least 50,000 Portuguese troops. But a 1970 offensive by Portuguese forces has successfully cleared large areas of Mozambique and silenced FRELIMO guerrillas effectively in many areas.

16. No book-length academic study of the war in Mozambique has been produced to date. English language coverage includes: Mondlane, *The Struggle for Mozambique;* Douglas L. Wheeler, "The Portuguese and Mozambique: The Past Against the Future," in Davis and Baker, *Southern Africa in Transition,* pp. 180–196; James M. Dodson, "Dynamics of Insurgency in Mozambique," and Kitchen, "Conversation with Mondlane," both in *Africa Report,* XII, No. 8 (November 1967), 31–32, 49–51, 52–55.

The first Portuguese reaction to the outbreak of fighting in 1964 was to retaliate with full fury. They razed rebel-held villages, burned crops, and sought to isolate the rebels from the populace. Eventually, the Portuguese actually attempted to create a no man's land between the two territories by clearing out villagers along the frontier (some 250,000 were moved), burning their dwellings and fields, and relocating them into 150 fortified villages.[17] The result was to precipitate an exodus to Tanzania, mostly of the Makonde people who inhabit both sides of the Ruvuma (about 120,000 in Tanzania and 80,000 in Mozambique). By 1968 totals had risen to 25,000 refugees in Tanzania and 2,700 in Zambia.

It is small wonder that Portugal and Tanzania have been brought to the brink of hostilities over the mutual boundary. It seems as if Tanzania has not sought to avoid a clash. Tanzania allowed military training camps for guerrillas to be constructed in the southern frontier area. No less than nine separate training bases have been reported in southern Tanzania. The Portuguese claim they have evidence that instructors from the Chinese People's Republic are operating at four of them.

This sort of policy led Portuguese Foreign Minister Alberto Franco Nogueira to suggest that the Portuguese might begin "legitimate retaliation" against countries like Tanzania which have allowed "terrorist" bases to be established along their frontiers. "There is now a new doctrine of legitimate retaliation," he said cryptically. "We are taking a very good note of this new doctrine." [18] A few bombing incidents within Tanzanian territory in late 1966 and early 1967 and the numerous Tanzanian charges that Portuguese military and civilian reconnaissance aircraft violate Tanzanian airspace appear to lend substance to Nogueira's warning.

In early 1969 two events occurred that would have shattered lesser nationalist movements. Dr. Mondlane, who stood virtually alone as FRELIMO's leader since its 1962 creation, was killed by a bomb in Dar es Salaam on February 3. No one is yet sure who mailed the package that contained the bomb, but the initial impact was staggering. A few weeks earlier, the deputy military commander of the FRELIMO forces, Samuel Kankonbe, had been assassinated in southern Tanzania. FRELIMO might have disintegrated in a leadership struggle based on

17. *Africa Diary*, VII, No. 5 (January 28–February 3, 1967), 3238.
18. *Nationalist* (Dar es Salaam), May 11, 1965.

ideological-ethnic-personal divisions. For years there has been talk of dissatisfaction among Makonde militants. Some Makonde members, whose people bear the burden of the battle in Mozambique, raided FRELIMO headquarters in Dar at least twice in 1968, sending some officials to the hospital with knife wounds. Then, in March 1969, Chief Lazaro Kavandame, a 65-year-old FRELIMO officer and the most prominent political leader of the Makonde, defected to the Portuguese. He claimed that FRELIMO had been using the Makonde as cannon fodder.[19]

These have been significant setbacks the results of which are still being felt. Collegial leadership has not worked. Accusations of tribal, regional, and religious favoritism have brought defection in the field and military and political retreat. The Makonde and Nyanja (most of whom live in Malawi) have constituted the bulk of FRELIMO fighters. This is, of course, a function of geopolitical accident rather than one of choice. It is possible to read into it, if one were from these groups, a conscious effort by a truly national leadership to exploit these peoples in the struggle. But the leadership still insists that its appeal is intended to be national in scope. Despite the efforts of President Nyerere and the OAU Liberation Committee, the three-man Council of the Presidency has broken up with the suspension of Rev. Uria Simango, thought to be Mondlane's logical successor. The Secretary of Defense and Commander of the Army, Samora Machel, and the Party's Secretary for External Affairs, Marcelino dos Santos, have taken over the leadership. The result of this political struggle in Dar has been a slowdown, if not actual sacrifice, of initiative to the Portuguese. The movement must somehow regain momentum if it is to achieve its political goals.

When considering the guerrilla movements in Portuguese Africa as a whole, it is necessary to bear in mind that Portugal herself is a poor European power of only nine million people. The average per capita G.N.P. is around $450 per year. This raises two fundamental issues. On the one hand, it is exceedingly costly for Portugal to sustain military forces amounting to at least 130,000 troops in three noncontiguous territories. On the other hand, however, Portugal's African possessions represent potential, if not actual as in the cases of Angola and Cabinda, eco-

19. *ARB*, VI, No. 4 (May 15, 1969), 1389BC–1390AB.

nomic assets to metropolitan Portugal. Without them the Portuguese economy would be even more retarded and depressed.

The combination of growing costs and larger troop demands have bedeviled Portugal. Defense expenditures now amount to around one half of the total governmental expenditures. The extent to which the economy can tolerate these expenses without outright collapse is debatable. It could be that external warfare, if kept within manageable bounds, might provide the stimulus for further profitable exploitation of her African possessions, as well as the impetus for generating long-needed growth in the metropolitan economy. On the other hand, this is an artificial and not necessarily efficient stimulation, far more effectively brought about by direct investment in capital-producing activities.[20] The problem of maintaining and increasing force levels is more perplexing. Portuguese use of African troops has not been altogether successful. Continued violent reprisal and repression against the peasantry will not help provide loyal African recruits. So, though Portugal may be able to sustain her present level of military operations in Africa perhaps long into the future, any significant increase in the intensity and scope of guerrilla activities may prove too costly in manpower and expenditures, and therefore it may lead to either a change in policy or a change in government in Lisbon.

In another respect, however, Portugal may not be able to afford to abandon all her African possessions. Portugal regularly shows an adverse balance of trade. Only in its African territories is a trade surplus recorded. Likewise, the balance of payments with her territories overseas is continually favorable. With the discovery of major oil reserves in Cabinda, the planned exploitation of the massive Cabora Bassa and Kunene River hydroelectric schemes in Mozambique and Angola, as well as the agricultural and mineral productivity of the African territories, especially Angola, Portuguese prestige and wealth (particularly that of some individual Portuguese capitalists) would suffer badly from the loss of these territories.

One way of prolonging and expanding Portugal's ability to mount a military defense of her African possessions is by combining with other

20. For conflicting positions on this issue, see Andrew Wilson Green, "Portugal and the African Territories: Economic Implications," in Abshire & Samuels, *Portuguese Africa,* pp. 345–363; and Chaliand, *Armed Struggle in Africa,* pp. 3–11. For the total extent of military costs see Martelli, "Conflict in Portuguese Africa," pp. 428–429.

states anxious to see a continued Portuguese presence in Southern Africa. Collaborative planning and actual assistance from Rhodesia and South Africa are well known. The Portuguese refer to this axis as ASPRO. Portugal's association with NATO is another case. In the following chapter we shall explore the ramifications of outside support, collaboration, and intervention. So far, at least in Portugal's case, NATO membership as well as the ASPRO linkage has helped relieve the pressure on an otherwise insecure colonial power.

D. *White-Settler Regimes on the Defensive:*
Rhodesia and South Africa

THE ZIMBABWE LIBERATION ACTIVITIES.[21] Rhodesian UDI found the nationalist liberation movements of Rhodesia—the Zimbabwe African Peoples' Union (ZAPU) and the Zimbabwe African National Union (ZANU)—in serious and open conflict with one another. This situation has changed little in the intervening years. Although violent internal resistance to the Smith regime has not been wanting, by and large internal African opposition lacks organization and coordination. It has essentially taken the form of spontaneous and sporadic outbursts with little long-range effect.

Likewise, the effectiveness of ZANU and ZAPU operating outside Rhodesia has been marginal. They have managed to infiltrate a few hundred guerrilla fighters into Rhodesia, but they have not been an insuperable challenge to the Rhodesian forces (strengthened by South African soldiers and police). The guerrilla campaigns began in August 1967 and were renewed in March 1968. Joint forces composed of ANC (South African) and ZAPU guerrillas crossed into Rhodesia from Zambia in a mass and then split into several units fighting in three separate areas. They were engaged by Rhodesian and South African forces and most were killed, captured, or fled into Botswana where some were apprehended and im-

21. See Colin Legum in *The Observer*, August 27, 1967; Colin Legum, "Guerrilla Warfare and African Liberation Movements," *Africa Today*, XIV, No. 4 (August 1967), 5–10; *Times* (London), March 11, 1968; and Rake, "Black Guerrillas," 23–25. Particularly useful for the international ramifications is John Day, *International Nationalism: The Extra-Territorial Relations of Southern Rhodesian African Nationalists* (London: Routledge & Kegan Paul, 1967).

prisoned. The 1968 infiltrations were not markedly more successful and largely followed the same pattern, although the nationalists appeared to be better armed and trained than earlier. What is so noteworthy is that the scale of the fighting is so small compared to the Portuguese territories, where thousands of nationalists are in the field.

But why do the Zimbabwe guerrillas have so little to show for their efforts? By far the most important reason has been the internecine struggle going on within and between the various movements. This competition has made it practically impossible to organize within the target territory. Contributing to this organizational problem has been the efficient informant network built up by the Rhodesian police (working in both Rhodesia and Zambia) which has taken full advantage of ZAPU-ZANU hatreds. Another explanation can be suggested by the nature of the boundary itself. Rhodesia is surrounded on three sides by Botswana, South Africa, and Mozambique. With only one flank open, and that a water boundary, the Rhodesian and South African security forces can be relatively concentrated. One can add to this the dilemma facing Zambia in dealing with Zimbabwean nationalists, too difficult to control or police within her own borders. Officially, Zambia denies harboring Zimbabnean guerrillas. She serves primarily as a transmission belt and jumping-off place for guerrillas coming from training in Tanzania and bound for Rhodesia and points south.

This in itself is enough to give alarm to the Rhodesian authorities, who have been secretive about the extent of the problem and the nature of their response. But they are upset by the prospect of an expansion in the fighting. More concrete measures for strengthening her forces and increasing cooperation with South African forces is an obvious reaction. There were no major incursions throughout 1969, but small-scale infiltration continued. In 1970, group penetration was again attempted, but the overall effect was militarily inconsequential.

Efforts to bring the two major revolutionary movements together have so far proved futile. The likely outcome is that one group will score a few startling field successes, and by so doing attract exclusive support of the OAU, Zambia, and perhaps the USSR. Without a nearby host territory, the other movement would atrophy, leaving just one effective movement in operation. So far, however, this outcome is far off. Intergroup struggle is the contemporary pattern and the lines of battle generally coincide with ideological divisions strongly interlaced with ethnic rivalries. ZANU is crudely identified with the Shona peoples of north and east Rhodesia, and ZAPU with the Ndebele of the south and west.[22] Nevertheless, their horizons are basically national (even if their membership is not), and their techniques and organization are modern. Heretofore, ZAPU has had the larger and more broadly based following, while ZANU has attracted much of the old nationalist leadership and the "intellectuals." Both fall into the II.D category of guerrilla movements. But the scars of the early 1960's in the townships of Rhodesia have not been easily healed, especially as long as the leadership personalities remain unchanged and unrepentant. Though the Rhodesian defense forces are not the most formidable in the world, the Zimbabwe nationalists have not reached a level of efficiency sufficient to test them. Barring radical changes, they are not likely to in the short run.

REVOLUTIONARY NATIONALISM FOR SOUTH WEST AFRICA.[23] In military terms, the impact of actual guerrilla activities in South West Africa is marginal. Engagements number no more than a dozen or two, many of which have not been confirmed. In a number of cases fighting was triggered by South African security forces that either stumbled upon infiltrating guerrillas or sought out guerrilla operatives. The effectiveness of guerrilla-launched strikes has been militarily negligible. Nevertheless, as the first concerted strikes within South Africa's immediate defense perimeter and as political gestures (in the Debrayian sense), their symbolic importance for inhabitants of South West Africa, for the immobilized United Nations, and for all the world to see, is not without significance.

Although SWAPO (the only active liberation movement operating directly within South West Africa) regards August 26, 1966 as the opening of the final stage of the liberation struggle, it would be useful to begin this description with the formation of the Ovamboland People's Organiza-

22. The ZANU position appears in the editorial, "Down With Tribalism!" *Zimbabwe News* (Lusaka), V, No. 4 (April 1970), 3–4, 9.
23. This account draws upon the following materials: Richard Dale, "South African Counterinsurgency Operations in South West Africa," presented to the Eleventh Annual Meeting of the African Studies Association, Los Angeles, October 16–19, 1968 (mimeo.); Richard Dale, "Ovamboland: 'Bantustan Without Tears?'" *Africa Report*, XIV, No. 2 (February 1969), 16–23; and Muriel Horrell, *South-West Africa* (Johannesburg: South African Institute of Race Relations, 1967).

tion in 1959. A year later it was transformed into SWAPO, seeking a territory-wide following. Its leaders, for their organizing efforts, were penalized by being returned to Ovamboland by the authorities. Sam Nujoma fled the country in 1961 and set up operations in Dar es Salaam. There, in limited concert with SWAPO leaders within South West Africa, he began to recruit guerrilla trainees, who were spirited out of the territory in small groups. They passed through Botswana, where the SWAPO office in Francistown expedited their passage to the Kongwa camp in Tanzania. From there, they fanned out to various training camps in other African states (Ghana, Algeria, and Egypt) as well as in Communist states (the Soviet Union, the Chinese People's Republic, and North Korea).

SWAPO men began returning to Ovamboland after September 1965. They established a training and base camp at Ongulumbashe. Here they functioned for several months without being detected. On August 26, 1966, the South African police, after having kept the camp under surveillance for several days, launched an attack on the base, killing two guerrillas and arresting nine.

There have been several incidents and minor engagements since then, but it is not exactly a record of intense confrontation or activity. Still, its importance as a catalyst must not be underestimated. SWAPO claims that fighting and South African countermeasures have led to the flight of some 4,000 refugees to Zambia, in addition to others in Botswana.[24] Particularly significant is the scene of battle and the composition of the participants, predominantly if not exclusively Ovambo. The Ovambo are the largest single population group in the territory—in 1966 an estimated 270,000, representing 45 percent of South West Africa's total. Ovamboland is in a situation particularly strategic for the struggle. Not only does it border on Angola, thus making it accessible to support and supply from abroad, but it is also a densely forested region (unlike most of South West Africa) conducive to guerrilla cover. A final consideration is that for years Ovamboland has been relatively isolated from the rest of South West African economic life. There are few white residents to mar the ethnic homogeneity of the region.

Despite ethnic homogeneity, there is by no means ideological or political agreement on the course that ought to be taken. In response to the

24. *Namibia News*, II, Nos. 4–6 (April–June 1969), 4–5.

Odendaal Commission report (1964) and following the nondecision of the International Court of Justice in July 1966, the South African Prime Minister offered to Ovamboland a form of carefully monitored self-government. Hand-picked Ovambo leaders accepted the offer and, in the process, asked the South African government for help in combatting guerrilla nationalists operating in Ovamboland. SWAPO officials and traditional Ovambo chiefs regularly trade insults and accusations, and there appears to be little hope of any collaboration between these two irreconcilable groups of leaders.

Another nationalist group, the South West Africa National Union (SWANU), was formed before SWAPO (in 1959), but it has been unable to gain either internal or external support. Its name was later changed to South West African National United Front (SWANUF), but today it is practically moribund. Generally identified with the less numerous Herero peoples (approximately 40,000) of the eastern part of the territory, its primary source of assistance is the Chinese People's Republic. OAU efforts to bring the groups together led to failure and, ultimately, to OAU-ALC exclusive support for SWAPO since 1965.

SWAPO still maintains party operations within South West Africa, although clearly overt activities are severely circumscribed. In all likelihood, external SWAPO cadres, with provisional headquarters in Dar es Salaam, three other offices in Africa (Lusaka, Cairo, and Algiers)[25] and three elsewhere (New York, London, and Helsinki), will be more effective in the necessarily clandestine struggle. They have managed to infiltrate, recruit, and train men within the target area and to politicize a few followers there. They have also convinced the OAU of the sole legitimacy of their movement in the territory, and they have solicited and secured assistance from the ALC and from bilateral sources, principally the USSR. And they alone have opened a front against the most formidable security force in Southern Africa—no small accomplishment considering their modest beginnings.

REVOLUTIONARY AFRICAN NATIONALISM AND SOUTH AFRICA.[26] Revolu-

25. There had been, at one time, other offices in Leopoldville, Accra, and Francistown.
26. The Republic of South Africa is one of those few African states with at least a modicum of primary materials and analytical studies of African protest and revolutionary involvements. Invaluable in the preparation of this section have been Gwen-

tionary guerrilla warfare has not been initiated in South Africa. Although it could be argued that the Bantu in South Africa are more politically attentive, as a group, than Africans elsewhere in Southern Africa, the policies of the white regime and their own strategic and tactical errors have served to deplete what following they once boasted, and to force into exile, execution, or prison the leadership material available. The result has been that the most overt form of organized political violence has been the terror and sabotage campaigns from 1961 to 1964.

By and large African nationalist organizations were not violently oriented before the tragic Sharpeville shootings of 1960.[27] But Sharpeville, compounded by the ruthless and unbending suppression of nonwhite nationalist organizations in response to the peaceful protests against Sharpeville, seemed to be the confirming lesson. African leaders learned that peaceful opposition was fruitless and that all legitimate channels for change were closed to their people. Apartheid was intransigent. Its spokesmen were willing to employ any means to defend it. African nationalists reasoned that they would have to be willing to use any means to destroy it. The questions remained when and how would violence be expressed and who would supply the leadership and structure to the cause.

Initially violence took multiple forms. Organizations earlier committed to nonviolent protest spawned clandestine movements dedicated to the violent overthrow of the racist system. In November 1961 *Umkonto we Sizwe* (Spear of the Nation) was formed and it went into action for the first time on December 16, 1961. It supported the African National Congress (ANC)—indeed was created by its leadership. But its chief pur-

dolen Carter, *The Politics of Inequality: South Africa Since 1948*, 2nd ed., rev., (London: Thames and Hudson, 1959); Edward Feit, *African Opposition in South Africa* (Stanford, Calif.: Hoover Institution, 1967); Edward Feit, *South Africa: The Dynamics of the African National Congress* (London: Oxford University Press, 1962); Leo Kuper, *Passive Resistance in South Africa* (New Haven: Yale University Press, 1957); and Govan Mbeki, *South Africa: The Peasants' Revolt* (Baltimore: Penguin Books, 1964). Mbeki is an ANC leader currently imprisoned in South Africa. See also Feit, "Urban Revolt," 55–72.

27. See Feit, *African Opposition*, which details the Western Area and Bantu Education campaigns of 1954–1955, and Kuper, *Passive Resistance*, which concentrates on the 1952 campaign for massive nonviolent opposition to apartheid and particularly the pass laws. On the matter of commitment to violence as a means, see Leo Kuper's definitive study, *An African Bourgeoisie: Race, Class, and Politics in South Africa* (New Haven and London: Yale University Press, 1965), esp. pp. 21–31 and 365–387.

pose was to recruit and train men in sabotage techniques and to launch a coordinated sabotage campaign throughout the Republic. Sabotage seemed to its leaders the sensible strategy, given the alignment of forces and the ends sought. Nelson Mandela, an ANC leader and one of the founders of *Umkonto we Sizwe*, felt that there were four alternative courses: sabotage, guerrilla warfare, terrorism, and open revolution. Despite the choice of sabotage because it "did not involve loss of life, and it offered the best hope for future race relations," the movement did provide for guerrilla training and planning.[28] *Umkonto we Sizwe* was effectively smashed with the arrest of seventeen top leaders at Rivonia in July 1963 and their subsequent trial and imprisonment. Smaller sabotage groups were even less active, and it soon became clear that sabotage was not an effective instrument for revolutionary change in South Africa.

The choice of terrorism, i.e., the calculated use of brutal and ritualistic violence aimed at persons, was taken up by numerous smaller groups. Chief among them has been *Poqo*, which emerged in 1962. The exact link between *Poqo* and the Pan-Africanist Congress (PAC) is not clear. More than likely, *Poqo* was formed by a breakaway group of PAC members. The PAC sought repeatedly to establish control over *Poqo*, without a great deal of success.

Even more concentrated and potentially more revolutionary in impact was the peasant uprising in Pondoland (the Transkei) in 1960. Aimed primarily at the system of Bantu authorities, the violence was carefully directed against the property and person of officials and supporters of the government. Councillors, headmen, and chiefs found their lives and property threatened, and assassinations were widespread. The movement established "mountain committees" to challenge the Bantu authorities and their puppets, the traditional chiefs, and to direct the program to ostracize or, if need be, punish collaborators. By August and October 1961, thirty Pondos were sentenced to death for their involvement in the uprising. Other much smaller and less well-organized resistance movements had occurred since 1946: in Witzieshoek, on the border of Basutoland; in Marico,

28. Nelson Mandela, *No Easy Walk to Freedom* (New York: Basic Books, 1965), p. 175. For a thoroughly different perspective on the movement, see the curiously self-critical account by Bruno Mtolo, *Umkonto we Sizwe: The Road to the Left* (Durban: Drakensberg Press, 1966). Once a member of the movement in Natal, Mtolo appeared as Mr. X, the chief state witness, at the Rivonia trial.

south of Bechuanaland; in Sekhukhuneland, in the northwest Transvaal; in Zululand; and throughout the Transkei. All were forcibly suppressed.

Both sabotage and terrorism, as well as open revolutionary protest, have been counterproductive in South Africa. Organization was weak, solidarity doubtful, competition among movements self-defeating. Acts of violence were generally uncoordinated and provided the government with further rationale to intensify repression of still legitimate dissent as well as a thorough destruction of the remaining African leadership pool within the country. Today a confident South African government can publicly declare, as did the Minister of Police and of the Interior, Mr. S. L. Muller, on August 31, 1969, and not without some justification, that at present there is not one known "terrorist" at large in South Africa.[29]

Nevertheless, outside the Republic planning and training and fighting go on. The PAC has been ineffectual and badly divided in Dar and Lusaka, but the ANC struck up an apparently mutually acceptable alliance with ZAPU.[30] Together their fighters have penetrated Rhodesia and engaged both the Rhodesian and South African military and police (since August 1967). It will be some time before the movement is ready to strike within the Republic, but guerrilla warfare is now the chosen medium and active preparation for that day goes on.

Guerrilla movements against white-settler regimes in Southern Africa have several characteristics in common. They have been unable, for a variety of reasons, to appeal to the black populations within the target territories. So far, at least, there have been no major uprisings within the three target territories in sympathy for or in support of the movements, which have been essentially exile movements whose primary bases of operations have been outside the targets. Since the movements have been driven underground and into exile few have been willing to risk sanctions to rally to their support. These movements have been embryonic in that they are still almost entirely dependent on host support and outside material and financial assistance. They are by no means self-sustaining. Even

29. As reported in *Rhodesia Herald* (Salisbury), September 1, 1969. Earlier the Minister had expanded on this theme, although insisting on the need for a network of legislation to be operative in order to maintain this condition. He thought the danger from external infiltration was far greater than that from an internal uprising.
30. ANC officials are enthusiastic about the *long-range* possibilities of such an alliance. Personal interviews, London, September 8, 1969.

within the refugee and exile communities from which they draw their memberships, there has been no voluntary rush to enroll or combine forces. To some extent, these movements might be regarded as heads without bodies, as the ranks are relatively thin. Refugee and exile status places tremendous psychological and physical demands upon individuals. It also presents certain problems, as well as opportunities, for the host countries.[31] But the fact remains that if a guerrilla movement is to make any impact, it must break out of the host-dependence syndrome and get into the field. Movements aimed at white-settler regimes have just begun to move hesitatingly in this direction. The responses they have received among their peoples have so far not been overwhelmingly supportive. This is not because there is an absence of sympathy for the cause. Dissatisfaction is acute and the conditions for unrest are and have been present. Rather, it is because the security force levels are high and the secret police networks have been convincingly efficient. The level of risk is too high and the likelihood for short-run success is too low for the ordinary citizen to commit himself to violence at this stage.

E. *Indigenous African Governments: The Congo and Sudan*

It is not easy to abstract briefly the specifics of the internal wars that have disrupted or are disrupting the indigenously-governed states of Black Africa. Many of the general conditions leading to guerrilla movements have already been discussed in the preceding three chapters, and there is little point in repeating those arguments here. It might be more fruitful to plunge into two individual cases, so that we might be able to trace, by further detail, the situations in these countries.

THE CONGO, 1964–1965. The Congo has been a crucible for a variety of disorders that new states are subject to. Army mutinies, anticolonial and anti-neo-colonial outbursts, racial, ethnic, religious, and regional unrest, provincial secession and national revolutionary warfare have plagued this state, particularly in its first five years of independence. It was not until 1964, however, that genuine guerrilla warfare spread throughout the

31. John Marcum, "The Exile Condition and Revolutionary Effectiveness: Southern African Liberation Movements," in Richard Dale and Christian P. Potholm (eds.), *Southern Africa in Perspective* (New York: Free Press, forthcoming). See also my article, "Host Countries."

country.[32] In 1964 the Congo underwent a massive internal war that enveloped at one point almost two-thirds of the country and prompted the intervention of not only several hundred white mercenaries employed by the central government, but Belgian and American armed units and assistance on the rebel side from Algeria, Sudan, Ghana, the U.A.R., the U.S.S.R., and China. In this instance, several supranational efforts were made to encourage, regulate, or contain civil war between rival domestic factions and forces.

The 1964–1965 guerrilla movements sought a radical transformation of the Congolese system, a "second independence," as some rebel leaders claimed. It grew out of economic deprivation and disparity, and the perceived prospect of improvement by violent insurrection. The absolute as well as relative decline of living standards among various categories of the population, particularly among the mass of laborers, the unemployed, and lesser civil servants, and in certain regions of the country—notably outside the Lower Congo and Katanga—fed the fires of dissent. Resentment mounted against the symbols of the establishment, the army and the police, the "intellectuals," the politicians, and the external exploiters of the Congo's resources.[33] But perceptions of deprivation and the extent of participation in the rebellion were also colored by local conditions and animosities, and assumed extremely complex patterns in the specific.

Starting in Kwilu Province in January–April 1964, then igniting in the eastern provinces in May and thence to the entire northeast and Nord Katanga region, the rebellion spread like a field fire. The small *Armée Populaire de Libération* (APL) routed an ineffectual and uninspired national army (ANC) and quickly occupied the eastern countryside. Rebel forces skillfully employed various forms of magic. *Simbas,* as the young, badly-armed, but exceptionally motivated rebel initiates were called, managed to snatch victory in the most "impossible" predicaments. Spurred on

32. This section was drawn from Anderson, von der Mehden, and Young, *Political Development*, pp. 120–142; Young, "Rebellion and the Congo"; Fox, "Traditionality and Modernity"; Fox, De Craemer, and Ribeaucourt, " 'The Second Independence,' " 78–109. The best documentary sources can be found in a series of volumes edited by J. Gerard-Libois and Jean Van Lierde for C.R.I.S.P. in Brussels, and titled simply, *Congo 1964, Congo 1965,* and *Congo 1966.* See also Benoit Verhaegen, *Rébellions au Congo,* I (Brussels: C.R.I.S.P., 1966).
33. We have treated these conditions more carefully in Section B of Chapter Two. See particularly Young, "Rebellion and the Congo."

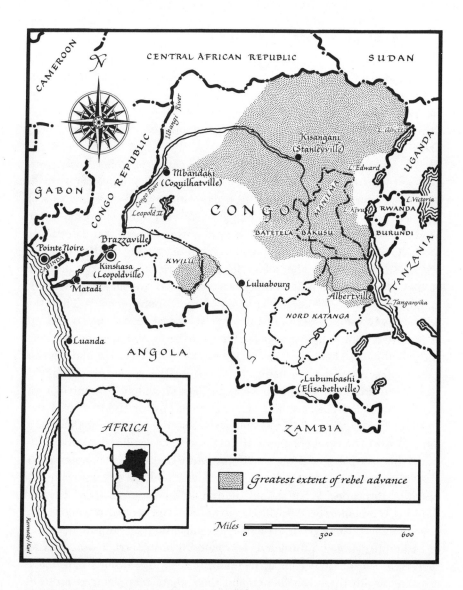

MAP 4

THE CONGO, AREAS OF GREATEST REBEL ADVANCE, 1964

Source: Charles W. Anderson, Fred R. von der Mehden, and Crawford Young, *Issues of Political Development* (Englewood Cliffs, N.J.: Prentice-Hall, 1967), p. 121.

by a ritualized form of magic or *dawa* that purportedly turned bullets into water and protected the *simbas,* both the government troops and the simbas became convinced of its effectiveness. ANC units fled because they believed their weapons were useless to combat simbas equipped with *dawa.*

But from this miraculous rise to prominence, the rebel forces were unable to govern the territory they occupied. The movements really foundered on a diffusion of purpose, organization, and leadership, as well as a dearth of qualified and experienced leaders. From their peak, in territorial terms around August 1964, they soon were dispersed and destroyed by ANC mercenary-reinforced counterattacks striking at the heart of rebel-held territories. The joint Belgian-American paratroop drop on Stanleyville (Kisangani) and other large towns in November 1964 served to point up the ephemeral character of these movements.[34] Thus this rebellion was really a series of uprisings staged at several levels and appealing to a wide range of peoples for a wide range of reasons. National and tribal-local, ideological and magico-religious, economic and psychological—the motives were many. But because the appeal was individualized and fragmented, the movements lacked widely attractive, transcendent and unifying symbols. The very reasons for the mercurial successes of the fragmented movements were also the reasons for their long-term failure. The rural character of the insurgency rendered a low-quality leadership incapable of dealing with the wider and more permanent problems of the management of a broadened war and the administration of liberated territories. What should be stressed in these paragraphs is that the Congo rebellion of 1964–1965 was not one but several rebellions that never achieved the type of leadership, organization, or purpose necessary to sustain a national, protracted, and modernized guerrilla war. It is for these reasons that the compartmentalization of the various movements associated with these rebellions (and their characters changed radically as conditions ebbed and flowed) is so difficult and must continue to be tentative.

THE SUDAN.[35] In comparison to the short-lived but brutal guerrilla wars

34. See my "The Stanleyville Rescue: American Policy in the Congo," *The Yale Review,* LVI, No. 2 (Winter 1967), 242–255; and Richard A. Falk, *Legend Order in a Violent World* (Princeton, N.J.: Princeton University Press, 1968), pp. 324–335.
35. The civil war in the Sudan has received relatively sparse coverage in the press and

in the Congo, the struggle in the Sudan has been drawn out, less confrontational, but no less bitter and cruel. Neither side has proven to be particularly efficient militarily or particularly effective politically or administratively, at least among the populace in the rebellious areas.

Division between the Arab north and the African south in the Sudan has been historical and profound, despite the continuing and long-standing interaction between the peoples. According to the 1955–1956 census, 39 percent of the Sudan's approximately 13 million people are Arab, 30 percent are southern, and the remainder are western, Beja and Nuba, Nubian, or foreigners. Of the total, 52 percent speak Arabic. Culturally, slightly over one-third are Arabic, slightly under a third are African, and the rest are admixtures of Afro-Arab culture.[36] The southerners, approximately four million, are racially Nilotic, Nilo-Hamitic, and Sudanic. Most practice their traditional religions, though significant numbers, especially among the dissident leadership elements, are Christian. Thus, Arab culture and language has served as the cement for the Sudanese state. But though they may unify the northern peoples, they have alienated southerners, who have been divorced from the centers of political, administrative, economic, and cultural life of the Sudan. Few southerners participated in the anti-colonial independence movements, often a consensus-building process for other African states. To some extent the British colonial administration contributed to the north-south split, as the northern leaders charge, but the division precedes the British entry and is far deeper than the superficial British impact on the three southern provinces, representing 300,000 square miles of Equatoria, Bahr el Ghazal, and Upper Nile.

---

scholarly journals. This account depends upon the following materials: Joseph Oduho and William Deng, *The Problems of the Southern Sudan* (London: Oxford University Press, 1963); Mohamed Omer Beshir, *The Southern Sudan: Background to Conflict* (London: C. Hurst & Co., 1968); George W. Shepherd, Jr., "National Integration and the Southern Sudan," *Journal of Modern African Studies*, IV, No. 2 (October 1966), pp. 193–212; Oliver Albino, *The Sudan: A Southern Viewpoint* (London: Oxford University Press, 1970). Lawrence Fellows, "The Unknown War in the Sudan," *New York Times Magazine*, September 22, 1968, pp. 25–27, 122–130; Al J. Venter, "Stalemate in the South," *News/Check*, August 22, 1969, pp. 31–33; Eric Pace, "Rebel Drive in South Sudan Appears to be Flagging," *New York Times*, January 31, 1969; and, "The Tragedy of the South Sudan," 2 parts, *East Africa Reporter* (Nairobi), VIII, Nos. 225–226 (November 29 and December 13, 1968), 12–13 and 14.
36. Shepherd, "National Integration," 196.

MAP 5

THE SUDAN, SOUTHERN PROVINCES

The cultural distinctions have complicated an unequal situation that has further disadvantaged the less-modernized southerners. The central government has intermittently attempted to Arabicize the southern peoples, imposing Arabic language instruction, new curricula, Arab teachers, and encouraging Arab immigration to the south and the Islamic religion in the region while discouraging Christianity. They have exploited the cheap labor from the south, given a disproportionately large number of senior positions in the civil service, the military, and the political élite to the northerners. Budgetary expenditures in economic and educational development schemes likewise favor the north. Small wonder that southern leaders refer to the Arab government in Khartoum as "imperialist." One southern leader declared that: "Imperialists don't always come from overseas and are not always white. . . . We learned quickly that freedom is another thing from independence. We lost our freedom when we gained our independence." The coercive Arabicization and the attendant repression has forced many southerners to flee the Sudan into neighboring states.

TABLE X

SUDANESE   REFUGEES, 1964-1968

Host Country	Jan. 1964	Jan. 1965	Jan. 1966	Jan. 1967	Jan. 1968	Aug. 1969
Congo (Kinshasa)	8,000	8,000	22,000	33,000	40,000	55,000
Central African Rep.	—	300	17,500	27,000	21,000	19,500
Uganda	5,000	12,000	44,000	55,000	60,000	71,500
Ethiopia	n.a.	n.a.	n.a.	n.a.	n.a.	20,000
Total	13,000	20,300	83,000	115,000	121,00	166,000

Sources: Various UN High Commission for Refugee publications.
n.a. = not available

The first major outbreak of violence occurred in July–August 1955 when a mob of southerners demonstrated against mass dismissals from a cotton-growing scheme. Soldiers sent to quell the demonstration panicked and fired into the crowd, as did northern merchants alongside them. Three weeks later, an Arab officer in the Equatoria Corps shot an unruly African soldier and a mutiny followed in which African soldiers brutally killed every northerner they could find. Northern troops were flown in to restore order in the rebellious south. Many of the rebels fled into the bush or into exile, thousands were imprisoned, and hundreds were executed or summarily killed. The military takeover in November 1958 led to six years of supression and injustice in the south. Violence spread, and by 1963 a full revolt erupted aimed at secession and independence from the Arab north. The revolution of October 1964, followed by the Khartoum Round Table Conference of March 1965, held promise for a reconciliation and the ascendance of moderate elements on both sides, but reforms never materialized and struggle continued in a low-key with sporadic flare-ups. Neither side was sufficiently large to pursue active and constant confrontation, but the rebellion was no less real and disastrous to the hapless civilian population that suffered from accessibility to both sides. One significant result of the Khartoum conference, however, was that the secessionist forces realized that other African states favored a policy of unity for the Sudan, and that independent Africa was unwilling to offer more than scant material assistance and sympathy to refugees and encouragement to moderate southern Sudanese politicians.

The proliferation of southern Sudanese political and military groups and factions is a source of confusion to observers and of weakness to the secessionist movement. From the Sudanese government standpoint, it has been difficult to know who speaks for the southerners and how to pursue a conciliatory policy. From the southern viewpoint, there has been a profusion of governmental and policy changes in Khartoum, so offers of amnesty and reform are seldom reliable or longstanding. For both contestants, fortunes shift rapidly. Each is as much concerned with maintaining itself within its own camp as it is in dealing with the obvious enemy. The southern movements are divided between military and political forces, separatists, federalists and reformists, those who function within the Khartoum arena, the southern arena, and the exile arena, and various personal and tribal factions thereof. In May 1969, the Anya'nya, which is the military wing of various provisional governments, shifted allegiance from the Southern Sudanese Provisional Government of Aggrey Jaden to the Nile Provisional Government of Gordon Mayen, with offices in Kampala.

The Anya'nya has been functioning within the Sudan since 1963. At times it has been relatively quiescent for want of ammunition, supplies, weapons, and recruits. There have been times when the Uganda army, in concert with the Sudanese government forces, has sought to eliminate

Anya'nya activity in Uganda,[37] but, otherwise, Uganda has unofficially provided the Anya'nya their chief vestibule for supplies and their chief sanctuary. In fact, on several occasions relations between Uganda and the Sudan have been strained because of Sudanese military incursions into and damage to Ugandan property. By and large, however, Uganda has sought to be fairly neutral in the conflict, protecting her own citizens and generously helping the thousands of Sudanese who have fled to Uganda. This has not been easy given the ethnic similarities between the refugees and the citizens of northern Uganda, whose sympathies lie clearly with the rebels.[38]

Many Anya'nya leaders are former Sudanese army men, either from the Equatoria Corps or more recent defectors. Their forces have been variously estimated at between 13,000 and 600, although the more common figure is around 5,000. It is opposed by around 17,000 Sudanese government troops. One thing is painfully clear for the Anya'nya; its units are uncoordinated and splintered, and leadership has been decentralized into geographic commands, with all the problems for future coordination and political unity that entails.

Where the Congolese rebellion attracted open and vital external assistance to each side, the Sudanese civil war has only recently attracted the attention of outside forces and with it interest and assistance. Ironically, the first external assistance to the southern separatists came as a fortuitous by-product of Sudanese governmental assistance to the Congolese rebels. When the rebels heard that Russian weapons were being funnelled through Juba to the Gbenya *simbas* in the eastern Congo, the Anya'nya ambushed some of the convoys. Then when the Congolese rebellion was later suppressed, the *simbas* who retreated into the Sudan were intercepted by Anya'nya units and relieved of their weapons. Others sold theirs. The central Congolese government willingly promoted this activity. So, by dabbling in Congolese affairs, the Sudanese provided their own dissident peoples with the modern weapons to make their own civil war more violent. In general, with the important exception of Egyptian help to the Sudanese forces, African states have followed a hands-off policy, as

37. See, *The People* (Kampala), January 28, 1967; and *Uganda Argus* (Kampala), October 7, 1968.
38. See, for example, the provocative statement by Mr. A. O. Okelo, National Assembly of Uganda, 3rd Session (1964/65), *Hansard*, 2nd Series—Vol. 42, p. 1181.

in the Biafran War. Except for the Malawi government and occasional politicians from Black Africa who publicly favor the southerners, the African governments are privately sympathetic to the southerners, and officially anxious to see the war terminated and Sudanese unity solidified.

Today the Anya'nya receive aid from a variety of sources, including Italy, France, West Germany, Scandinavia, Belgium, Israel, and many of the private humanitarian organizations formerly associated with the Biafran relief program. Despite this variety, the extent of aid is not great, and certainly has not made the movement successful. The Israelis, of course, deny their involvement, but their help seems to be obvious to on-the-scene observers.[39] The Anya'nya have been strongly anti-Communist, a rare orientation given the general temper of guerrilla movements in Africa. The Sudanese get the bulk of their assistance from Egypt and Russia, particularly since the government of Major-General Nimeiry has been more vocally pro-Arab in the Middle East crisis than earlier Sudanese governments. So far, with the exception of charges of Egyptian pilots flying bombing missions into the south, no direct outside participation is evident.

The positions of both sides seem firm. The southerners demand the acceptance by the central government of the principle of secession for the southern provinces and the Sudanese demand agreement on the unity of the state before they will agree to reforms, cease-fire, and open negotiations. But by periodic concessions the Sudanese may be able to slice away secessionist support within the southern Sudan and among the refugees, and thereby reduce the Anya'nya to a hard core of isolated irreconcilables. Military conflict is stalemated, and the war appears to be a fixture of Sudanese politics into the distant future, subject to periodic contraction and expansion in scope and intensity.

F. *Conclusions*

From Eritrea on the Red Sea to Senegal and Mauritania in the west is a girdle of states with ethnically and religiously divided populations, African/Arab-Berber-Moor and non-Muslim/Muslim. In some territories non-black governments prevail (Mauritania, Sudan) and in other Africans

39. See Venter, "Stalemate in the South," 32–33.

dominate (Chad, Ethiopia, Kenya, and Mali). Internal conflict along these lines has already erupted in Chad, Ethiopia, Kenya, and the Sudan. The generally nonnegotiable character of the issues in each instance suggests a long period of low-keyed guerrilla conflict in these states. Depending on the abilities of leadership elements, the extent of external involvement and sanctuary, and the physical conditions in the contested areas, this class of guerrilla conflict may be the future pattern. If it is compounded and reinforced by economic and ideological stratification and by the insinuation of cold war issues, we can almost be certain of widespread guerrilla conflict. However, since these are clearly regionally divided states, the appeal of these movements is bound to be restricted, regardless of their ideologies, organization, and techniques. Though this serves to narrow the territorial arena of conflict, it tends to demand constant policing in the face of regular, practically institutionalized dissatisfaction.

In conclusion, there are built-in limits to the long-run future of guerrilla wars for independence against white colonial regimes. All Portuguese territories are presently involved (except for Cabinda) in such engagements. Likewise, wars against independent white-settler regimes are inherently restricted to the three territories discussed above. Rather, categories III and IV—secessionist and revolutionary movements against indigenous black governments—would appear to be the wave of the long-run future. Practically all African governments are subject to dissident minorities (and in some cases majorities, depending on how we group, particularly if we consider economic stratification). Depending on the breadth of their bases, all governments are in varying degrees insecure and not especially well-equipped, militarily and administratively, to subdue or prevent general uprisings. After all, the Sudan and the Congo have two of the largest and best-equipped armed forces in Black Africa. Their field records, however, are not impressive against relatively weak internal enemies. The prospect, then, for long-smouldering, perhaps low-intensity guerrilla conflict is great in the next thirty years. The only real defense that the established central governments have is effective, efficient, and representative government; and representative government is not always possible in deeply divided countries. A better look into the future demands a consideration of several additional factors to be examined in the following chapter.

Chapter Six

THE FUTURE
OF GUERRILLA
WARFARE IN AFRICA

So far, we have considered the general variables which affect the total magnitude of political violence. But guerrilla warfare is a distinctive sort of organized political violence. With few exceptions, African states are ripe for political violence, if I might paraphrase. This does not mean, however, that Africa is ripe for revolution, or that political violence will be expressed in the mode of guerrilla warfare. The chances for guerrilla warfare and its potential for military and political effectiveness depend upon additional variables that ought to be considered in this segment of our analysis. These include: (1) technological change and weapons development; (2) the extent of cooperation among guerrilla and revolutionary movements (within and among territories); (3) the extent of cooperation among antiguerrilla forces; (4) external involvement; and (5) developments in the configuration of interstate power outside of Africa.

First, let us summarize the probable patterns of domestic politics relevant to guerrilla warfare. Most African states are comprised of societies with multiple stratification contours. To some extent these are reinforcing (e.g., when economic stratification hardens ethnic divisions), and to other extents they are crosscutting and tend to proliferate as well as transcend fragmentational patterns. If we assume that primitive societies tend to develop into traditional societies, traditional into modern, and modern into neo-modern,[1] not necessarily at an even pace or in a linear direction, and that some nation-states are composed of societies at various levels of development, and, further, that the nation-state will continue to be the primary unit of international politics for at least the next three or four decades, we can see that African states especially will be subject to the continuation of profound incompatibilities between the nation-state and the social groupings that reside therein. The essence of this tendency, however, is the uneven pace and distribution of development, in both domestic and interstate terms. Uneven development provides the seeds for exploitation and conflict in both arenas. In African states we find the coexistence, not always voluntary or compatible, of elements of all four types of societies—primitive, traditional, modern, and neo-modern. It is this *asynchronie*, as Argentine sociologist Gino Germani called it, that is at the root of much of the political violence in Africa, because it is difficult in this context to develop mutually beneficial and symmetrical interaction among disparate groups. Only if the lines of exchange and the outlets for movement from level to level within the system are clear and open for all significant societal groups, and if movement is encouraged rather than compelled, can the essential conditions for violence be minimized.

Added to these cleavages are distorted sets of material expectations created during the political struggle for independence and immediately thereafter, and the inability of most governments to provide the services or the symbols to maintain their legitimacy. The uneven reward patterns based on limited resources and on external economic and cultural penetration further contributes to *asynchronie* and the potential for political violence. This all too brief discussion provides us with a springboard into those crucial variables that are ostensibly independent of the domestic factors conducive to guerrilla warfare.

A. *Technological Change and Weapons Development*

There has been a steadily growing interest among the established powers over the past decade in applying scientific innovations to weapons devel-

1. This terminology has been developed by Galtung, "Future of International System," 305–333.

opment, especially in the field of counterinsurgency. One evident example has been the use of helicopters in the Algerian War. These developments have increasingly favored the antiguerrilla side. The guerrilla flourishes where the regime forces are immobile, uncoordinated, and unable to amass quickly a concentration of fire power greater than that of the guerrillas. The helicopter and other innovations in air and water craft, sensitive electronic detection devices, sophisticated and more transportable communications systems, and the application of medical, chemical, and biological innovations to counterinsurgency have improved the ability of status quo forces to neutralize the advantages of surprise, intelligence, mobility, and popular support that the guerrillas might otherwise enjoy. By and large, however, most African governments cannot afford these latest developments in weaponry and matériel without military assistance from abroad. So, while the ingredients for more effectively combatting guerrillas exist, they can only be obtained at the price of greater dependence on foreign, usually Western, governments, a political liability that might not always offset the possible military advantages.[2]

With still more limited resources, this expensive equipment is even less available to guerrilla movements. In a military sense, as the century wears on, the relative military effectiveness of guerrilla forces is likely to be diminished by technological innovations applied to counterinsurgency operations. This will by no means assure the success of governments against guerrillas, for the political factors are still most vital to the outcome of any conflict. It appears, further, that the application of technological innovations to political activity for preventative purposes is far removed in time from most of twentieth-century Africa, except in the matter of political socialization, which will be treated subsequently.

B. *The Extent of Cooperation among Guerrilla Movements*

We have seen that in some territories more than one nationalist or revolutionary organization functions, to the detriment of the movement as a

2. The extent and nature of this foreign military assistance and dependence is examined in Geoffrey Kemp, "Arms Traffic and Third World Conflicts," *International Conciliation*, No. 577 (March, 1970), 1–80; John L. Sutton and Geoffrey Kemp, *Arms to Developing Countries, 1945–1965*, Adelphi Papers No. 28 (London: Institute for Strategic Studies, October 1966).

whole, and that it is exceedingly arduous to gain unity, even within single movements. This general tendency is understandably repeated and compounded when one extends the analysis to joining several movements from different territories. Despite entreaties by men like Kwame Nkrumah that African revolutionaries should establish a unified military force, nothing of this sort has emerged.[3] The OAU, and particularly its African Liberation Committee (ALC), has sought to pressure various factions within movements, and contending movements within territories, and other African states as well, to coordinate and cooperate in common revolutionary endeavors. The results have been marginal. There is also an OAU Military Commission and periodic conferences of "military experts," but little progress ensues. What military coordination there has been has come essentially from the nationalist movements themselves. Since the summer of 1967 ZAPU-ANC forces have operated jointly in Zimbabwe. There have also been reports of joint COREMO-PAC infiltration routes through Mozambique, and MPLA-SWAPO cooperation in southeast Angola. So far these efforts have been ad hoc (the ZAPU-ANC linkage is getting firmer) and on such a small scale as to be little more than symbolic. In fact, some infiltrating insurgents have been faced by the hostility of a few black governments and by tightened regulations on their activities in other states. In addition to the meager level of cooperation, there are occasionally reports of violent clashes between movements (GRAE-MPLA, ZAPU-ZANU, for example) in both host and target territories.

Nevertheless, "alliances" of a sort have been struck up, although the measure of actual military planning and cooperation undertaken is conjectural. They have mostly grown up in exile and their existence has not been reflected by field successes. Among them are CONCP, the "Khartoum Alliance," and the "Congo Alliance." These groupings were constructed largely as a reaction to OAU and ALC immobilism, and as bargaining organizations vis-à-vis the ALC, which had been initially assigned responsibility for the coordination of strategies. The nationalists found themselves victimized by political disputes among independent African states. ALC and other OAU member states and host countries have been unable and unwilling to overcome their own intra-African squabbles in order to assist the liberation of their brothers to the south.

3. See Nkrumah's *Revolutionary Warfare.*

Realizing this, nationalist movements, on the basis of one movement per country (after all, they too have many petty as well as profound divisions that prevent all-out coordination), pooled their leverage. There is still some question, however, as to how much cooperation exists beyond the superficial conference sort. The resulting "alliances" have so far been functionally and organizationally loose, but at least the idea of the necessity for regional coordination has been implanted.

Another possible unifying force would be the rise of a charismatic and forceful leader, combining leadership and organizational skills with a magnetic personality. Such an individual could possibly play on the potential ideological appeals of racial and class factors. To date, however, neither shared racial injustice nor common economic exploitation has provided sufficient incentive to achieve unity. But racial and class consciousness are variables that can be gained or lost with a startling rapidity. The likelihood for their growth in the next few decades is high. Low cooperation does not necessarily mean less guerrilla warfare, just less focus and intensity, and less likelihood for military and political success. The convergence of widespread racial and class ingredients would serve to expand the guerrilla wars beyond the scope of the target territories and beyond Africa as well.[4] The deliberate conduct of a racial crusade on the part of blacks would further internationalize a conflict that already has a central racial component thanks to white Southern Africans who have made race the organizing principle for their states and for social, and hence economic, policies. The chances for such a surfacing of incipient attitudes and a hardening of political divisions along racial lines are high, thereby facilitating greater coordination among liberation movements and their allies.[5]

4. See Harold R. Isaacs, "Color in World Affairs," *Foreign Affairs*, XLVII, No. 2 (January 1969), 235–250; and Locksley Edmondson, "The Challenges of Race: From Entrenched White Power to Rising Black Power," *International Journal*, XXIV, No. 4 (Autumn 1969), 693–716.
5. I would argue that the policies of President Banda, Chief Jonathan, President Tsirinana, and others notwithstanding, in the long run will see a hardening of political divisions along racial lines. See my "Southern African Bridge Builders and the Rationalization of International Tokenism," prepared for a conference on "The Role of Public Policies in the Elimination of Racial Discrimination," Aspen, Colorado, June 7–9, 1970 (ditto, 12 pp.).

c. *Cooperation among Antiguerrilla Target Regimes*

The extent of the coordination of antiguerrilla activities in white Southern Africa has been fairly high. The reason is clear—their futures are jointly bound up with one another. Geopolitical factors seem to be emphasized by each of the white partners. For example, speaking in January 1968, a South African official said that it was time South Africans realized that if the soldiers Portugal had in Angola and Mozambique were to be withdrawn, South Africa could become involved in a "terrorist war" within weeks. He went on to add that the Portuguese territories and Rhodesia had become South Africa's first line of defense.[6] This is but one expression of an attitude that has been recognized in South Africa for several years.

The Defense Act of 1913 provided that South African armed forces would serve in Southern Africa, both inside and outside the Union, but the effect was to restrict their service to the High Commission Territories, South West Africa, and Southern Rhodesia.[7] Later, in 1939, Minister of Defence Oswald Pirow presciently argued that the purpose of the Union Defence Force was limited to helping settler communities in British Africa, should Africans revolt.[8]

Since the outbreak of the war in Angola, however, initial misgivings about the reliability of Portugal as an ally have been overcome. Although many Afrikaners still have their doubts about a too close association with the "British" in Rhodesia, to say nothing of the Latin Portuguese (who are, after all, Roman Catholics, and who publicly profess multiracialism), South African officials have sought to foster greater military cooperation, in planning and practice, with their regional white neighbors. Claims of an "unholy alliance" have been in the news since about 1961. Despite a 1967 statement at the United Nations by South Africa's Foreign Minister, Dr. Hilgard Muller, that a "mutual security arrangement" exists among the white regimes of Southern Africa and the black governments of Botswana, Lesotho, and Malawi,[9] officials of Portugal, Rhodesia, and South

6. Speech by T. J. A. Gerdener, at the time Administrator of Natal Province, reported in *Africa Diary*, VIII, No. 3 (January 14–20, 1968), 3753.
7. J. E. Spence, *Republic Under Pressure: A Study of South African Foreign Policy* (London: Oxford University Press, 1965), p. 8.
8. *Ibid.*, pp. 7–8.
9. *New York Times*, October 5, 1967.

Africa repeatedly deny the existence of any such formal alliance. On one such occasion, Prime Minister Vorster said: "We are good friends with both Portugal and Rhodesia, and good friends do not need a pact. Good friends know what their duty is if a neighbour's house is on fire. I assure you that whatever becomes necessary will be done." [10] And this is generally believed to be true—by whites in the region and by African nationalists, too—that South Africa will do whatever is necessary to try to prevent revolutionary nationalists from nearing her borders. Although rumors persist, whether or not the alliance has been formalized is not crucial. In practice collaboration is extensive.

We have seen how the various nationalist liberation movements are aware of the possibilities open to them through protracted guerrilla warfare, and how some military thinkers and planners in the southern sphere are also alert to such possibilities. Not only have Portugal, Rhodesia, and South Africa concentrated on training and equipping their security forces for counterinsurgency operations, but they have gone even further. Commandant Neil Orpen of South Africa, for example, in his book *Total Defense*, advocates that South Africa begin to build up her irregular forces and train them in commando resistance, a tactic used with success by the Boers. By and large, however, the white regimes have probably extended themselves to the limit in personnel terms, in amassing contemporary military superiority[11] (see Table XI). Black Africa and Africans within white-governed states have barely begun to tap the human resources at their disposal. On the other hand, they do not as yet possess the economic resources to sustain larger standing armies or irregular forces.

On the matter of cooperation, evidence seems to point clearly to a higher degree of existing cooperation among antiguerrilla forces in white Southern Africa than among guerrilla units, and a prospect that such cooperation will continue and even expand in the future. Less likely is increased cooperation between antiguerrilla forces in black-governed Af-

10. *ARB*, IV, No. 8 (September 15, 1967), 845C. For a similar Portuguese statement, see *ibid.*, VI, No. 6 (July 15, 1969), 1452B–C.
11. A discussion of force levels in the region will appear in my forthcoming study of international relations in Southern Africa. Up-to-date data on forces can be found in various publications of the Institute for Strategic Studies, London, particularly the annual studies, *The Military Balance* and *Strategic Survey*.

TABLE XI

APPROXIMATE MILITARY FORCE LEVELS
IN SOUTHERN AFRICA, 1966–1969

	Regular Army	Fully Trained Reserves	Air Force	Navy	Police	Police Reserves	Armed Militia or Guerrillas
Rhodesia	4,500	12,500	900	n.i.	6,400	28,500	n.i.
Port. Angola	60,000	n.i.	3,000	3,500	5,000	n.i.	15,000
Port. Mozam.	40,000	n.i	2,700	3,500	3,000	n.i.	7,000
So. Africa	28,000*	45,000	4,700	2,500	34,437	20,000	58,000
Congo (K)	36,300	—	600	100	20,800	n.i.	n.i.
Tanzania	7,900	4,000	300	100	8,500	n.i.	n.i.
Zambia	4,000	1,000	300	—	7,000	1,600	n.i.
Malawi	850	n.i.	n.i.	n.i.	3,000	n.i.	n.i.
Mozambique	—	—	—	—	—	—	8,500
Angola	—	—	—	—	—	—	(GRAE) 3–8,000 (MPLA) 5–7,000
Zimbabwe	—	—	—	—	—	—	200–500

Sources: Wood, Armed Forces of African States; Legassick, "African Guerrilla Activity"; Vernon McKay, "Southern Africa and Its Implications for American Policy," in William A. Hance (ed.), Southern Africa and the United States (New York: Columbia University Press, 1968), pp. 1–32; The Military Balance, 1968–1969 (London: Institute for Strategic Studies, 1968), and various other disparate articles.
n.i. = no information
* includes Citizen Force under training at the time

rica. Unless the OAU or some similar standing organization can be renovated to provide for central coordination, it is not likely that ad hoc organizations will develop. This is largely because guerrilla movements directed against established black regimes are themselves disjointed, territorially narrow, and politically parochial. The issue of the extent of cooperation on either side does not necessarily lower chances for guerrilla uprisings and incursions.

In some respects it is pointless to detail the distribution of military power in the context of revolutionary warfare. This seems to be the case in Africa especially. A classic military confrontation involving the armed forces of State A against State X is not likely in the short run (five to ten years), nor is a frontal clash between two sets of formal or informal (but entirely committed) allies, A-B-C against X-Y-Z.

What good, hypothetically, is the knowledge that State A can mobilize

30,000 well-armed and reasonably well-trained soldiers, a squadron of jet fighters, 25 helicopters reinforced by 15,000 police, if, at the outbreak of hostilities, its social and economic fabric may collapse because of a lack of popular support for the government or the war? Since most of the states in Africa cannot be sure of unquestioning support for a military undertaking of a general magnitude, this is one factor that would require more complete country-by-country surveys. Most discussions of military force levels generally assume an essential stability of the political and economic systems necessary to sustain forces in the field. In the context of the African states, this assumption should not go unquestioned. Likewise, although it seems likely that non-African actors will participate in any general conflict in Southern Africa, no one is quite sure what the alignments and the extent and nature of the respective external activities will be. Thus, again, the unknowns leave too much to conjecture. Finally, and most importantly, is that experience of the past three decades shows that apparent superiority in the traditional components of military power are not alone adequate to defeat a well-organized and determined liberation movement, particularly if the latter employs guerrilla tactics. The classic components of military power are not to be minimized entirely, for they serve as useful deterrents to potential rebels or to outsiders considering the prospects of intervention. Still, modern theories of guerrilla warfare clearly indicate that to the traditional factors of warfare must be added others which are far less quantifiable and yet may work to the advantage of insurgent elements.

D. *Extent and Nature of External Involvement*

Guerrilla warfare can be said to be at least as much a function of international as it is of national politics. To ignore this is to blind ourselves to a perspective vital to understanding the future of guerrilla warfare. No state in Africa is "unconditionally viable" in that it cannot prevent the foreign imposition of a drastic political and social change inside its own borders.[12] A major revolutionary guerrilla war for supremacy in a strategic territory is like a mortally wounded animal; it attracts the buzzards of international politics ready to feed on the carrion. The actual

12. See: Boulding, *Conflict and Defense*, pp. 58–79.

character of the war tends to determine the behavior and makeup of the international actors that become involved. Since today's international environment is unstable, guerrilla movements and their opponents tend to assume the ideological coloration of (or are at least regarded as replicating) the principal adversaries of the global contest.[13] Major states see an opportunity to participate in unauthorized violence, and this leads to a further deterioration of the norms and procedures designed to safeguard the autonomy, independence, and legal equality of sovereign states.

There are a number of possible alternatives relating to external involvement in guerrilla wars. Regarding the number of actors, there may be no intervention, or unilateral or multilateral participation. Another scale ranging from passive to active participation can include strategies such as votes in international bodies and recognition, acting as a host territory, providing material assistance, and direct military intervention with or without an invitation. The historical patterns indicate that in certain circumstances limited involvement has a spiraling effect leading to increasing involvement—what American journalists have called the "slippery slope" syndrome.[14] Involvement of one great power in the East-West competition or in that between the USSR and the Chinese People's Republic, usually though not always, has the effect of compelling the opponents to intervene. Revolutionary intervention often gives rise to counterrevolutionary intervention or vice versa; or it may inspire further revolutionary intervention by another power seeking to gain influence in the movement. In other words, intervention in what is regarded as a globally important guerrilla war has a symmetrical character that in turn raises the stakes and expands the war. This is only in those territories that are regarded as strategically vital to the great powers or where the powers sense that an important ideological conflict is at issue. Ironically, once an external force has become involved actively, it could well be subject to a further set of complications. The established regime has a tendency to rely more and more upon the external force. As this occurs, the external

13. See the excellent essay in Richard A. Falk, *The Status of Law in International Society* (Princeton, N.J.: Princeton University Press, 1970), pp. 60–83.
14. For a brief discussion of this phenomenon, see Adam Yarmolinsky, "American Foreign Policy and the Decision to Intervene," *Journal of International Affairs*, XXII, No. 2 (1968), 231–235. This entire issue is devoted to "Intervention and World Politics."

force becomes enmeshed in the tasks of client management. The host government possesses authority but little power, and the external ally possesses power without authority. Both actors become dependent on as well as imprisoned by one another.[15] The United States-Vietnamese pattern is illustrative. It is still a question of how much the United States people and their governments have learned from their Southeast Asian experiences, and whether this will have a spill-over into their future African policies. Unless their involvement can be surgically "clean," as in the Stanleyville rescue operation of 1964, which would be unusual, the morass of involvement in guerrilla warfare in Africa could be enervating.

The exact level of foreign involvement in Africa's guerrilla wars is not easy to determine. On the guerrilla side we find that the Communist countries supply the bulk of financial and material assistance for Southern African nationalist parties. Since May 1968 there has been a significant increase in Chinese assistance. The fundamental competition for allegiance among guerrilla movements is increasingly between the two Communist powers rather than between Communist and anti-Communist sources.[16] Movements heavily dependent on Chinese aid are the smaller SWANU, UNITA, and COREMO, with PAC, ZANU, and FRELIMO also drawing upon the Chinese. The chief recipients of Russian assistance are MPLA, ANC, ZAPU, FRELIMO, and SWAPO. These sources of aid are likely to expand tremendously in the future, with greater Chinese assistance and perhaps a less impressive increase in Russian aid. This is not to say that the influence of these countries will grow proportionately, however. In contrast, direct bilateral aid from the West is practically nonexistent and tends to stigmatize the movement it seeks to support. The only other source of assistance that could in some measure offset the concentration of supplies from Communist sources comes from the host countries (as in the case of GRAE) and from the OAU itself.

The African Liberation Committee was created in 1963 by the OAU.

15. See the excellent paper by Yashpal Tandon, "The Internationalization of the Civil War: Lessons from the Congo, Nigeria and Vietnam," presented to the Conference on "Africa in World Affairs: The Next Thirty Years," Makerere University College, Kampala, Uganda, December 13–15, 1969 (mimeo., 25 pp.); as well as James N. Rosenau (ed.), *International Aspects of Civil Strife* (Princeton, N.J.: Princeton University Press, 1964).

16. See Patrick Keatley's series of articles in the *Manchester Guardian Weekly*, July 24 and 31, August 7 and 14, 1969.

Its assignment was to coordinate aid and to grant legitimacy of a sort to acceptable revolutionary movements. The imprecise criteria for recognition and assistance applied by the ALC relates to: (1) demonstrated field success; (2) a willingness to establish "common action fronts"; and (3) political and ideological reliability. The first criterion seems to be the most important although it has been loosely applied to include not only military success but a broadly-based popular following, particularly in territories where guerrilla warfare has been limited or nonexistent. This policy has given a distinct advantage to movements that have already been able to attract external support and/or to have initiated hostilities. Thus the overall impact of Russian and Chinese assistance is magnified, since an OAU endorsement is likely to follow military effectiveness or activity.

Although the ALC has also sought to establish itself as the coordinating agency for all forms of external assistance, it has been unable to do so. Its annual budget of approximately $1.7 million is only about one-tenth of the total assistance received by revolutionary movements. The ALC has reluctantly delegated responsibility to host countries bordering on target territories. In fact, this devolution of responsibility merely represents the legitimization of the central role of host governments.

OAU recognition is of capital importance. Only recognized parties are eligible for ALC aid. Criteria are applied unevenly. In some territories (Mozambique and Namibia) only one movement has been sanctioned and assisted. In others (Zimbabwe and Angola) multiple recognition prevails, although in reality assistance is concentrated in one movement.

Lately, the ALC policy seems to have favored more "radical" parties. Parties with linkages to the West have been rejected, and distribution of OAU support reflects this. Revolutionary members of the ALC have gained the upper hand since about 1965. But with or without ALC support, guerrilla movements have found by experience that the cooperation of a sympathetic host government ultimately is the most helpful form of external assistance.

So far, OAU assistance has been little more than symbolic. It is not likely to be increased in the short run. The organization itself is too conservative, and it has little effective power to enforce its decisions upon member states. Moreover, the OAU is not in a position to prevent intervention in Africa by external forces. Its policies during the Nigerian and Congolese civil wars bear out these generalizations. The possibility of future OAU involvement on the antiguerrilla side, that is in support of established black regimes, must not be ruled out.

What about UN participation in African guerrilla wars? Politics within the United Nations seem to make participation unlikely, unless changes in the configuration of power in the General Assembly and Security Council should enable those organs to arrive at substantive decisions including active military intervention or assistance. The experience of the Congo is enlightening. During the early months of the 1960 disorder there was a modicum of international cooperation to direct an organized UN participation in Congolese affairs. But the consensus broke down quickly thereafter, and the Soviet Union was eased out of the decisional process for UNOC operations. A new coalition of United States and moderate Afro-Asian governments permitted UNOC to function. But the financial weakness, as well as the operational infirmities of the United Nations, led to an attitude within the Organization of caution about deep entanglement in domestic civil politics. Whether this reticence can be overcome depends more on the distribution of power within the Organization and upon the relationship of that power to the overall constellation of world power, than it does to experiential reservations. For the next five to ten years it appears that the United Nations will not be equipped or willing to indulge actively in African civil wars. Nor is there any indication that African statesmen would want the United Nations to get involved. Rather, they would argue that the OAU is better suited and able to settle disputes without the possibility of foreign great power entrée into the continent.

The question of external support has so far been considerably more important for the nationalist movements than for the white regimes of Southern Africa. Without a host country and material and financial assistance, few nationalists would be able to operate at any level of effectiveness. In contrast, the problem for the white governments is not financial—they can find funds for defense expenditures—but political. Thus, in the formal sense, it is incorrect to describe any sort of military relationship (except for those between Portugal, Rhodesia, and South Africa and between Portugal and NATO) with external governments as assistance or aid. Their task, though no less difficult, is to convince foreign governments to permit arms manufacturers in their own countries to sell war materials to the white regimes.

For the Republic of South Africa this is not all that easy. A 1963 Security Council resolution called for a total embargo on the sale of arms, ammunition, and military vehicles to the Republic, to which the United States, Canada, Switzerland, and West Germany acceded. Britain and France maintained the right to sell arms provided they are "not suitable for dealing with internal troubles." Simply put, if a state unilaterally determines that a particular class of weapons are primarily for defense against external enemies, then it permits licensing for the sale. Is the ANC, then, an external enemy? If we accept the position of the South African Minister of Police that not a single "terrorist" is at large in the Republic, then any arms sale would be legitimized since all enemies are, *ipso facto*, external. At any rate, these are virtually meaningless distinctions since South Africa is practically self-sufficient in the manufacture of the less sophisticated weaponry of counterinsurgency. More expensive and complex weapons systems, however, are supplied from abroad, embargo notwithstanding. The embargo has been easily evaded, though with some public defensiveness, by suppliers. Moreover, the UN embargo came a bit too late to have a deep short-run effect. From 1960 to 1964 South Africa had undertaken a major renewal and expansion in heavy military equipment. Only when one considers selected strategic materials or a long-term arms embargo to extend beyond the period of obsolescence of her present weapons stock, can one justifiably talk about South African vulnerability.[17]

By far more significant is Portugal's NATO association.[18] Without it she would be militarily incapable of sustaining the level of counterguerrilla activity she now mounts in Africa. This is for several reasons. First,

17. For discussion of this question, see William F. Gutteridge, "The Strategic Implications of Sanctions against South Africa," in Ronald Segal (ed.), *Sanctions Against South Africa* (Baltimore: Penguin Books, 1964), pp. 107–115; and several other selections in this somewhat outdated book.
18. Fairly complete coverage of this issue can be found in S. J. Bosgra and Chr. van Krimpen, *Portugal and NATO* (Amsterdam: Angola Comité, October 1969). This pamphlet successfully documents the importance of this relationship and concludes that NATO members and NATO as an organization are crucial accessories to the Portuguese military effort in Africa.

some armaments which Portugal has acquired as a member of NATO have been employed in her African wars. How much is hard to say. Although in such instances her NATO partners insist that NATO armaments are to be used exclusively for defense in the North Atlantic area, these provisions of the treaty have been difficult to enforce. Nevertheless, it is clear that some NATO weapons are used in Africa. It is equally clear, however, that Portugal's main benefit from NATO membership is that her domestic-European military requirements are secured, freeing her own less impressive resources for full use in Africa. A second benefit related to the first is that through her NATO membership Portugal can more easily purchase weapons from manufacturers in NATO countries. Norway has refused any sales to Portugal. All other member states permit sales but usually seek to extract a promise that such weapons will not be used outside the treaty area. Portugal herself maintains that such weaponry is used only for defensive purposes "within Portuguese territory." This, of course, enables her to claim that her African possessions are "overseas territories," not colonies, and thus an "integral" part of metropolitan Portugal, clearly within the North Atlantic.

Additional benefits come to Portugal in financial terms. Under a cost-sharing formula, each NATO state pays what it can in infrastructure costs. In Portugal's case this amounts to only 0.28 percent of the total. But since a number of NATO installations are in Portugal, an estimated $6 million in additional NATO funds are spent in Portugal annually. Add to that the $10 million per year pumped into the Portuguese economy (mostly from the Azores base) by the U.S. military, and the approximately $500 million spent by the U.S. military there between 1959 and 1965.[19] West Germany, France, and the United States continue to be the chief military suppliers for Portugal. And their pooled knowledge of and experience with guerrilla warfare has been transmitted to Portuguese officers and military planners as well.

Both Portugal and South Africa have expended considerable energy trying to convince NATO military men that the most vulnerable flank of

19. A summary discussion of U.S.-Portuguese military relations can be found in Marcum, *Angolan Revolution,* pp. 272–277 and 182–187. See also Robert A. Diamond and David Fouquet, "Portugal and the United States," and Basil Davidson, "Arms and the Portuguese," both in *Africa Report,* XV, No. 5 (May 1970), 15–17 and 10–11.

NATO is the South Atlantic and particularly Southern Africa.[20] Playing upon the idea that Britain's withdrawal of forces east of Suez has created a vacuum that the Soviet Union and especially her naval forces seek to fill, both countries have appealed to the obsessive anti-Communism of the United States, and to some elements in France and the United Kingdom, and have pushed for the creation of a SATO as part of, or coordinated with, NATO. Whether or not NATO likes it, South Africa regards herself as part of an organization to defend Western European civilization against Communist and racial incursions. In South African eyes it is just a matter of time before the rest of NATO recognizes South Africa's strategic importance and comes to respect and support her defensive contribution. Whether or not that support will be forthcoming is an important question. To a large extent, insofar as the United States is concerned, an answer depends on the extent to which such a decision will be based upon Cold War images and the relative measure of influence of military men or political men. Given the "slippery slope" syndrome and an initial decision by civilian politicians to aid white Southern Africa in a small, material way, it would appear that further incremental decisions by military men or by politicians dependent on military intelligence and advice could drag a reluctant government into another quagmire. Depending on the degree of Communist leverage over the guerrilla movements, the ability of South African publicists to play on this and the racial issue, and the capacity of American investors in white Africa and conservative pressure groups to influence policy, this is possible. In the short run, the prospect of direct U.S. military assistance is not likely. But in the short run, normal and cordial economic and social relations may serve the white Southern African purposes adequately.[21] Meanwhile, the long run depends on de-

20. Abdul S. Minty, *South Africa's Defense Strategy* (London: Anti-Apartheid Movement, October 1969), pp. 20–31. A representative official viewpoint was expressed in a speech by the Commandant-General of the South African Defence Force, General R. C. Hiemstra, "Containing Communism," Africa Institute *Bulletin* (Pretoria), VII, No. 9 (October 1969), 387–402.

21. Professor George W. Shepherd, Jr., argues cogently that according to every interaction variable he surveys (between white Southern Africa and the West European and North American powers) "the policies of the core states [Europe and North America] are strengthening Southern African states and integrating them more closely into the sub-system. . . . It is hard to avoid the conclusion that step-by-step the systemic relationship with Southern Africa is dragging the core nations into supporting the South African Whites in the counter-revolutionary struggle." See his "The White

velopments too complex to foresee in American domestic and international politics.

Apparently, the European powers would rather continue "business as usual," and should guerrilla confrontation escalate, they might wash their hands of the military struggle, attempt to play it completely by ear, and try not to alienate either side too much so that commercial doors would remain open regardless of who wins. If the United States could possibly avoid being placed in a Cold War ideological bind, she might well prefer the latter course, too. In Southern Africa, the United States has preferred to defer to Great Britain in policy initiation. She has done so on the Rhodesian question, and may perceive the South African situation similarly. In this case, however, a Conservative government in London might be more willing to trade in arms with the white Southern Africans, and to resist sanction and boycott efforts of international bodies. Future intervention by the United States is likely to take the course of attempts to control preventatively the political situation in a more subtle fashion—to prevent open warfare and to encourage reformist and proximate solutions to problems that, as presently conceived in Southern Africa, do not admit of half-measures.

e. *The Global Distribution of Power*

About all that can be done in this section, given its thoroughly speculative character, is to sketch some probable developments in world politics over the next three decades, and to attempt to suggest how they might affect the future of guerrilla warfare in Africa. The global configuration of power seems to be turbulent. Although the basic bipolarization of power has not disintegrated markedly, there is evidence indicating not only a breakdown in political bipolarization, but a growing and potentially challenging nuclear power in China. Moreover, with the increasing usage of localized force, the super powers have not been able to have their way throughout the world. Unprecedented nuclear capability has not been translated into global hegemony in the sense that their words

Atlantic Sub-system and Black Southern Africa," presented to the Colloquium on International Law and Development in Southern Africa, U.C.L.A., April 8, 1970 (mimeo.), pp. 36–37.

are fiat in their spheres of influence, however defined. As long as nuclear force is distributed so as to deter its activation by either side even in geopolitically remote areas, the smaller power can function in no great fear of nuclear attack. But a so-called nuclear umbrella is no guarantee against great power involvement in its affairs in other ways. Likewise, the presence of large standing or volunteer armies in a regional context has taken on a new significance either for encouraging or discouraging guerrilla operations. The arms race has been so politically and financially expensive that weapons development could well take a radical turn in three decades' time. Long-term forecasting, at best, can do little more than attempt to provide a rough estimate of shifts in power relations between states. It cannot expect to forecast specific events or series of events. Even so, there is always a chance that some fortuitous event can ignite a chain reaction which will radically alter the tempo and direction of international processes, or at least destroy the basis on which forecasts were undertaken. These caveats apply to long-term forecasting in primarily stable international systems. Saul Friedländer maintains that in unstable systems, long-term forecasting must be regarded as impossible.[22] It is just such an unstable system that exists and will probably continue to exist in the latter quarter of this century. If this is the case, forecasting is futile. Nevertheless, conjecture is important, and could be helpful.

It is likely that the next three decades will continue to see the growth of Chinese power, first on a regional and then on a global scale. This force will further enable the Chinese to become more actively involved in guerrilla movements in Africa, and to encourage African militancy at the expense of the Soviet Union's professed leadership of the Communist revolutionary movement internationally. Indeed, continued Russian economic development might well turn her into a status quo force in areas beyond her periphery (where she already acts as a conservator of the postwar territorial allocations). The possibility remains that the Soviet Union might seek to reassert herself as champion of the revolutionary forces in the less-developed world, but this appears less and less likely as Chinese rhetoric and activism is supplemented by Chinese economic and military power. So the possibility of an arrangement, formal or informal, between the United States and the Soviet Union is not so prepos-

22. Friedländer, "Forecasting in International Relations," 43.

terous. Regarding Africa, this may come either in the form of a distribution of influence areas where competition is limited or eliminated entirely, or in the form of a less ambitious formalization whereby the two powers agree that competition will continue in Africa, but they will not allow the issues to drag them into a direct nuclear or military confrontation. If hegemony in Africa passes to the USSR, guerrilla warfare in Southern Africa will probably ensue on a larger scale. If hegemony devolves to the United States, prospects for successful guerrilla warfare diminish measurably. If both keep hands off in an hegemonial sense, the likelihood of guerrilla warfare will not be radically affected, since both pledged not to go to the brink of direct conflict.

We will probably see a further proliferation of nuclear weapons, some of them rather crude devices without credible delivery systems.[23] Within a decade, the Republic of South Africa could possess nuclear weapons capable of regional application. Despite the South African vote in the General Assembly in June 1968 which "commended" the Nonproliferation Treaty, the explanation of her vote by Ambassador Botha did not bespeak of all-out approval.[24] However, the Republic fears direct external intervention in an area in which she feels she has a proprietary right. She would probably avoid using her nuclear weapons for more than propaganda purposes. The Western and Russian nuclear umbrella could thereby shield the black states of Africa from all but the most irrational usage, not an unthinkable contingency given the religious fervor and ideological constitution of white South Africa.

Throughout this era, the relative military and economic weakness of the black states of Africa seems likely to continue, with selected exceptions thereafter. Nigeria and the Congo may be likely candidates for medium power status. They have geographical advantage, are surrounded by smaller states, have the unexploited resources that the rest of the world values, and have the extensive populations necessary to develop them. A modicum of economic development could be parlayed into continental power, even in the face of an industrialized and strategically situated South Africa. But invariably this prospect would necessitate

23. John P. de Gara, "Nuclear Proliferation and Security," *International Conciliation*, No. 578 (May 1970).
24. United Nations, General Assembly Res. 2373 (XXII), June 12, 1968; and United Nations Doc. A/C.1/PV. 1579, June 5, 1968, 11.

new and radical leadership capable of transcending conditions described earlier. With strong bases for operations (the Congo would be more valuable locationally) the various guerrilla movements could be more formidable, provided, of course, that the governments could be enlisted in active support. Speculation about such alterations in the overall global distribution of power enables us to make some brief and very general projections about the future of guerrilla warfare in Africa.

F. Short-Run Trends (Five to Ten Years)

In black-governed Africa, it appears that the conditions for political violence persist. It is not likely that most governments will be able to eliminate those conditions. That being the case, what is necessary for this to be transformed into guerrilla struggle are generalizable ideologies, astute leadership, and external assistance during the earlier stages of the movements. By and large, however, in Black Africa guerrilla movements have been parochial in appeal and will continue to be until a revolutionary popular base can be hammered out to transcend primordial loyalties. Objectively, the base is there. Subjectively, the base is not conscious of its potential unity or power. Likewise, massive external assistance for guerrillas is even less likely than assistance for the established governments' antiguerrilla forces. Until the Southern African issue is resolved, help for guerrilla movements against black regimes will be difficult to attract. So, the picture looks to be one of continued and even more widespread guerrilla struggle in Black Africa, but efforts will probably be indecisive, sporadic, localized, and generally of low intensity, ebbing and flowing as a series of relatively isolated actions and reactions.

Against white Southern Africa, guerrilla warfare will probably continue to smoulder and increase in focus and intensity. The issues are indeed generalizable and uncompromisable in these territories. Without the possibility for remedial change to dissipate incipient support for hardening guerrilla positions, it will be increasingly easier to attract support and recruits from and in target territories. Guinea (Bissau) will probably be almost entirely liberated (if not entirely), although PAIGC may not be able to get Portugal to negotiate her final departure or to deliver the military *coup de grâce*. Portugal might look for a face-saving alternative by negotiating with a more moderate or malleable party, such as FLING, and then withdrawing, forcing FLING to deal directly with the PAIGC forces. In Southern Africa, guerrilla forces will likely concentrate on Portuguese Africa and Rhodesia, temporarily postponing the Republic of South Africa for geopolitical and other practical reasons. In Angola and Mozambique, the war probably will be spread territorially although, barring unity in the movements, it will continue to sputter. In Zimbabwe, the long-term enfeebling effects of economic sanctions (even though they have been porous),[25] a growing internal unrest, and more widespread and effective guerrilla raids may combine to frighten many settlers southward and to cut down on the inflow of white settlers from Europe and the dominions. It is quite possible that a general panic may set in that could lead to a majority government before the end of the decade. Retreat is still possible to South Africa, and with such an option, one's threshold of tolerance for sacrifice and danger is usually lowered. Even though guerrilla struggles are more advanced in the Portuguese territories, political and economic factors combine to indicate that majority government may well be achieved in Zimbabwe before the independence of the Portuguese territories. In fact, the Portuguese territories, especially Angola, might still act out the Rhodesian experience of a unilateral declaration of independence by a white-settler minority dissatisfied with the support from Lisbon. So far, the magnitude of the Portuguese military effort in her territories diminishes this prospect immensely.

It might be useful at this point to explore the potential effects of the establishment of black governments in any of the territories adjacent to the Republic of South Africa. Most of the principals, black and white, have assumed so far a classic "domino" stance: if any single vital territory were to change government (in racial terms), then it would be impossible for the white regimes to maintain the status quo in the rest of the area. But this is a simplistic overview of regional politics. So much

25. Johan Galtung, "On the Effects of International Economic Sanctions: With Examples from the Case of Rhodesia," *World Politics*, XIX, No. 3 (April 1967), 378–416.

depends on the character of the newly established black regime. Admittedly, if it attained power in the crucible of guerrilla struggle, it would be awkward to abandon its revolutionary posture and policies toward the remainder of white Southern Africa. Nevertheless, the exigencies of economic survival might necessitate a working relationship with the ideological enemy. To be sure, the degree of maneuverability open to states in situations where their linkages to neighboring states are intensive and extensive is a matter of perception as well as objectivity. The different responses of Malawi and Zambia to roughly analogous situations is a case in point.[26] So, if a black government were set up in Mozambique or Zimbabwe, it is not altogether clear that it would be completely free to assist revolutionary forces operating against neighboring white regimes. The color of those in governmental positions is no guarantee of militancy in regional politics. Angola is sufficiently independent of her white neighbors (in economic terms) to enable a black government to be true to her ideological predispositions. It should be stressed, however, that objective economic factors alone do not determine policy. Nor are we saying that an economically dependent or penetrated black state cannot assist revolutionary movements. What is being suggested is that the fall of a white regime in a given territory and its replacement by a black regime is no assurance that, ipso facto, the revolutionary cause will be aided, in the aggregate, although such an event is still necessary if revolution is to be ultimately achieved throughout the region. The fall of one white regime does not necessarily presage the fall of all white regimes. If, however, a black government were fully determined to assist revolutionary forces, it would be exceedingly difficult to prevent serious instability in target territories. South Africa is obviously the core of the regional political system. Serious instability in that state would almost assuredly lead to the downfall of all regional white regimes. The reverse, though likely, is not necessarily the case.[27]

26. A discussion in detail of this issue appears in Kenneth W. Grundy, "The Foreign Policies of Black Southern Africa," a paper presented to the Symposium on International Law and National Development in Southern Africa, held under the auspices of the African Studies Center of the University of California, Los Angeles, February 25, 1970 (mimeo., 56 pp.). Further details on regional economic relations are treated in Chap. III of my forthcoming study of international relations in Southern Africa.
27. Larry W. Bowman, "The Subordinate State System of Southern Africa," *International Studies Quarterly*, XII, No. 3 (September 1968), 231–261.

G. *Long-Run Trends* (*Thirty Years*)

The possible short-run trends sketched for Black Africa in the preceding section might well continue throughout the succeeding decades. Or we might suggest a modified set of alternative futures. But, first, we must remember that we are dealing with some three dozen states and the range of variables and alternatives open to them is immense. So when attempting to preview the future, we refer merely to possible general patterns and contours.

Within three decades we could probably expect some boundary readjustments and territorial arrangements that might provide the opportunity for remedial governmental changes that might reduce the possibility for the organized and violent expression of primordial dissatisfactions. Through successful consolidation and the actual elimination of nonviable states, obvious sources of challenge to central governments might be diminished. In the remaining states, *modus vivendi* and *operandi* between central governments and their geographical components could reduce some of the causes for further strife. Large, structural state and governmental modification may provide the basis for continuing incremental changes, thereby sapping dissident movements of their constituencies. Added to this is the further possibility for greater political socialization within individual states. This may be brought about by conscious politicization of the masses, the control of education, expanded literacy, growing wealth, declining inequalities of income, and advancing urbanization and industrialization. Moreover, the armed forces should grow in efficiency and especially in their counterinsurgency skills. If these developments take place, revolutionary units might be more inclined to rely upon military intervention and the coup d'état as the most efficient and reliable avenue for governmental change.[28] So, depending upon the adaptability of African regimes, an alternative future is for a decline in the use of guerrilla warfare in Black Africa. The fact that no guerrilla movement has displaced or achieved independence from a Black African government to date is a lesson not lost on many African revolutionaries.

The future of the white governments of Southern Africa depends largely on the external environment. One must be aware that it is prob-

28. Edward Luttwak, *Coup d'État: A Practical Handbook* (New York: Fawcett, 1969).

ably misleading to regard all of white Southern Africa as a unit. Although it is apparent that the present trend is toward greater collaboration in a common defensive posture, there are, on the other hand, certain seeds of disintegration among the white inhabitants of these territories, mostly based on national and religious prejudices. It is quite possible that in the face of enduring extensive and intensive pressure, the front might collapse.[29] Should the Western great powers support the white regimes, the latter could still be in power thirty years hence. If they remain ostensibly neutral or continue to support indirectly these governments through economic, political, and social association, guerrilla units might have a difficult time initiating and conducting hostilities in an even more efficient and thoroughly repressive milieu. It could be argued that within these states there still exists a potential for internal resolution—that within the various segments of these societies regenerative forces exist which might encourage compromise and cooperation between the races.[30] While I am not a specialist on South Africa, my view is that international intervention in some form is needed to compel whites to negotiate a settlement, assuming that such nonviolent alternative is indeed still alive. If, on the other hand, the Western great powers actively oppose the white regimes, the latter would likely be removed or at least renovated, not necessarily by externally supported guerrilla forces, but by the combination of a credible threat of widespread and intense political violence and great power pressure. Such a change may possibly see the great powers attempt to provide guarantees for the white minorities in the region, through constitutional and legal arrangements or perhaps through some sort of international agreement involving the major powers and the contending regional parties. The range of possibilities, from integration to separation, are many.[31] It could be then that guerrilla warfare may de-

29. For example, in a simulation exercise at M.I.T. dealing with crisis in Southern Africa, the Republic of South Africa was willing to trade off the white regime in Rhodesia in order to prevent the outbreak of war in the region and the likely military intervention of the USSR. Robert H. Bates, *A Simulation Study of a Crisis in Southern Africa* (Cambridge, Mass.: Arms Control Project, Center on International Studies, Massachusetts Institute of Technology, n.d.), Publication C/69-20 (mimeo., 19 pp.). See also Bowman, "The Subordinate State System," 251–253.
30. See the argument in Kuper, *An African Bourgeoisie*, pp. 386–387; and in his "Nonviolence Revisited," in Rotberg and Mazrui, *Protest and Power*, pp. 788–804.
31. See the systematic and reasoned article by Austin T. Turk, "The Futures of South Africa," *Social Forces*, XLVI, No. 3 (1966), 402–412.

cline in usage in the latter decade or two of the twentieth century. In other words, the use of guerrilla warfare may peak by 1980 or 1985.

All this being said, let me offer a demurrer. It is clear that "correct prediction" is impossible given the subject matter. We should be satisfied with the mere anticipation of some of the most general alternative futures and contingent crises. About the only "correct prediction" we might venture at this point is that we can expect, with absolute assurance of contradiction, that a good many of these previews will necessitate radical revision in the forthcoming years.

It is because of the very tentative nature of this endeavor and the treacherous reality of the situation in Southern Africa, however, that we feel compelled to go a step further, this time to look into the future in more normative and prescriptive terms. Thus may we relate the empirical-descriptive substance of the preceding chapters to the value preferences touched upon in the Preface and in Chapters One and Three.

Chapter Seven

TOWARDS A
MORE ACCEPTABLE
FUTURE IN
SOUTHERN AFRICA

So far the discussion has concentrated upon the subject of guerrilla warfare. It is not entirely fortuitous that this interest has brought us to an ultimate focus on Southern Africa, because it is there that guerrilla warfare is most likely to be consciously and convincingly pursued in the coming decades. In terms of a preferred world order it is in Southern Africa that a resort to violent instruments of change seems most acceptable. In order to understand how guerrilla warfare can be a serious component of change in Southern Africa, however, it is necessary to discuss the future of the region in a broader context.

The futures suggested in the preceding chapter have been based upon perceived trends and forces currently operative in Africa. The result has been the presentation of what one could call counterutopias. We have seen, if I may summarize, a developing pattern that includes: (1) a weapons technology that continues to favor white status quo regimes; (2) cooperation between guerrilla movements and between these movements and independent Black Africa that is competitive, weak, or nonexistent; (3) high level collaboration between the white regimes that is growing stronger; (4) external involvement of North America and Western Europe in the military infrastructure and the general economies of white Southern Africa that is, in varying degrees, vital and growing; and (5) a configuration of international power distribution that threatens to intensify and diversify (via the rise of the Chinese People's Republic as a world power deeply interested in Southern Africa, particularly through Tanzania and Zambia, and via the proliferation of nuclear weapons, probably to include the Republic of South Africa within a decade or two). Certainly for the overwhelming majority of the people in the region, and for that part of the world community aware of the fundamental injustices suffered by the black majorities, the prospect of continued minority rule and exploitation, or of a major world war (even if it may be a limited nonnuclear struggle à la Vietnam) fought in Southern Africa is a counter-utopia, upsetting and unacceptable.

Before continuing, let me say that this chapter is a human and, hope-fully, a humanistic endeavor. It is subject to the frailties of any individual and hence prejudicial exercise. It is not easy to avoid a shrill tone in dealing with emotional issues. Though I shall not consciously shuck off my academic garb, I shall, in this chapter, write as a morally concerned human being. In such a context, many writers have a tendency to moral-ize. The fact is that this entire chapter is, in effect, a sermonette. This being so, let me bare my preferences rather than mask them as scholarly findings.

I find any political system based upon the conscious degradation and exploitation of an entire class of people odious. This is the case whether the regime so based is a minority or a majority regime. The world has known and knows today an astounding variety of tyrannies. That the majority exploits a minority only means that a smaller proportion of people are directly degraded by the system. It is still a tyranny and it still does damage sociopsychologically to both ruler and ruled. Systems stratified by biological criteria that cannot be transcended—for example, race, sex, color of eyes, caste—are even more repulsive, for they mark someone as permanently subhuman. They come to be regarded, in the words of Erik H. Erikson, as pseudo-species.[1] In that fashion they be-

1. "Insights and Freedom," the Ninth T. B. Davie Memorial Lecture, University of Cape Town, 1968. See also his *Gandhi's Truth: On the Origins of Militant Nonvio-lence* (New York: W. W. Norton & Co., 1969), pp. 431–434.

come ready and rationalized targets for exploitation, physical abuse, warfare, and even extermination.

In this chapter we are to address ourselves solely to the future of Southern Africa. It is no easy task for, as we have seen, the imponderables are complex. Personally, I find the white regimes of Southern Africa particularly offensive because not only do they present a system where a minority dominates the majority of the population of the region, but because they have raised to the level of preferred values (or are raising in the case of Rhodesia) the principles which I, and most contemporary civilized men, find distasteful. They have institutionalized racial and cultural arrogance.[2] It is easy for me to subscribe to the Lusaka Manifesto on this point:

> We are not hostile to the Administrations in these States because they are manned and controlled by white people. We are hostile to them because they are systems of minority control which exist as a result of, and in the pursuance of, doctrines of human inequality. . . .
>
> Our stand toward Southern Africa thus involves a rejection of racialism, not a reversal of the existing racial domination. We believe that all the peoples who have made their homes in the countries of Southern Africa are Africans, regardless of colour of their skins; and we would oppose a racialist majority government which adopted a philosophy of deliberate and permanent discrimination between its citizens on grounds of racial origin.[3]

Because my own country has profound racial difficulties, I find the Southern African phenomenon to be symbolically important and politically significant. It represents, in many ways, a microcosm of the future of international relations in the next few generations, and therefore cries out for an equitable solution.

Our first order of business is to sketch out a hypothetical, albeit credible, description of Southern Africa in the 1990's. It cannot be a com-

2. See Chapter II of my forthcoming study of international relations in Southern Africa for a discussion of the racial component.
3. The "Manifesto on Southern Africa" was adopted at the Fifth Summit Conference of East and Central African States held in Lusaka, Zambia, April 14–16, 1969. Reprinted in U.S. Congress, House, Committee on Foreign Affairs, *Report of Special Study Mission to Southern Africa*, 91st Cong., 1st sess., October 10, 1969, pp. 39–42.

plete picture. It will not necessarily be an ideal order for all people or even for this author. But an effort will be made to create a regional order that will be at least more tolerable than the present order, one that is attainable, and one that in large measure defuses the cataclysmic racial struggle of potential worldwide dimensions toward which we now seem to be stumbling. This preferable future will be tendered in scenario form. Using that scenario, we shall attempt to fashion various ingredients in the strategic-political path to our alternative future. Finally we will add two additional transitional scenarios that lead us up to the conditions necessary to make the following representation more tenable.

A. *A More Acceptable Future—1998*

It is now over one hundred years since John Fiske wrote:

> No one can carefully watch what is going on in Africa today without recognizing it as the same sort of thing which was going on in North America in the seventeenth century; and it cannot fail to bring forth similar results in the course of time. . . . Already five flourishing English states have been established in the south . . . . Who can doubt that within two or three centuries the African continent will be occupied by a mighty nation of English descent . . . ?

In 1994, after many tense and turbulent years, that dream has been laid to rest. To be sure, there are still the commandoes, thousands of irreconcilables who insist that they will never obey a nonwhite. But at present they are "underground." On the surface, they obey the laws or try to avoid contact with the authorities. But someday, so they say, they will rise up to reclaim their "rightful" place in South Africa. The likelihood is that the commandoes will die a slow death. They realize that if they strike now, there is little hope to gain power. International involvement is too menacing. Their followers have mostly fled the country, and the chances are that most commandoes would prefer to leave as soon as they can make liquid their assets. Occasionally, one of them gets into a fracas with an African. The African complains to a local official and the offender is expelled from the country after a brief imprisonment. There were a lot of these sorts of incidents after the new government was inaugurated. Some were even worse, particularly the disturbed violent ones. At least forty or fifty armed individual whites have run amok killing blacks on sight. One Afrikaner in the Krugersdorp shopping mall machinegunned twenty-six Africans before he was shot. In contrast, there have been no bombing reports, aimed at either white or black, in over a month. The Interpol contingent sent by the United Nations put an end to that.

Hundreds of thousands of whites, mostly urban English speakers, and many of the more militant Afrikaners, fled the country. "Off to Australia" has been a catchword these past ten years, for Australia opened her doors to "political refugees," as she called them. She even offered them cheap land in the Out Back. A joke making the rounds in Luthuli, as the capital is now known, is that the government plans to erect a monument to the Kangaroo, the Savior of South Africa. Argentina and Brazil absorbed many of the remainder. Those who went off to relatives in England, the United States, and Western Europe were required to make public testimony to their opposition to racial separation and exploitation before they were permitted to enter.

Strangely, many of the Afrikaners who survived the struggle for majority rule stayed on, hoping that, as a chosen people, somehow they would regain their past power. The majority of them, however, either fled or adjusted doctrine and behavior to accommodate to the sociopolitical changes around them. Many still resist or avoid social and economic intercourse with nonwhites, if they can; but one by one those who persist in the old patterns are being weeded out.

So, of the almost five million whites who lived in South Africa in 1988, the peak year, there are still about three million today. Throughout the late 1980's and the early 1990's there had been an influx of Rhodesian settlers, and the Lourenço Marques Flight of 1991 swelled the numbers of whites. But these were difficult times for the *verkrampte* Afrikaner who didn't really appreciate the new European stock.

As for the Africans, Indians, and Coloreds, their lives have been deeply effected by the establishment of the new government. Most of them still live on the old Bantustans, though the drift to the city has been practically impossible to slow down since the Citizenship Law and the government decrees that revoked "job reservation" and established equal pay for equal work. The Africanization of the civil service has also tempted many Africans into the towns and administrative centers. The Omnibus Civil Rights Act of 1994 also broke down all enforced segregation barriers in public accommodations and facilities. But by and large, economic stratification still coincides with racial differences. And this ramifies into all facets of public and private life. In this respect the new government has been temperate in dismantling the "private" apartheid structure. They don't really have the funds to make massive changes, nor can they mobilize enough skilled and reliable bureaucrats to enforce all the new laws. But that will come now that the corner has been turned. Their reticence to act vigorously also results from a realization that the economy somehow survived the transition, and that it needs certain skills that Africans and other nonwhites as yet do not possess in sufficient quantity.

The choice of the Transitional Cabinet, with Jannie De Wet as Prime Minister, was a surprise to almost everyone. Many ANC Africans resented the selection of a Colored P.M., but no one can challenge his *bona fides* as a nationalist fighter with a long and courageous record. It has proven to be a stroke of genius, for De Wet understands the Afrikaners, and is able to communicate with them and to convince many that their future still lies with Suid Afrika. That he is a "conservative" in the context of nonwhite politics has not been helpful, but the presence of large-scale American, British, and UN aid has made his leadership more palatable to those who have sacrificed and suffered so much the past two decades.

It has not been an easy four years. Every governmental decision has been a sensitive one. The coalition is tenuous, particularly on the economic issues. The P.M. has consistently held that "the hemorrhage must be stopped." No more nationalizations. No more group expulsions. No pogroms. He has even prosecuted gangs of African young people that have from time to time terrorized the European quarters. Who would have thought that a "law and order" P.M. would have emerged?

But the fact is that the economic dislocations, though disturbing, have somehow been tolerable for most people. The *ngawethu*, formerly the Rand, is still strong on the currency market. Productivity, though down about 25 percent from the 1985 figures, is now stabilized. The extent of external financial and technical assistance, and of the replacement of capital has been heartening. Unemployment is not unmanageable, despite the initial capital flight—and it looks like South Africa will survive. Even the ANC militants admit that the economy has come through amazingly well, though they are contemptuous of the pace and the direction of change. Today, they represent the chief threat to continued stability. The regime has not been able to disarm or "neutralize" the "external army"—mostly ANC groups that have lost some of their earlier discipline —though they are still disenchanted. It was primarily international pressures that enabled the De Wet coalition to assume power. It is probably international backing that enables it to withstand a complete radicalization, even if temporarily.

So the forces confronting the country are still ominous—the white commandoes (both inside and outside the country); the British, American, UN, and Chinese interests and pressures on various elements within the country, especially on the business community; the "external army" that is now dispersed in South Africa; and the factions and private groups coinciding mostly with economic and ideological subdivisions among the people. At least the apartheid system has been repudiated and defeated, and the government reflects a sort-of majority rule. To add to that, the economic machinery seems to be contributing to almost everybody's benefit.

In retrospect the vital decade was the 1980's. The surprisingly easy collapse of Rhodesia in 1985 broke the logjam. After the governmental collapse in Portugal, her withdrawal from Mozambique in 1991, and Angola immediately thereafter, was smooth. Then the well-timed Durban uprising and the external incursions led to the final demise of the Nationalist government. The *verkramptes* were right on this point; once you relax some of your controls, once the lid is off, you lose everything. Nevertheless, it did not come easily. Thousands died in the struggle in Durban. Some likened it to the Warsaw ghetto uprising. But this time the rest of Africa, the "external army," the great powers, and the United Nations pitched in. The Nationalists' threat to use their nuclear missiles against African cities was nullified by a joint United States-Russian counterthreat to level, by strategic nonnuclear bombings, sections of heavily white cities. The international response to the white regime made the difference and showed the Nationalists that they were alone. Those among the government who called for an Armageddon were repudiated, and the government, resigned to its fate, stepped down, almost miraculously.

The armed forces were never given the opportunity to resist. The call-up that followed the Durban uprising and the external incursions failed to materialize. Many whites were too interested in protecting their families by getting them out of the country. So only about one-half of the expected mobilizable white males reported for duty. Those who reported were sent to the borders to deal with the infiltrators. The police were thought to be able to handle the urban uprisings. While the army was occupied, swift airborne invasions by African and UN troops proceeded to occupy the cities. UN tactical bombers had earlier immobilized the South African military airports before planes could take off. From there on the white units suffered from even higher desertion rates. This was the genesis of the commando units, too.

Ritual group murders followed during the next few weeks, but the efficient UN units made that practice an increasingly suicidal one. The failure of the attempted march on Pretoria by the mobile 2nd Army and the staunch defense by the joint U.S.-Ethiopian forces led to a relatively swift collapse of the rest of the defense forces. A decree that enabled the white soldiers to lay down their arms in return for safe and escorted passage through the country to their homes and thence to a port of embarkation proved sufficient to deter all but the most irreconcilable. The cities were occupied by the international brigades. The white South African soldiers had not realized how divorced they had become from the South African countryside; their isolation on the frontiers led many to seek the quickest way out of the crisis—flight. Perhaps the full impact of the changes had not yet hit the majority of South African nonwhites. Perhaps their political maturity explains their behavior. But they did permit their armed enemies to opt for escape, and the entire country benefited by nonwhite tolerance.

Those few weeks of fighting were in fact horrible. The retaliations on both sides were widespread. An estimated 70,000 lost their lives. The populace has still not been entirely disarmed. But a new nationalism has been forged in those brief weeks of struggle, and, on occasion, racial cooperation. Whether that national spirit can carry South Africa through the difficult times ahead remains to be seen.

B. *Steps toward Change*

That the preceding scenario or something similar to it will ever be a reality does not seem likely if present trends continue. But the more acceptable future constructed may not be impossible. To be sure, racist societies are resilient. Nevertheless, if we are ever to reach a more desirable world, there is some necessity to plan and think through possible developments. History need be neither inevitable nor entirely fortuitous.

What I should like to discuss, in a most general way, are a number of the ingredients that can contribute to arriving at the future sketched above. There is no guarantee that the various elements in our action plan will necessarily lead to a satisfactory change. It could be that only one or even none of the changes suggested would be necessary. They merely represent several fronts along which efforts to shape the future may be pursued. They have been presented from the least activist and least violent, to the most. To those who would like more detail, we can only respond that this is simply impossible. Our enterprise here is conjectural. When more comprehensive examinations of a given alternative are available, efforts have been made to integrate those findings into the proposals and to cite the works involved. We seek merely to suggest what we think should be done in order to redirect what is at present an unacceptable pattern of change.

The first level of activity cannot in itself be expected to bring down white minority governments in Southern Africa or force significant reform upon them. Rather, such activities are designed to accent the universal rejection of racialism, to discourage private and governmental relationships that strengthen or legitimize white minority regimes, to weaken racist regimes, and to set the stage for more militant and vigorous antiapartheid activities.

To begin with, it is necessary to reeducate the American and West European peoples to the state of life for nonwhites in Southern Africa. Once aware of the conditions in these countries, it should be easier to activate and focus popular feelings toward more actively antiracist foreign policies. In the United Kingdom and the United States, black cultural and political groups should concentrate on the black communities. Various religious groups, such as the World Council of Churches and the University Christian Movement, various national and international sectarian bodies and organizations of the clergy could take it upon themselves to educate and involve their "constituencies" and wider publics. Groups such as Peace Corps returnees, the League of Women Voters, and trade union political action bodies might join in. Student associations and, ultimately, public and parochial educational systems should be encouraged to make the study of Southern Africa a part of the curriculum. Committed bodies might be able to make educational materials available to teachers, and to brief them periodically on Southern African affairs. Television and radio networks as well might be enlisted in this informational campaign. If interest is sufficiently high, programming can eventually be made to conform to popular concerns. Unadulterated information should be adequate to interest people in the affairs of Southern Africa. In all cases, the false and often implicit arguments based upon racial affinity should be refuted. Then efforts should be made to demonstrate how conditions in Southern Africa relate to one's own country's domestic and foreign affairs. Once aware of the problems of Southern Africa, the citizenry might be prepared for political action and organized into groups designed to take more active steps to pressure private and public bodies that contribute to the continuation of racist rule in Southern Africa. It must be shown that it is or may be politically advantageous, domestically and internationally, and in the long-run economically profitable, to do what is right in Southern Africa. United States officials, since the Eisenhower years, have consistently maintained that they are opposed to racist political systems and that the Southern African situation may at some later time threaten world peace. Such governmental statements can be cited frequently in the informational program in the United States.

Building on this foundation, Western governments might then be more inclined to undertake a series of steps to reorient Southern African policies away from deep involvement in white Southern African economies and regimes and toward more vigorous support for the independent states of black Southern Africa. Such a change in policy necessitates both positive and negative steps. The positive steps are intended, on one hand, to give greater aid to black Southern Africa (in order to strengthen independent black Southern Africa's ability to withstand economic and political pressures from the white South and to provide an alternative example of fruitful race relations) and, on the other, to offer rewards that might serve as a prod toward reforms within white-governed states in the region.[4]

The black states in the region had been British colonies and protectorates, and Britain continues to be an important trading partner and source of developmental assistance. In the case of the former High Commission Territories and Malawi, Britain is their chief financial crutch. Only in the case of Zambia has the relative importance of British assistance been lessened since UDI.

Despite the high proportion of assistance coming from one country, its total magnitude is inadequate to the tasks of development. Little of the bilateral assistance goes toward long-range economic development and capital expenditure. Only Zambia and Tanzania, among regional states, have found other sources of aid, among them Italy, the Chinese People's Republic, and other Eastern-bloc countries. For a variety of motives, the CPR has intensively cultivated relations with Tanzania and Zambia. The Tan-Zam railway project, to cost in the range of $400 million, will have political ramifications far beyond the developmental impact it will make— and that will by no means be minor. Just as UDI severed long-standing economic links between Britain and Rhodesia and etched stronger ones between Rhodesia and South Africa and Mozambique, so UDI has prompted Zambia to change the pattern of her extracontinental as well as continental relations.

Another important source of bilateral assistance for economic development might be the United States. In fact, however, U.S. assistance has been marginal. None of the black states in the region have been designated "emphasis countries," i.e., bilateral aid is no longer extended and only regional or multidonor aid is permitted. Instead, in 1968 a regional AID office for Southern Africa was established in Lusaka. But recipient governments are inclined to see the regionalization of aid as, in reality, an

4. Some excellent general and specific suggestions at this level are advanced in John Marcum, "Southern Africa and United States Policy: A Consideration of Alternatives," in George W. Shepherd, Jr. (ed.), *Race in United States Foreign Policy* (New York: Basic Books, forthcoming).

abandonment of black Southern Africa. This may well be the present case. The pretentious geographical scope of the U.S.'s Southern African assistance program cannot hide the meager amounts allotted to these countries. It is not difficult to conclude that, except for Great Britain, Europe and the United States have abandoned black Southern Africa to the economic hegemony of white Southern Africa, and even the magnitude of British aid means, in effect, continued economic weakness. It is this apparent orientation that must be modified. Indeed, a good case can be made that, given the long-range volatility of the Southern African issues, practically all of United States and West European aid to Africa ought to be directed toward black Southern Africa, thereby providing it with the developmental potential to become really independent of South Africa. This is of course a long-range strategy, but a start must be made somewhere.

Likewise, governmental and private humanitarian policies might be launched to assist refugees and exiles from white Southern Africa. Health, education, and welfare programs could be opened, instead of abandoning refugees to host countries and international bodies that are not prepared, financially or administratively, to render adequate assistance. This would, moreover, serve the dual purpose of enabling the West to make a contribution to African development and to offset the inordinate influence of Communist countries in assisting refugee and guerrilla movements.[5] Even if such aid were filtered through some international body, as it should be, it would still serve these purposes.

In concert with these positive steps to assist white Southern Africa's black neighbors and the direct victims of regional repression, a number of "negative" steps could be taken to withhold Western support from Southern African racism. Before discussing the specific sorts of policy steps, governmental and private, that might be attempted, it is necessary to do two things: (1) to explore the extent to which Western involvement bolsters the white regimes in Southern Africa,[6] and (2) to outline a case

5. See my "Host Countries," and also Marcum, "The Exile Condition."
6. Fortunately the extent of Western support for Southern African racism has been well documented. See "A Special Report on American Involvement in the South African Economy," *Africa Today*, XIII, No. 1 (January 1966); "Allies in Empire: The U.S. and Portugal in Africa," *Africa Today*, XVII, No. 4 (July–August 1970); "Apartheid and Imperialism: A Study of U.S. Corporate Involvement in South Africa," *Africa Today*, XVII, No. 5 (September–October 1970); Bosgra and van Krimpen, *Portugal and NATO*; Segal, *Sanctions Against South Africa*; William A. Hance (ed.),

for "disengagement" and withdrawal from activities that are wittingly and unwittingly supportive of racism.

The Western world supports Southern African regimes in at least seven important ways: (1) by direct and indirect investments; (2) by maintenance of the international gold standard; (3) by extensive and expanding trade relationships; (4) by diplomatic and political relationships; (5) by technical and scientific exchanges; (6) by cultural and educational exchanges; and (7) by direct and indirect military cooperation and assistance. Although much of this may be repetitious, let me at least outline the effects of these sorts of involvements. Despite increased international awareness of the nature of apartheid and related racial exploitation in Rhodesia and Portuguese Africa, foreign investment continues to flow into white Southern Africa. Total foreign investment in South Africa now exceeds approximately $7 billion.[7] The latest 1968 figures indicate an increase in total foreign liabilities of some 65 percent over the 1956 data. Foreign investment in South Africa thus has increased at roughly 5 percent per year during the last decade. In many instances this is a higher rate of increase of domestic investment than in the countries from which investment capital flows into South Africa. Most of the rise in foreign liabilities took the form of direct investments, increasing almost $2 billion between 1956 and 1968. Data on investments from individual countries in South Africa have not been published since 1966, but UN figures for that year indicate that the United Kingdom owned 57 percent of foreign investments in the country, the United States owned 13 percent, and France, Switzerland, and West Germany totalled 12 percent. Though the British share of this total declined throughout the 1960's, the U.S. share was rising steadily, from $140 million in 1948 to $528 million in 1965 to

Southern Africa and the United States (New York: Columbia University Press, 1968); United Nations, Unit on Apartheid, Department of Political and Security Council Affairs, Industrialization, Foreign Capital and Forced Labour in South Africa (New York: United Nations, 1970); and U.S. Congress, House, Committee on Foreign Affairs, United States-South African Relations: Hearings Before the Subcommittee on Africa, Parts I–III, 89th Cong., 2d sess., 1966, esp. pp. 15–26, 48–51, 489–495. Numerous shorter articles on these subjects can be found throughout the issues of Africa Report, Africa Today, Africa Digest, Africa Confidential; indeed, even in the Rhodesian and South African news releases and governmental information materials distributed throughout the Western world.

7. This data and that which follows were drawn from United Nations, Unit on Apartheid, Industrialization, Foreign Capital, pp. 58–89.

TABLE XII

IMPORTANCE TO SOUTH AFRICA OF TRADE
WITH MAIN TRADING PARTNERS

	Exports (excluding gold)				Imports			
	1963		1968		1963		1968	
	U.S. $ Millions	%	U.S. $ Millions	%	U.S. $ Millions	%	U.S. $ Millions	%
United Kingdom	449.6	35.1	666.5	31.6	506.0	30.0	629.3	23.9
United States	124.3	9.6	146.2	6.9	286.3	17.0	465.9	17.7
Germany (Fed. Rep.)	69.5	5.4	141.8	6.7	181.6	10.8	355.2	13.5
Japan	99.3	7.7	286.2	13.6	79.0	4.6	173.5	6.5
Italy	69.4	5.4	60.1	2.9	47.7	2.9	109.3	4.1
Africa, total	150.1	11.7	348.7	16.6	119.1	7.1	168.7	6.4
Total	1,282.1	—	2,103.4	—	1,684.1	—	2,629.2	—

Source: Tabulated from Tables B7, 8, 9, 10 of United Nations, Department of Political and Security Council Affairs, Unit on Apartheid, *Industrialization, Foreign Capital and Forced Labour in South Africa* (New York: United Nations, 1970).

approximately $945 million by 1969. The largest portion of U.S. investments are in manufacturing and vital petroleum exploration. The multinational corporation has been a boon to the South African and Portuguese African economies. A significant example of the importance of this nexus grew out of the aftermath of the 1960 Sharpeville shootings. This event shook confidence in South Africa's stability, and with that South Africa faced a serious financial crisis. A group of American financiers helped to save the Republic by raising a $150 million loan from the International Monetary Fund, the World Bank, Chase Manhattan Bank, First National City Bank, and a group of unidentified American financial leaders. Most of these investments are tremendously profitable. For the British economy, with its perennial balance-of-payments problem, income received from South Africa (approximately £60 million per year since 1964) is important. The private sector has not been the only recipient of needed foreign capital. Germany, Italy, Switzerland, and the United States alone have lent the Republic's government over $112 million between 1964 and 1968.

Trade data is no less revealing. The South African economy is highly

TABLE XIII

IMPORTANCE OF TRADE WITH SOUTH AFRICA (1964 & 1968)
TO MAIN TRADING PARTNERS
(Percent of total trade)

	1964		1968	
	Exports	Imports	Exports	Imports
United Kingdom	4.7	3.0	4.1	3.5
United States	1.5	0.7	1.3	0.4
Germany (Fed. Rep.)	1.4	0.5	1.4	0.7
Japan	1.7	1.5	1.3	2.2
Italy	1.1	0.8	1.1	0.6

Source: Calculated from Table B11 of United Nations, Department of Political and Security Council Affairs, Unit on Apartheid, *Industrialization, Foreign Capital and Forced Labour in South Africa.*

dependent on external trade (see Table XII), though not as much as it once was.[8] The bulk of this trade is with Europe, which buys over half of South Africa's exports and provides over half of its imports. The value of both imports and exports are each equal to roughly one quarter of the South African gross domestic product. Table XIII shows instead the small role that trade with South Africa plays with most of her main trading partners.

Given the added vulnerability of the South African economy with regard to an inability to produce import substitutes and to redirect exports to the domestic markets, the South African economy is dependent upon the world economy, and yet her economic and social policies make South Africa an object of virtually universal condemnation. Likewise, the particular composition of imports, and growing trade deficits that are offset only by continuing exports of gold, render her economic picture serious despite ostensibly impressive economic development since World War II.

Thus, there are several ways to pressure South Africa at levels below conventional sanctions.[9] For example, two "historical anachronisms" have survived South Africa's withdrawal from the Commonwealth. The Republic still enjoys preferential treatment from Commonwealth members for

8. *Ibid.*, pp. 38–57.
9. See the *Star* (Johannesburg), Weekly Air Edition, September 5, 1970, p. 7. These proposals were developed by Miss Barbara Rodgers, formerly a high-ranking member of the British Foreign Office's Southern Africa Department.

her exports. She thereby receives duty-free entry for almost all her products. This is especially helpful in that it includes Great Britain, her main trading partner. South Africa is also listed among those countries (all others belong to the Commonwealth) that are exempted from Britain's Exchange Control Act of 1947. This means that British investors in the South African economy are not subject to the harsh restrictions that prevent unlimited investment into other countries. If these advantages were to be removed, pressures and counterpressures within the white community in South Africa might lead to a relaxation in some aspects of apartheid.

A further, more sweeping step short of sanctions might be to reverse this process. First, remove "most favored nation" treatment for South African products in the Commonwealth and then among other UN nations. Then, an escalated graduated tariff might be considered for South African and Portuguese products. If these countries did not arrive at agreements with the United Nations regarding South West Africa and the Portuguese African territories, the tariffs could be raised perhaps 5 percent per year. If the balance of payments problem grew unacceptable, these countries might be forced to establish import restrictions themselves. Conversely, reductions in these penalties would be directly linked to positive steps regarding racial policy on the part of these South African governments.

Continued diplomatic, political, and military relationships have in various ways contributed to a growing identification of the Western world with Portugal and South Africa. In Chapter Six we discussed Portuguese-NATO links and efforts to create a SATO involving Europe and America. Despite South African boasts that they presently have sufficient supplies of weapons and ammunition to repulse an invasion and maintain internal stability, and the fact that most light arms and ammunition as well as light aircraft and military vehicles are manufactured or assembled in the Republic, the fact remains that for the sophisticated weaponry South Africa and Portugal must shop abroad. The South African air force is composed of British-made Buccaneers, Canberras, and Shackletons, and French Mirage fighters. Helicopters are largely of French manufacture. The navy employs ships manufactured in Great Britain and the first of three French submarines has been delivered. Rocketry is predominantly of French design. Continuing need for parts and new devices renders South

Africa and Portugal vulnerable to a complete, long-term arms embargo. Even though they may learn to make do without foreign-made weaponry, it would be at a reduced level of effectiveness and at a more expensive price.

In the field of technical and scientific development South Africa has made impressive strides and devoted much capital. Nevertheless, for advanced training and for increasingly expensive and vital equipment, she has been dependent on close ties with Western, and particularly American, scientists and scientific institutions.[10] These relationships are mainly on an individual basis, but U.S. government research organizations are also involved, among them NASA, the National Institutes of Health, and the Atomic Energy Commission. Often U.S. government funds support the American share of joint private activities.

Thus, in a multitude of ways, Western governments and private groups have woven an intricate pattern of involvement and hence support for the racist structures of white Southern Africa. We have in effect become, though the realization of it may be psychologically repressed because it is contrary to all our professed values, partners in apartheid and racial exploitation, partners in the bloody repression of a colonized people, partners in the defense of a regime representing but a quarter-million in a total population of approximately five and a quarter million. In the white-governed territories of Southern Africa there are approximately 4.1 million whites among 35.4 million people. Even if we assume that white citizens are united in their support for governmental racial policies, this would represent government by at best 12 percent of the population. Nowhere in our professed political heritage could we countenance such a situation. If we were to reverse the situation and argue that America's blacks, approximately 11 percent of the population, should control the American political system to the total exclusion of her whites, should command wages ten times higher than her whites, should regard her whites as inferior, culturally, intellectually, biologically, and spiritually and treat the whites accordingly, you would be ready for the battlements. How can we in conscience and consistency, therefore, maintain that somehow or other "European civilization" must be maintained at all costs in Southern Africa?

10. See D. S. Greenberg, "South Africa," Parts I and II, *Science*, CLIX, Nos. 3941–42 (July 10 and 17, 1970), 157–163 and 260–266.

Southern African white minority regimes do not embody the ideal features of European civilization, but rather some of its trappings and some of its worst characteristics. It is for this reason that they do not deserve the support of the West. A minimal policy of disengagement is in order. It may be that by such policies the United States, or even the United States in concert with Western Europe, could not actually alter the situation in Southern Africa significantly. I happen to think that it could. But even if it could not, such policies set the West on the right track, morally and ideologically. Policy would then complement pronouncement. Such policies at this level are neither militant nor violent. They are within the range of possibility in the 1970's, given domestic political situations throughout the West. They represent in many ways an alternative approach to combatting Russian or Chinese influence in Africa, despite what the South African and Portuguese governments, and various conservative organizations in Western countries, say. Rather, these policies would establish, as we should have done a decade ago, a friendly image in the independent states of Black Africa, immensely sensitive to the racial ramifications of Western policies. Heretofore, the white regimes had been convinced that humanistic tendencies in the West were an aberration, a transitional malaise. It is time we informed them in no uncertain terms that we are not going to defend their right to exploit others simply on the basis of the spurious criteria of racial similarity, and that until they redirect the entire basis of state organization, Western countries will support only those regimes that repudiate racialism, as in the Lusaka Manifesto. Then and only then could we deal with them to mutual advantage. Even if this necessitates some economic sacrifice for the West, it is a small price to pay to actualize our own, often repeated, principles.

Precedent for active policies of disengagement already exists. The Scandinavian countries have opposed apartheid in a variety of ways.[11] If demands of antiapartheid movements are made specific and focus on the relevant agencies, it may well be that, one by one, private groups and governmental bodies can be made to curtail involvement. If governments became truly interested in disengagement, it would be relatively easy, even in capitalist countries, to discourage new investment in and trade

11. See Sven Skovmand, "Scandinavian Opposition to *Apartheid*," in United Nations, Unit on Apartheid, *Notes and Documents*, No. 23/70 (October 1970).

with white Southern Africa by tax penalties or by tax incentives and tariff adjustments, and to encourage greater investment in and trade with Black Africa. The Swedish government and possibly other European governments have taken steps to prevent investment in the Cabora Bassa hydroelectric scheme on the Zambezi. Similar pressures might prove equally effective if made clearly, rationally, and with sufficient credibility to be economically and politically persuasive.

Fundamentally, policies of disengagement need not necessarily lead to the total isolation of white Southern Africa. On the contrary, cultural and educational exchanges that do not lend legitimacy to the regimes and that serve to enlighten both sides could be encouraged. They help to face the regimes with sticky policy questions—witness the Arthur Ashe and Congressman Diggs episodes in 1969–70—and they force the white populations to divide on these issues and, hopefully, to break down parochialisms that presently prevent change. Similarly, insofar as the black states of Southern Africa are actually compelled to deal with their white neighbors, these states can continually pose dilemmas within white Southern Africa and especially among Afrikaners. The struggle against apartheid can thereby go on on more than one front. Those Africans who oppose it by force can do so. Those African states that feel that contact can open doors may attempt their approach, provided their activities do not strengthen the white South militarily or economically and do not become too widespread. Dual policies may thereby serve within white Southern Africa to negate a consistently racist attitude toward Black Africa and perhaps toward domestic blacks.[12] In order to defend racism, such regimes must become less racist in foreign policy. This poses immense problems for regime ideologies and for the white citizenry. Inconsistencies and dilemmas thereby weaken racist governments.

The second level of activity might be invoked if the first level appears to be fruitless and commitment to change is waxing. By this time, frustration tends to be growing, the educational campaigns in the West have sown the seeds for the acceptance of more active antiracist policies, and

12. Elsewhere I have argued that such "token" approaches toward South Africa will not by themselves weaken racist regimes measurably (see "Southern African Bridge Builders"), but in combination with continued and growing militancy by other black states and groups and hostility in Western quarters, South Africa's dealings with her neighbors are complicated. It forces her out of adamant, uncompromisable positions.

Western governments are aware of the political implications of a failure to take seriously the demands of domestic and international pressure groups. Policies at this level involve a strengthening of the UN's capacity to aid Black Africa and to invoke universal or near-universal sanctions against white Southern Africa. Whereas in the past two decades there had been considerable interest in the use of sanctions to bring about changes in Southern Africa, the short-run failure of UN sanctions against Rhodesia has led to a reduction of interest. According to Hance, among the explanations for the lowered interest are:

1. doubts regarding the legal justification for sanctions;
2. doubts regarding the ability to secure approval for mandatory sanctions in the Security Council;
3. doubts regarding the effectiveness of sanctions as a weapon against apartheid . . . ;
4. fears regarding the impact and outcome of sanctions:
   a. on South African whites . . .
   b. on South African non-whites . . .
   c. on such heavily dependent countries as Lesotho, Botswana, Swaziland, Malawi, and even Zambia . . .
   d. on South Africa's major trading partners and investors . . .
   e. on the United Nations.[13]

Galtung mentions two additional reasons: (1) inability to define clearly the purpose of sanctions; and (2) inability to recognize that in economic warfare adaptive measures are devised, and upper limits to withstand value deprivations tend to rise, and could well contribute to greater political integration within the target state.[14]

These possible objections notwithstanding, we are referring now to sanctions in an era when presumably a more nearly universal effort is likely. If first-level approaches have been invoked by the Western powers and have been recognized as less than successful, it is possible that such governments may be willing to attempt the next level of a still nonviolent policy. With U.S., U.K., and perhaps USSR collaboration, a sea blockade

---

13. William A. Hance, "The Case For and Against United States Disengagement from South Africa," in Hance, *Southern Africa and the United States*, pp. 107–108.
14. Galtung, "International Economic Sanctions."

of Southern Africa might even be attempted and, provided that sanctions are linked to clear-cut policy changes in the direction of long-run majority rule, such a policy might prove successful. This policy might also be supplemented by carefully announced rewards to the minority governments for any positive steps toward majority rule. In other words, if, for example, in the case of Rhodesia the constitution were to be amended to give equal representation to nonwhites, and a timetable were set up to lead to representation on the basis of one-man one-vote, then the present regime would be granted recognition by member states, would be seated in the United Nations, and would be afforded most-favored-nation tariff treatment. If a higher quota of Africans were admitted to the University College, Salisbury, assistance to the University would be made available. If residential housing patterns were desegregated, or school expenditures were equalized and schools desegregated, and so forth, directly compensatory reward structures might be established. Remember that this is not so much a reward to those who have been racist in the past, but rather an effort to improve the lives of the indigenous population and to remove what can be regarded as a potentially explosive threat to the peace. Ultimately, of course, this must mean majority rule. The South West African issue might also be dealt with in this fashion. Nevertheless, the prospects for such a policy of rewards is not bright in light of the records of inflexibility of the regimes, particularly of the pre-UDI Smith regime in bargaining with the Wilson government. It must be made clear, at any rate, that the purpose of sanctions and of level-one policies as well, is not to punish the established regimes. This would make such policies counterproductive. The purpose is rather to discourage further racism and to encourage positive and recognizable steps in the direction of equitable majority rule.[15] Throughout such an "escalation," if it can be called that, contacts must be kept open with the target regimes so that they might know that certain significant changes in their policies would bring almost immediate relaxation of international pressures and perhaps meaningful benefits.

Each of the above levels of activity, though not directly a part of guerrilla efforts against white Southern Africa, would serve to weaken

15. Detailed discussions of the nature and potential effects of sanctions against South Africa can be found in Segal, *Sanctions Against South Africa.*

and isolate the minority regimes, and to make more difficult their ability to resist internal and international coercive pressures. In this respect they are preliminary steps to level three, which is clearly linked to the principal subject of this volume—guerrilla struggle. Level three entails various measures contributory to expanding and making more efficient nationalist military efforts aimed at bringing to power regimes that at least pay lip-service to majority rule, legal equality, and government in the interests of the total populace. Simply put, at this level we seek to answer the question, What would it take to improve the chances for African nationalist military success against minority regimes in Southern Africa?

Much of what is written here will not be new, nor can it be written with absolute assurance of correctness. Much of what we know about the causes and effects of guerrilla struggle is still subject to debate. Nevertheless, from African experiences we can suggest several ways in which the chances for military and political field success by the nationalist movements might be enhanced by the movements themselves. These are not necessarily presented here in order of importance.

First there is the need to widen the base of support for nationalist liberation movements, to "popularize" the struggle. Though the phrase "peoples' war" has obvious and unfortunate ideological connotations in international politics today, it is applicable to the African scene. It is no accident that the struggle that has become most popularized, that of the PAIGC, is so far the most successful in both political and military terms. Thus it is important to be constantly aware that, though the tools of struggle appear at first blush to be military, the ultimate ends are political —to gain independence and to build a nation. To these ends, political means should not be minimized. It is not easy for liberation parties that are primarily exile organizations to grasp this, much less to implement it. Political education and peasant mobilization are difficult enough in underdeveloped countries where, at least, the regime has been legitimized and is, in military terms, unchallenged in its territory. But, nevertheless, field activities must be emphasized. PAIGC leadership operates primarily in nationalist "occupied" areas, constantly explaining, educating, directing the struggle and relating to its constituents. In short, it is not an exile organization, it is a participant movement. This is one reason why groups such as the ANC, SWAPO, ZAPU, and ZANU have had such a difficult time. At the first opportunity, the theater of operation for the top leadership must be in the target territory. Prior to this, leadership must develop and utilize links with supporters in the field. In these ways, moreover, the leaders can by example and effort solidify their own positions within the struggle. They become identified with risk, sacrifice, and integrity, and the level of their popularity and appeal can be raised. To date, few leaders have been able to create and maintain such an image. Their behavior in exile is often associated with expensive living, dishonesty, petty and fratricidal quarrels, nepotism and tribalism, "conference-mongering" and globetrotting, and the distribution of meaningless sinecures. Those in the field, if they don't desert, may look upon exile leadership with contempt.[16]

Another facet of the "popularization" of the struggle relates to the "nationalization" of the war, not necessarily in geographical terms (though this would ultimately occur if field success is achieved), but in terms of broadening participation and leadership beyond a narrow tribal, ethnic, or class base. Those opposing the guerrilla movements have an interest in playing upon and exacerbating tribal animosities, and in instigating them where few existed in the past. It is instead absolutely imperative that parochial images be abandoned, even if this necessitates the relinquishing of a certain amount of control or the sacrifice of immediate, short-range gain on the part of those who, heretofore, have taken the risks. Ethnic and class cleavages must be transcended as soon as possible in the struggle, or they will be a continuing source of strength for the status quo. In exile, even more than in struggle, these communal differences seem to be the most petty and debilitating to the movement.

Even though it is necessary to establish governments in exile and to undertake the business of quasi-diplomacy—and also to provide services for refugees and exiles, bargaining, security, and fund raising abroad— perhaps a form of rotation for all officials between foreign capitals, training camps, and in-field political-military assignments might serve the twin purposes of identifying the leaders with their people and testing the dedication and loyalty of those more inclined to the relative comfort and safety of life in exile. Though some might argue that this is too egalitarian in that those with specialized skills ought to be used where they are best suited, one could reply that if the ultimate purpose is the creation of an

16. See Marcum, "The Exile Condition."

independent and viable nation-state, skills must be transmitted to many people. But more importantly, there is a credibility gap in these organizations between the leaders and the led. This policy represents a relatively quick and inexpensive way to solve this problem and to acquaint all segments of the organization with the challenges of other segments.

It has been said hundreds of times and in almost as many ways that the struggle for the liberation of Southern Africa is a regional struggle and must be dealt with in regional, not territorial terms. If the forces of the status quo see the necessity to collaborate and to subscribe to a sort-of "domino theory" of the Southern African war, an almost mirror image of regional geopolitics exists on the black side.[17] This involves not only the establishment of greater links and more cooperation between various liberation organizations within a given territory and among all of the territories, but also a more active and helpful role for the independent states, regionally and continentally. Ideally, a single movement for the entire region, massively supported by the OAU, is in order. Present steps in this direction have been slow in developing. There is no easy way to do this. Hard work and a willingness to compromise are demanded—even to the point of concentrating all forces in a single target area until that territory is liberated, or until sufficient portions are effectively administered and relatively secure so that the movement there has a momentum of its own and thus can carry the struggle through to satisfactory conclusion. Heretofore, it has been difficult enough to find numbers of men willing to take risks in order to liberate their own homelands. To inject the added demand that they must fight to secure independence for other men's lands, to defer the values for which they fight, may indeed be asking too much of liberation groups at their current level of consciousness.

Here, then, emerges the need for dynamic, dedicated, and skillful leadership, and for a persuasive and realizable ideology. There are no such ideology and leadership presently on the scene. But it does not follow that the requisite leadership and ideology cannot arise quickly and take effect soon. If the end of the twentieth century is to see majority rule in Southern Africa by means of guerrilla struggle, these ingredients must be soon provided. It might be that by a kind of Darwinian process, by a non-

17. See, for example, the interview with Emile Apollus of the UN's Council on Namibia, in *News/Check* (Johannesburg), IX, No. 7 (October 2, 1970), 12.

physiological survival of the fittest, only the most dedicated and skillful leaders will in fact assume control of only the most representative movements, and from these bases form wider and wider movements capable of waging guerrilla struggle successfully. This may happen, but only if the psychological toll of repeated defeat and steady subjugation can be overcome; if the risks of engagement do not assure that participation will be physically destructive; if dedication to change outweighs the temptations of inertia. So much depends on the qualities of leadership and ideological appeal. The assumption throughout the preceding section has been that only when the political facts of nationalist movements can be changed, will the military aims of the struggle be more assuredly achieved. To some extent much of what I have written here appears to be conventional wisdom, frequently stated, seldom detailed, even less often fulfilled. But until such time as fruitful efforts are made to bring about the dictates of conventional wisdom, there is little point in embellishing on the grand outlines. There is no ready formula for breathing life into the plan, for it is, as I mentioned, an essentially political endeavor and that, in turn, is in many ways a human art form. One does not follow a blueprint for building a viable nationalist movement (though we know that certain materials and tools are needed) any more than one has guidelines for writing a *Hamlet* or designing a Chartres Cathedral.

The final level of action—direct external military intervention—demands the highest measure of commitment from external actors, and thus is least likely on the basis of current political values and configuration. Nevertheless, various aspects of this sort of policy deserve consideration. It is widely thought that in the short run the military capabilities of Africa north of the Zambezi are not sufficient to pose a grave threat to the military forces of white Southern Africa.[18] Moreover, there appears to be little inclination on the part of Black Africa's leaders to test this speculation, that is, to launch direct military operations against the racist regimes to the south. Even with massive support in arms and material, the logistical and physical problems would be imposing. Nothing short of a highly coordinated, well-planned and directed, and convincingly efficient

18. Illustrative of this viewpoint are William Gutteridge, "The Military in Africa," *African Affairs*, LXIX, No. 277 (October 1970), 366–370; and Deon Fourie, *War Potentials of the African States South of the Sahara* (Johannesburg: The South African Institute of International Affairs, 1968).

operation would be necessary to succeed and to deter counteraction and reprisal that would be destructive of innocent lives and of the existing productive property that would be of value in building a postindependent state. Only a thoroughly credible and convincing threat would assure minimal resistance and, hence, relatively successful and acceptable use of force.

There are, of course, numerous problems that must be considered. One pertains to questions of international law. It might be argued, for example, that simply because the situation in Southern Africa does not meet with our approval, we are not empowered, nor is any body, public or private, national or supranational, to utilize force to upset the status quo.[19] Such an argument might be further extended to contend that international law, in regard to the issues of internal war or externally instigated internal war, dictates that third powers pursue one of two policies: (1) either display an attitude of impartiality regarding the contending parties; or (2) discriminate in favor of the "legitimate," i.e. recognized, regime. The fact is that international law has a built-in bias in favor of the status quo, and that most commentators on the law do approve of this conservative bias. But in situations where there are two or more claimants to legitimate authority, and where an undeniably coercive struggle for power is in progress, international law is not as clear as some would have us believe. There are no undisputed legal standards to govern outside participation in internal war. Rather, in its present state, the basis of international legal theory is ideological. It is not an "operative code of conduct." [20] International law provides wide latitude to decision makers to intervene or not to intervene on the basis of policy preferences. No less an authority than Vattel maintained that third states had a third option—to intervene on the side or faction that, in their view, is pursuing the juster cause.[21] Since justice is a political and ideological concept as much as it is a legal one, this serves, in effect, to sanction support of either revolutionary or conservative elements. If the intervening power is inclined to be squeamish, there is adequate precedent for mobilizing international or suprana-

19. See, for example Charles Burton Marshall, *Crisis Over Rhodesia: A Skeptical View* (Baltimore: Johns Hopkins Press, 1967).
20. See Falk, *Legal Order*, pp. 99–108.
21. Emmerich de Vattel, *The Law of Nations* (1958), quoted in Falk, *Legal Order*, p. 106.

tional consensus through the United Nations, the OAU or, as in the case of the 1965 U.S. intervention in the Dominican Republic, some other regional body. Though the Western powers show, at present, a preference for intervention at the invitation and in support of the incumbent faction, that requirement has not always been necessary. Simply put, there are no uniform standards of interventionary behavior. Actions and legalistic rationalizations have invariably reflected ideological predispositions, and not, as it is frequently and sanctimoniously contended, some abstract standard of immutable law.

In the cases of Rhodesia and South West Africa this sort of debate may be even less relevant. A case can be made that until the current Rhodesian government is accorded international legitimization by at least some segment of the international, nation-state community, sovereignty still formally lies with the United Kingdom. Regarding South West Africa, though its present legal status is still unclear, it is widely recognized that it has a somewhat unique international status. Even the Republic of South Africa, though unwilling to admit of the United Nations' jurisdiction growing out of the transition from Mandate to Trust Territory status, does not regard South West Africa legally as an integral part of the Republic. Though actual policy appears to bring the administration of South West Africa progressively closer to actual integration with the Republic, at least its international status is admitted. Insofar as various UN organs have attempted to interpret that status, direct UN military intervention or UN-sanctioned military intervention would not necessarily be condemned in legalistic terms in most of the world. In that respect, there are sound legal arguments favoring certain types of intervention against the present regimes in both Rhodesia and South West Africa.

A second subject of conjecture centers around the matters of finance, logistics, and tactics. Using the Congo operation as a basis for cost projections, a force of some 20,000 Western troops could be supported in Southern Africa for approximately $200 millions per year.[22] It is likely that

22. Average yearly costs for the UN Congo Operation were approximately $100 million. Troop salaries accounted for one-fourth of the total. African and Asian troops, comprising 82.4 percent of the total manpower, were paid salaries equal to about 3 percent of the total costs. Projecting these figures, and assuming the same relationship of troop salaries to total costs, the costs for an American force would be about double that of the UN forces in the Congo. See E. W. Lefever and W. Joshua,

a "surgical" operation in Rhodesia or South West Africa would involve the troops of Western nations less than a year. Intervention in South Africa or Portuguese Africa would, under the present circumstances, force military and human costs far higher.

Let's look at the matter of a hypothetical U.S. intervention in Rhodesia. Assuming British support and OAU or UN approval, the operation might be considered this way. Rhodesia is, in area, the smallest white-governed territory in the region. Its white population is roughly a quarter of a million and it is highly concentrated in urban areas (over 80 percent), particularly in two cities, Salisbury and Bulawayo. In addition, the Rhodesian armed forces are comprised of between 4,000 and 5,000 regulars and approximately 12,500 reservists. Rhodesia's terrain is a relatively flat and open plateau that would be suited to a Western-style army. Logistically, an entirely airborne operation concentrating on the chief cities would be in order, and support and supply, though difficult without Portuguese cooperation, would not be impossible. White emigration would be high, especially with the proximity of South Africa, and if the Zambian or Kenyan examples are any indication, we can expect a loss of about 74,000, or one third of the European population, in the five years after the establishment of a majority government.[23] In Rhodesia this estimate might be too high given the high proportion of landed, "permanent" settlers in comparison to Kenya or Zambia. The idea of resettlement allowances for Europeans might be considered in that it may blunt domestic opposition in the United States.

In regard to the external reactions to such an intervention, unless Western governments were willing to admit the insincerity of previous pronouncements, they would be forced to pay at least lip service in support of intervention. But the real question is not what would other governments say, but what would they do. It is unlikely that any state would attempt to obstruct physically the United States, Britain or the United Nations in the conduct of such an operation. South African interference

---

United Nations Peacekeeping in the Congo, prepared for the U.S. Arms Control and Disarmament Agency (Washington: Brookings Institution, 1966), pp. 22 and 39–40.
23. For some thoughts on these issues see James R. Scarritt, "The Adjustment of Europeans to Zambian Independence and Its Implications for Southern Africa," a paper presented to the 1970 Annual Meeting, African Studies Association, Boston, October 1970 (mimeo.).

is not likely since she has nowhere to turn for help but the West, and so far she has been careful to avoid provoking external action, sanctions, or military intervention against her. Nor would any Communist state stand in the way of intervention. If they oppose at the United Nations, they risk the ire of the Third World and thereby precipitate a policy victory for the West. If the operation were launched with OAU approval regardless of the UN position, the Communist countries would not likely be in a position to oppose physically the West in this region. If they did oppose intervention under these circumstances, then the West would find itself in the novel posture of befriending Third World militants, with "imperialist obstructionism" emanating from Communist states. Certainly the Communist countries would try to convince the Third World that such Western intervention was an imperialist ploy—an effort to establish a client state and thereby to prolong imperialist interests regionally. The effects of these arguments would depend on the ability of the Western states to convince African states of the sincerity of their purposes. In order to do this, African officials would have to be included early in the planning stages.

African statesmen have, since before UDI, been calling upon Western governments to use force in suppressing the Rhodesian regime. President Kaunda has repeatedly offered Zambian territory as a base for British troops seeking to depose the Smith government. African states realize that they need Western assistance in these operations. To avoid the charge that this is traditional paternalistic great power intervention, it would be wise for the West to cloak the operation in the legitimizing mantle of the United Nations or the OAU, preferably the latter. Perhaps the OAU's African Liberation Committee, or some such representative nationalistic body, should be included early in the planning. With whites taking the risks and doing the work and blacks participating in the administration, the imperialist image of American foreign policy might be diminished. Likewise, if administration of the occupied territory were quickly turned over to some African body—perhaps Zambia (with strong UN and Western support) or some committee of the OAU or the Zimbabwe nationalists (if they could cooperate)—many of the initial reservations of African states might be dispelled. African governments are not likely to be put off by arguments of precedent, or consistency, or "law." They tend to see through arguments based on formality and to look for the more telling considerations of ultimate purpose and eventual result. If such an intervention means the defeat of a minority government and its replacement by an African government dedicated to majority rule, they would be inclined to support it.

To many the preceding discussion, especially of level-four actions, may seem rather ethereal and academic. I would be the first to agree, except that this discussion presupposes a fundamental alteration of governmental attitudes toward Southern African affairs in the West, growing out of efforts to implement particularly first and second-level activities. The chief task is educational. Level one takes precedence. The populations in Western Europe and North America must be able, in their minds, to encourage and support their governments to move in this direction.

c. *The Transitional Period*

This final section will be devoted to presenting the prominent features of two scenarios in a chronological format that could dovetail into the scenario of South Africa provided in Section A. Many of the tactics and instruments for change that may be employed have already been suggested and discussed, so less detail is necessary than might otherwise be the case.

Rhodesia/Zimbabwe

1983—Isolated unrest and sporadic incidents of violence have marked the almost twenty years of independence since UDI. By and large, the regime has maintained order, although the economy has not blossomed and white immigration has remained steady, but at an extremely low level. So far, not a single state has formally recognized Rhodesia's independence. But at least five states, including South Africa, Portugal, Greece, Taiwan, and Spain, have quasi-diplomatic representation in Salisbury.

1984—Early in the year the existence of a secret, antigovernment white vigilante group is disclosed. It calls itself the Citizens' Defence League (or the League for short). Despite a steady drift to the Right (as Center critics were silenced or emigrated), the Rhodesian Front is still in power. But the R.F. has been constantly pushed by a Right-wing party, the Rhodesian Alliance, for the last five years. Whether or not there is a direct organic link between the vigilantes and the R.A. is not definitely known. But the League is popularly suspected to be the militant wing of the R.A.

January 1984—Fifty-two African "terrorists" are excuted by the Rhodesian authorities. The UN and the OAU condemn Rhodesia, as do most of the governments of the member states. Secret talks begin between some members of the OAU's Liberation Committee and high officials in the UN Secretariat.

February 1984—The League was formed in response to the bombing of the Cecil Rhodes Statue in the middle of Jameson Avenue. In retaliation, League operatives are believed responsible for seven isolated murders of apparently innocent African pedestrians around the Kopje and Harari areas of Salisbury. The bomb and shooting "war" between secret militants of both races escalates. Africans bomb the main office of the Standard Bank, the Parking Garage on Union Avenue, and the General Post Office. In turn, whites, with far more effect, attempt to destroy the football stadium at Mufakose, and a single-man's hostel in Harari. In the latter bombing, forty-four Africans have lost their lives.

In Lusaka, the government in exile, a product of the ZAPU-ZANU coalition (now called the Zimbabwe Union) that had been formed in 1981 (after Nkomo's death), has taken up a petition by Africans in Salisbury and Bulawayo and has transmitted it to the OAU for its April heads of state meeting in Lagos. The petition requests the United Nations to intervene militarily in order to protect Africans from "unprovoked and irrational attacks by white citizens aided by the criminal minority government of the Rhodesian settler party, and constituting acts of genocide in contravention of the (redrafted) Genocide Convention of 1980."

April 1984—The OAU summit resolves to place its full diplomatic weight behind the African peoples' petition. The OAU Secretary-General and the UN Secretary-General meet in New York to discuss an overall strategy for the Rhodesian situation.

May–June 1984—White citizens of Rhodesia are also alarmed now by the basic lack of safety in Salisbury and Bulawayo. They petition the government to legitimize and assist their vigilante activities, or to reassign some army units (heretofore almost exclusively in the Zambezi Valley or the Wankie areas) to police the cities and outlying townships.

October 1984—General election in Rhodesia brings about the fall of the Rhodesian Front government and its replacement by the Rhodesian Alliance.

November 1984—Debate begins in the Security Council on a resolution that would authorize UN armed intervention in Rhodesia unless a timetable for the establishment of majority rule by December 1985 is announced by December 31, 1984. After two weeks of debate a resolution passes in only slightly modified form.

December 1984—While awaiting reaction from Salisbury (no official reaction is expected), the secretaries-general of the OAU and the United Nations, and the heads of mission of the Chinese People's Republic, Great Britain, the United States, and the Soviet Union, collaborate in planning the UN effort. Although China is reluctant to approve UN intervention without massive Chinese participation, complete OAU approval of the action convinces the Chinese to participate in the planning efforts and it is agreed that they are to supply up to 1,000 troops for the UN stand-by force.

March 1985—In a joint OAU-UN announcement, it is revealed that in implementation of the Security Council Resolution on Rhodesia, the United Nations is prepared to occupy Rhodesia and administer the territory until the provisional Zimbabwe government assumes control at the earliest date. A stand-by force of some 30,000 troops, consisting of about 5,000 Scandinavians, 7,000 Europeans (Austrian, Irish, and Yugoslav), 8,000 Africans (Congolese, Ethiopian, and Nigerian), and 10,000 Asians (mostly Indian but also Ceylonese, Indonesian, and Japanese) is readied for action. Great Britain, the United States, Japan, and the Soviet Union are to provide all logistical support and supplies. The OAU-UN announcement urges the R.A. government to comply with the directives of the UN Commander in Chief, and to command its armed forces and its citizens not to resist the occupation.

April–May 1985—Two months of hurried diplomatic activity find the Rhodesian government appealing to the Republic of South Africa. The latter, however, disavows any desire to become directly involved in an open war with the United Nations over Rhodesia. She does agree to serve as an intermediary on behalf of Rhodesia, but in this effort she is thwarted at every turn. *Time* reports a secret trip by the Special U.S. Presidential Assistant for Foreign Affairs to Pretoria (two weeks before the Rhodesians approached the South Africans) in order to assure South Africa that the intervention will be limited to Rhodesia. Great power solidarity on this issue is surprisingly tight, and the Rhodesians quickly realize that resistance at this point would be futile and suicidal.

Meanwhile plans for a multiracial transitional government are advancing apace. The OAU, in concert with the UN Economic Commission for Africa, agrees to supply high level administrative and technical personnel to assure unbroken provision of governmental services.

July 10, 1985—The airlift of the first contingents of UN forces to Salisbury, Bulawayo, Kariba, Fort Victoria, and Umtali meets with no resistance from the Rhodesian armed forces. The top officers surrender with ceremony in Salisbury. Government officials are granted political asylum in South Africa. There is some token resistance from League branches, but casualties are limited.

Portuguese Africa

January 1985—The United States declares that all her military arrangements with Portugal, both bilateral and multilateral, will be terminated within twelve months unless Portugal agrees to set a timetable for the independence of and majority rule in her African territories. The Portuguese Premier responds by demanding the immediate cessation of U.S. operations in the Azores and a rapid withdrawal of forces.

January–March 1986—Other NATO powers pressure Portugal to reconsider her expulsion of American forces from the Azores.

March 1986—Lisbon announces her intention to terminate her NATO membership unless other NATO powers publicly support Portugal in "her" African territories.

April 1986—The wars in Angola and Mozambique continue at a rising level. There are 125,000 Portuguese troops in the former and 95,000 in the latter. Defense expenditures now consume some 62 percent of the Portuguese budget and total Portuguese combat deaths for 1985 were set at 7,500. In spite of the increase in revenues from oil production, there has been little welfare progress in metropolitan Portugal. Domestic opposition begins to surface in massive proportions. The public funeral for the 42 troops killed in an eastern Angola ambush, which the government sought to use to arouse patriotic sentiments, turns into an antigovernment demonstration and riot. The world's press records the violent police repression in which 18 lost their lives. Seething anti-regime discontent grows in importance and openness throughout 1986 and 1987. The General Directorate of Security becomes an increasingly independent governing agency with widespread arrests and detentions. On four occasions troops are rushed to the campus of the University of Lisbon to suppress antiwar rallies. Finally, the university is closed down and evacuated.

June 1987—FRELIMO establishes a new headquarters in Salisbury.

1987–1988—The war heats up in Mozambique. The Portuguese troop level climbs to 200,000. Desertions increase. One entire unit of about 35 predominantly African troops "disappear." Speculation that they defected to FRELIMO is ended when they turn up two weeks later at a press conference in Salisbury calling for the Portuguese to lay down their arms and rally behind a majority government in Mozambique.

March 1989—The Portuguese Premier is assassinated in Coimbra.

April–June 1989—Governmental instability erupts in Lisbon.

July 1989—Rioting occurs throughout Lisbon. Police and domestic security forces are unable to maintain order. The Acting Premier recalls 7,000 troops from Luanda.

August 1989—Although domestic order is shakily restored, the people now demand an increase in educational and economic opportunities. They insist that the war makes domestic development impossible.

September 1989—Spain agrees to serve as intermediary to negotiate with PAIGC forces. Negotiations, which had been going on secretly in Madrid for two months, are publicly disclosed.

October 1989—Portugal agrees to grant independence to Guinea (Bissau) and a peaceful transition takes place in Bissau. In point of fact, PAIGC has controlled all but the city of Bissau and its immediate environs since about 1983 and Portugal merely holds on to the enclave city in order to convince the world of its 'legitimate" claim to the entire territory.

Twenty thousand Portuguese troops are evacuated from the city and assigned immediately to Angola.

February 1990—Unrest hits Lisbon again. Troops brutally suppress anti-war demonstrations. Large segments of the populace and press demand an absolute end to the wars in Africa. The U.S. Secretary of State announces that if Portugal withdraws from Africa and orients her foreign policy toward Europe, a consortium of NATO states are prepared to grant substantial economic aid and to sponsor Portuguese entry into the Common Market and her readmission into NATO.

June 1990—Junior military officers in Lisbon force the government to resign and a new government is formed, dedicated to a rapid withdrawal from Africa and peace with the African nationalist movements. The new government discloses that some 3,200 political detainees will be released and that the Chief of the General Directorate of Security has been arrested and will be brought to trial. Negotiations open with MPLA in Rio de Janiero and with FRELIMO in Rome. After a few days, cease-fire agreements are reached. Both nationalist movements pledge their commitment to multiracialism and urge Portuguese settlers and troops to remain in Africa and build their nations together.

January 1991—All Portuguese troops leave Mozambique. In a week, over 15,000—mostly Europeans, Chinese, and mulattoes—flee from Lourenço Marques by auto caravan, air lift, and chartered ships to Durban. Nevertheless, racial tensions are surprisingly low in the city.

March 1991—Portuguese troops and officials depart Angola with the assistance of NATO air forces. Citizenship clauses in the new Angolan and Mozambican constitutions automatically grant citizenship to all Portuguese citizens of the territories unless by December 31, 1991, they made a public announcement of their desire not to become Angolans or Mozambicans. Except for those who fled, few decline citizenship.

I have attempted in this chapter to provoke, suggest, and elaborate upon various possible approaches to altering the status quo in Southern Africa. Current trends do not presage the futures sketched herein. It is clear, however, that there is a multiplicity of lines toward change. Various combinations of policies and efforts may be undertaken. Results may be uneven. Perhaps outcomes may be different from those envisioned by policy makers. But unless steps in the direction of radical sociopolitical change are underwritten, the pessimistic futures sketched in Chapter Six seem all too likely. We would be then left, at best, with a deteriorating situation in which our alternatives would be even more constrained than at present and our consciences contorted by the human misery we have contributed to by our policies and by our inaction.

APPENDIX 1

ABBREVIATIONS USED IN THIS BOOK

ALC—African Liberation Committee (of the OAU)

ALN—Armée de Libération Nationale (Algeria)

ANC—African National Congress (South Africa)

ANC—Armée Nationale Congolaise

APL—Armée Populaire de Libération (Congo)

CNL—Conseil (sometimes Comité) National de Libération (Congo)

CNRA—Conseil National de la Révolution Algérienne

CONCP—Conferência das Organizações Nacionalistas das Colônias Portuguêsas

COREMO—Comité Revolucionário de Moçambique

CRUA—Comité Revolutionnaire d'Unité et d'Action (Algeria)

FARP—Forces Armées Révolutionnaires du Peuple (Guiné-Bissau)

FLING—Frente de Luta pela Independência Nacional da Guiné

FLN—Front de Libération Nationale (Algeria)

FLNA—Frente Nacional de Libertação de Angola

FRELIMO—Frente de Libertação de Moçambique

GRAE—Govêrno Revolucionário de Angola no Exílio

KAU—Kenya African Union

KCA—Kikuyu Central Association (Kenya)

MPLA—Movimento Popular de Libertação de Angola

MTLD—Mouvement pour le Triomphe des Libertés Democratiques (Algeria)
NATO—North Atlantic Treaty Organization
OAS—Organisation Armée Secrète (Algeria)
OAU—Organization of African Unity
OPO—Ovamboland People's Organisation (South West Africa)
OS—Organisation Spéciale (Algeria)
PAC—Pan-Africanist Congress (South Africa)
PAFMECA—Pan-African Freedom Movement of East and Central Africa
PAFMECSA—Pan-African Freedom Movement of East, Central, and Southern Africa
PAIGC—Partido Africano da Independência da Guiné e Cabo Verde
PPA—Parti Populaire Algérien
SATO—South Atlantic Treaty Organization
SWA—South West Africa
SWANU—South West Africa National Union
SWANUF—South West African National United Front
SWAPO—South West Africa Peoples' Organization
UDI—Unilateral Declaration of Independence (Rhodesia)
UNITA—União Nacional para a Independência Total de Angola
UNOC—United Nations Operation in the Congo
UPA—União das Populações de Angola
UPC—Union des Populations du Cameroun
ZANU—Zimbabwe African National Union (Rhodesia)
ZAPU—Zimbabwe African Peoples' Union (Rhodesia)

APPENDIX 2

FACTUAL SUMMARY OF THE MAJOR GUERRILLA
ORGANIZATIONS CURRENTLY OPERATING IN AFRICA

ANGOLA—*MPLA*

Leader, Agostinho Neto
Military Campaign Officially Launched, February 6, 1961
Number of Armed Troops in Target Territory, 5–7,000
Principal Headquarters, Lusaka
Principal Sanctuary, Zambia
Principal Training Grounds, internal
Principal Source of Funds and Material, USSR
Recognized by the OAU
International Organizational Affiliations, CONCP, Khartoum Alliance

GRAE/FLNA

Leader, Holden Roberto
Military Campaign Officially Launched, March 15, 1961
Number of Armed Troops in Target Territory, 3–8,000
Principal Headquarters, Kinshasa
Principal Sanctuary, Congo (K)
Principal Training Grounds, Congo (K)
Principal Source of Funds and Material, Congo (K)
Recognized by the OAU (de jure)
International Organizational Affiliation, Congo Alliance

UNITA
Leader, Jonas Savimbi
Military Campaign Officially Launched, February–March 1966
Number of Armed Troops in Target Territory, 1–1,500
Principal Headquarters, internal
Principal Sanctuary, Zambia
Principal Training Grounds, internal
Principal Sources of Funds and Materials, Chinese People's Republic
Not recognized by the OAU
International Organizational Affiliations, none

CHAD—*FROLINAT* (Chad National Liberation Front)
Leader, Secretary-General Dr. Abba Siddick
Military Campaign Officially Launched, 1965
Number of Armed Troops in Target Territory, 2,000
Principal Headquarters, Tripoli
Principal Sanctuary, Libya and Sudan
Principal Training Grounds, internal
Principal Sources of Funds and Materials, none
Not recognized by the OAU
International Organizational Affiliations, none

ETHIOPIA—*ELF* (Eritrean Liberation Front)
Leader, Sheik Idris Mohammed Adum
Military Campaign Officially Launched, September 1, 1961
Number of Armed Troops in Target Territory, 1,500
Principal Headquarters, Damascus
Principal Sanctuary, Sudan
Principal Training Grounds, Syria
Principal Source of Funds and Materials, Syria
Not recognized by the OAU
International Organizational Affiliations, none

GUINEA (BISSAU)—*PAIGC*
Leader, Secretary-General Amilcar Cabral
Military Campaign Officially Launched, early 1963
Number of Armed Troops in Target Territory, 10,000
Principal Headquarters, Conakry

Principal Sanctuary, Guinea
Principal Training Grounds, internal and Guinea
Principal Source of Funds and Material, USSR
Recognized by the OAU
International Organizational Affiliations, CONCP, Khartoum Alliance

MOZAMBIQUE—*FRELIMO*

Leaders, since the 1969 assassination of Eduardo Mondlane, a Presidential Commission now consisting of Samora Machel and Marcelino dos Santos
Military Campaign Officially Launched, September 25, 1964
Number of Armed Troops in Target Territory, 8,500
Principal Headquarters, Dar es Salaam
Principal Sanctuary, Tanzania
Principal Training Grounds, internal and Tanzania
Principal Source of Funds and Material, USSR and Chinese People's Republic
Recognized by the OAU
International Organizational Affiliations, CONCP, Khartoum Alliance

COREMO

Leader, Paulo Gumane
Military Campaign Officially Launched, October 24, 1965
Number of Armed Troops in Target Territory, 250–300
Principal Headquarters, Lusaka
Principal Sanctuary, Zambia
Principal Training Grounds, internal
Principal Source of Funds and Material, Chinese People's Republic
Not recognized by the OAU
International Organizational Affiliation, Congo Alliance

RHODESIA (ZIMBABWE)—*ZANU*

Leader, Rev. Ndabaningi Sithole (imprisoned)
Military Campaign Officially Launched, April 29, 1966
Number of Armed Troops in Target Territory, 200–300
Principal Headquarters, Lusaka
Principal Sanctuary, Zambia
Principal Training Grounds, Tanzania

Principal Source of Funds and Material, Chinese People's Republic
Recognized by the OAU
International Organizational Affiliations, Congo Alliance

ZAPU
Leader, Joshua Nkomo (imprisoned)
Military Campaign Officially Launched, August 13, 1967
Number of Armed Troops in Target Territory, 250–500
Principal Headquarters, Lusaka
Principal Sanctuary, Zambia
Principal Training Grounds, Tanzania
Principal Source of Funds and Material, USSR
Recognized by the OAU
International Organizational Affiliations, ZAPU/ANC Alliance, Khartoum Alliance, Associate Member of CONCP

SOUTH AFRICA—*ANC*
Leader, Acting President Oliver R. Tambo
Military Campaign Officially Launched, December 16, 1961
Number of Armed Troops in Target Territory, no information
Principal Headquarters, Morogoro (Tanzania)
Principal Sanctuary, Zambia
Principal Training Grounds, Tanzania
Principal Sources of Funds and Materials, USSR
Recognized by the OAU
International Organizational Affiliations, Khartoum Alliance, Associate Member of CONCP, ZAPU/ANC Alliance

PAC
Leader, Acting President Potlako K. Leballo
Military Campaign Officially Launched, no information
Number of Armed Troops in Target Territory, no information
Principal Headquarters, Dar es Salaam
Principal Sanctuary, Zambia
Principal Training Grounds, Tanzania
Principal Sources of Funds and Materials, Chinese People's Republic
Recognized by the OAU
International Organizational Affiliation, Congo Alliance

SOUTH WEST AFRICA (NAMIBIA)—*SWAPO*
Leader, Samuel Nujoma
Military Campaign Officially Launched, August 26, 1966
Number of Armed Troops in Target Territory, 100–150
Principal Headquarters, Dar es Salaam
Principal Sanctuary, Zambia
Principal Training Ground, Tanzania
Principal Source of Funds and Materials, USSR
Recognized by the OAU
International Organizational Affiliations, Khartoum Alliance, Associate Member of CONCP

SWANUF
Leader, F. J. Kozonguizi
Military Campaign Officially Launched, no information
Number of Armed Troops in Target Territory, no information
Principal Headquarters, formerly Dar es Salaam
Principal Sanctuary, no information
Principal Training Grounds, no information
Principal Source of Funds and Materials, Chinese People's Republic
Not Recognized by the OAU
International Organizational Affiliations, none

SUDAN—*Anya'nya*
Leader, Gordon Mayen (Head of Nile Provisional Government), Gen. Tafeng Lodongi (military)
Military Campaign Officially Launched, 1963
Number of Armed Troops in Target Territory, 5,000
Principal Headquarters, Kampala (NPG), Military Headquarters internal
Principal Sanctuary, Uganda (only for refugees)
Principal Training Grounds, internal
Principal Sources of Funds and Materials, Israel, France, Italy
Not recognized by the OAU
International Organizational Affiliations, none

INDEX

Accra Conference on Positive Action and Security, 31, 32
Achebe, Chinua, 20n.15
Addis Ababa conferences, 32, 103
Adum, Sheik, *see* Idris
African Liberation Committee, *see* ALC
African National Congress, *see* ANC
ALC (African Liberation Committee), 111, 130; history and policy of, 137–138
Algeria, 14, 31, 35, 59, 66, 110, 116; struggle for independence of, 83–89; training of guerrillas by, 53
Algiers, 111
All-African Peoples' Conference (in Accra), 31, 32
ALN (*Armée de Libération Nationale*), 50, 66, 85, 89
American armed intervention in the Congo, 116, 118
ANC (African National Congress), 32, 33, 34, 50, 63, 72, 78, 107, 111, 112, 114, 116, 118, 130, 137, 174; factual summary of, 194; its identification with Marxism–Leninism, 69n.56
Angola, 3, 35, 56, 67, 69, 70, 92, 110, 132, 138, 147; guerrilla organizations in, 191–192; unrest in, 94–97
antiguerrilla target regimes, *see under* target regimes
Anya'nya, the, 66, 78, 122–123, 125; factual summary of, 195
apartheid, 112, 170; defeat of (in scenario), 159
APL (*Armée Populaire de Libération*), 116
Apollus, Emile, 69
Arab-African divisions in the Sudan, 119–120
Armée de Libération Nationale, see ALN
Armée Populaire de Libération, see APL
Ashe, Arthur, 171
ASPRO, 107

assimilation (*assimilado*) policy of Portugal in Portuguese Africa, 91–92
asynchronie, 127

Bakongo, the, 56, 96
Baluba (Nord Katanga), 78
Bantu, the, 56, 61, 112, 113; policy of South Africa toward, 4
Basutoland, 113
batuni, 80
Bechuanaland, resistance movement in, 114
Belgium, 124; intervention in the Congo by, 116, 118
Berber speakers, 84, 89
Biafra, 37
Biafran relief program, 124
Bissau, 97, 98, 99; *see also* Guinea (Bissau)
Bosgra, S. J., on Portugal and NATO, 140n.18
Botha, Minister of Defence P. W., 70
Botswana, 14, 107, 108, 110, 132
Boulding, Kenneth E., 21
Brazzaville, 14
Britain, 140, 142; economic aid to black states by, 163; *see also* Great Britain *and* United Kingdom
Burundi, 14

Cabinda, 105, 106, 125
Cabo Delgado, unrest in, 94
Cabral, Secretary-General Amilcar, 67, 98, 99, 102, 192
Cairo, 32, 111
Cameroons, the, 14, 59
Canada, 140
Central African Republic, 14
Chad, 14, 78, 125; guerrilla organizations in, 192
Chase Manhattan Bank, 166
Che Guevara, 47–48, 54
China, Chinese People's Republic, 111, 116; aid to Africa guerrilla movements

by, 51–54, 110, 137, 192, 193, 194, 195; growth of power of, 144; as a nuclear power, 143; relation of Mao's guerrilla strategy to foreign policy of, 48–49
Chinh, Truong, 47
Chou En-lai, 37
CNL (*Conseil [Comité] National de Libération* [Congo]), 78
CNRA (*Conseil National de la Révolution Algérienne*), 89
colons, the, opposition to France's policy in Algiers of, 88
Comité Revolucionário de Moçambique, *see* COREMO
Comité Révolutionnaire d'Unité et d'Action, *see* CRUA
Commonwealth, the, relation between South Africa and, 167–168
Communist guerrilla ideas and practices in Africa, 49
Communist literature, distribution among African guerrillas of, 54
Communist revolutionary thought, 63
Conakry, 98, 192
CONCP (*Conferência das Organizacões Nacionalistas das Colônias Portuguêsas*), 130, 191, 193, 194, 195
Congo, the, 14, 56, 59, 60, 67, 72, 125, 191; guerrilla warfare in, 115–117; medium power status of, 145–146; political unrest in, 16, 18–19; salaries in, 18
Congo Alliance, 130, 194
Conseil (sometimes *Comité*) *National de Libération* (Congo), *see* CNL
Conseil National de la Révolution Algérienne, *see* CNRA cooperation, among guerrilla movements, 129–131, 133; *see also under* target regimes
COREMO (*Comité Revolucionário de Moçambique*), 103, 130, 137; factual summary of, 193
corruption in Africa, 68–72
counterguerrilla thinking in Africa, 68–72
counterutopia, 28
CPR, *see* Chinese People's Republic
CRUA (*Comité Révolutionnaire d'Unité et d'Action*), 84, 89
Cuba, guerrilla training of Africans in, 51
Cuban academies of Marxism–Leninism, Agitation, and Guerrilla Warfare, 51

cultural and educational exchanges, encouragement of, 171
cultural heterogeneity, 22–23

Dahomey, 14
Damascus, 192
Dar es Salaam, 110, 111, 114, 192, 193, 194, 195
dawa, 61, 77, 118
Debray, Regis, thesis of guerrilla warfare expressed by, 8, 64–65
Defense Act of 1913, 132
de Vattel, *see* Vattel
De Wet, Prime Minister Jannie (in scenario), 158
Diggs, Congressman, 171
discontent, channels for expression of, 21–22
disengagement, as a suggested policy, 170–171
domestic policies of African states, patterns of, 127–128
Dominican Republic, the, intervention by the United States in, 179
domino theory, of African revolutionaries, 69; of white African international politics, 69; of black and white regional politics, 146–147
dos Santos, Secretary Marcelino, 105, 193
Durban uprising in Africa (in scenario), 159

economic deprivation in Africa, 13–19
economic welfare as an immediate end, 3–4
Egypt, 110, 124; *see also* U. A. R.
ELF (Eritrean Liberation Front), factual summary of, 192
Embu, the, 80, 82
ends-means dilemma, 2
Erikson, Erik H., 154
Eritrea, 124
Estado Novo, 91
Ethiopia, 14, 58, 125; guerrilla organization in, 192
ethnic factors, 23
Exchange Control Act, exemption of South Africa from, 167
external factors as a cause of political unrest, 10
external involvement, extent and nature of, 135–143
external military intervention, 177–178

Fanon, Frantz, 2n.1, 30, 58, 61n.42, 62, 65
FARP (*Forces Armées Révolutionnaires du Peuple*), 98
First National City Bank, 166
Fiske, John, 156
FLING (*Frente de Luta pela Independência Nacional de Guiné*), 147
FLN (*Front de Libération Nationale*), 66, 78, 79
FLNA (Frente Nacional de Libertação de Angola), factual summary of, 191
FLN–ALN independence fighters, 89
force capabilities, 9
Forces Armées Révolutionnaires du Peuple, see FARP
foreign investment in white Southern Africa, 165–167
foreign involvement, *see* external involvement *and* external military intervention
Fox, 60–61
France, 124, 140, 141, 142; aid to Sudanese guerrillas by, 195; investment in South Africa by, 165
FRELIMO (*Frente de Libertação de Moçambique*), 35, 53, 56, 64, 67, 78, 103, 104, 105, 137; factual summary of, 193
Friedländer, Saul, 27n.1, 144
FROLINAT (Chad National Liberation Front), factual summary of, 192
"From Gandhi to Mandela," 33
Front de Libération Nationale, see FLN
frustration, *see* systemic frustration

Gabon, 14
Galtung, Johan, 172
Gambia, 14
Gandhi, Mohandas K. (Mahatma), 30, 33–34
Gandhism, African, 32, 33
Gbenye-Soumaliot regime, 38
Ghana, 14, 110, 116
Giap, General Vo Nguen, 47
Gikuyu na Mumbi, 79
global configuration of power, effect on future guerrilla warfare in Africa of, 143–146
"Glorious Military Thought of Chairman Mao," 43
governmental ineptitude, 18–20

GRAE (Government of the Angolan Republic in Exile), 96, 97, 102, 130, 137; factual summary of, 191
GRAE/UPA, 78, 97, 102
Great Britain, 143, 164; *see also* Britain *and* United Kingdom
grievances, *see* discontent
gross national income per capita of African countries, 14
guerrilla movements, purposes of, 28; typology of African, 78; against white settlers in Southern Africa, characteristics of, 114–115; *see also* guerrilla warfare
guerrilla organizations operating in Africa, factual summary of, 191–195
guerrilla training, of Africans, 51–55; sites in Africa, 53
Guerrilla Warfare (by Che Guevara), 54
guerrilla warfare, wars, African theories of, 55–72; analysis of future African, 124–128; Communist theories of, 42–54; foreign involvement in African, 135–143, 177–178; as a form of political violence, 7; as a form of political and military warfare, 25–26; in the indigenous African states, 115–125; projection of long-run trends for African, 149–151; projection of short-run trends for African, 146–148; and World Order series, 3; *see also* guerrilla movements
Guevara, *see* Che Guevara
Guinea (Bissau), 14, 146; guerrilla movement in, 96–102; guerrilla organization in, 192–193; *see also* Bissau
Guinean socialism, 102
Gumane, Paulo, 193

Hajj ben Ahmed Messali, *see* Messali
Hance, William A., 172
Hanrahan, 45
Hegel's Unity of Opposites, 43
Helsinki, 111
heterogeneity of the African population, 22–24
High Commission Territories, 163
Ho Chi-minh, 47
humanitarian policies, need of launching, 164
Huntington, Samuel P., 25, 26

ideological indoctrination of guerrillas in Africa, 64
ideology, and revolutionary behavior, 11–12
Idris Mohammed Adum, Sheik, 192
indigenous African governments, internal wars in, 115–124
ineptitude, *see* governmental ineptitude
international law, in regard to use of force in Southern Africa, 177–178
International Monetary Fund, 166
intervention in Rhodesia, suggestions for, 179–182
Israel, 70–71, 124, 195
Italy, 124, 163; aid to the Anya'nya by, 195; investment in South Africa by, 166, 167; trade between South Africa and, 168
Ivory Coast, 14

Jaden, Aggrey, 122
Japan; investment in South Africa by, 167; trade between South Africa and, 168
Jenmin Jih Pao, 49

Kampala, 195
Kankonbe, Samuel, 104
Kasanje, 94
Katanga, 78, 116; Copperbelt, 19
Katzenbach, 45
KAU (Kenya African Union), 79, 82, 83
Kaunda, President Kenneth D., 31, 32, 33, 52, 181
Kavandame, Chief Lazaro, 105
KCA (Kikuyu Central Association), 79, 82, 83
Kenya, 14, 35, 58, 59, 90, 125; Mau Mau revolt in, 78–83
Kenya African Union, *see* KAU
Kenya Defense Council, 83
Khartoum Alliance, 130, 191, 193, 194, 195
Khartoum Round Table Conference, 122
Kikuyu, 61, 78, 79, 81, 82, 90
Kikuyu Central Association, *see* KCA
Kimathi, Dedan, 81
Kinshasa, 14, 19, 191
Kisangani, *see* Stanleyville
Kozonguizi, F. J., 195
Krimpen, *see* van Krimpen

Kuper, Leo, 112n.27
Kwili Province, 116; *see also* Mpeve
Kwili rebellion, 58, 64

"Land Freedom Army," 80
Lari Raid, 80, 81
Lawrence, T. E., and guerrilla warfare, 42
Leabua, Chief Jonathan, 29
leadership, as a factor in revolutions, 12, 131
leadership attitudes, 37–38
League of Women Voters, 162
legitimacy of a regime, and dissidents, 9–10
Lesotho, 14, 29, 132
"liberated" territory, problems of administration of, 60
Liberia, 14
Libya, 14, 192
Lin Piao, 48–49
Lodongi, General Tafeng, 195
London, 111
Lower Congo, the, 19, 116
Luanda, 94
Ludorf, Justice, 54
Lumumba, Patrice, 30
Lusaka, 111, 114, 163, 191, 193, 194
Lusaka Manifesto, 155

Machel, Secretary of Defense Samora, 105, 193
Madagascar, 14
magico-religious thought, 61–62
Makonde, the, 56, 104, 105
Malagasy, 78
Malawi, 14, 124, 132, 148, 163
Mali, 14
Mandela, Nelson, 32, 113
"Manifesto on Southern Africa," 155n.3
Mannheim, 28
Man of the People, A, 19n.15
Mao Tse-tung, 64; contribution to African guerrilla thought by, 72; and guerrilla warfare, 42, 43–48
Marcum, John, 94
Maria's War, 94
Marico, resistance movement in, 113–114
Matthews, Joe, 63
Mau Mau movement, the, 77–83; compared with the Algerian, 90–91; ideology of, 58

Mauritania, 14, 124
Mayen, Gordon, 122, 195
Mazrui, Professor Ali A., 15–16, 23, 32
Mbeki, Govan, 112n.27
Mboya, 31, 35
Meru, the, 80, 82
Messali, Hajj ben Ahmed, 83
military and police forces in Africa, 20
military space, symbolic expression of, 45
military time, awareness by guerrillas of, 68
Mondlane, Eduardo, 35, 64, 67, 68, 103, 104, 193
Morocco, 14, 85
Mouvement pour le Triomphe des Libertés Démocratiques, see MTLD
Movimento Popular de Libertação de Angola, see MPLA
Moyo, Jason, 28
Mozambique, 56, 64, 70, 108, 132, 138, 147, 163; guerrilla war in 103–105; guerrilla organizations in, 193
Mpere, 78
MPLA (Movimento Popular de Libertação le Angola), 78, 94, 96, 97, 130, 137; factual summary of, 191
Msonthi, J. D., 32
MTLD (Mouvement pour le Triomphe des Libertés Démocratiques), 84
Mtolo, Bruno, 113n.28
Muingi, see Uigana wa Muingi
Mulele, Pierre, 58, 64
Mulelists, 78
Muller, Minister of Police S. L., 114

Nairobi, 79
Naivasha, 81, 82
Namibia (South West Africa), 138, 195
nationalism, African, causes in Portuguese Africa of, 92–93
"nationalization" of guerrilla wars, 175
national liberation movements, need of widening base of support for, 174–175
NATO, Portugal's membership in, 107, 139, 140–142
Ndebele, the, 109
"negative" steps to assist white Southern Africa's black neighbors, 164, 166–168
Neto, Agostinho, 191
New York, 111
Niassa, 103
Niger, 14

Nigeria, 14; medium power status of, 145–146
Nkomo, Joshua, 194
Nkrumah, 2n.1, 31, 37, 130; principle of "positive action" of, 30, 33
Nogueira, Foreign Minister Alberto Franco, 104
nonviolence, doctrine of, 30, 31, 33; reasons for, 33–34
Nord Katanga, see Baluba
norms relating to violence, 10
North Korea, 110; guerrilla training of Africans in, 51
Norway, 141
nuclear power, 143, 144, 145
Nujoma, Samuel, 110, 195
Numeiry, Major-General Gaafar, 124
Nyanja, the, 105
Nyerere, President Julius K., 1–2, 31, 32–33, 35, 105

OAS (Organisation Armée Secrète [Algeria]), 90
oathing among the Kikuyu, 79–80
OAU (Organization of African Unity), 5, 32, 102, 103, 108, 111, 130, 134, 137, 176, 179, 191, 192, 193, 194, 195; policy of, 138–139
OAU Liberation Committee, 105
Odendaal Commission Report, 111
Omnibus Civil Rights Act of 1994 (in scenario), 158
Ongulumbashe, 110
Organisation Spéciale, see OS
Organization of African Unity, see OAU
Orpen, Commandant Neil, 133
OS (Organisation Spéciale), 84
Ovamboland, 110, 111
Ovamboland People's Organization, 109–111

PAC (Pan-Africanist Congress), 113, 114, 130, 137; factual summary of, 194
PAFMECA (Pan-African Movement of East and Central Africa), 31, 42
PAFMECSA (Pan-African Movement of East, Central, and Southern Africa), 31, 32
PAIGC (Partido Africano da Independência da Guiné e Cabo Verde), 64, 67, 78, 98–99, 102, 146–147, 174; factual summary of, 192–193

Pan-Africanism, 28, 29
Pan-Africanist Congress, *see* PAC
Parti Populaire Algérien, see PPA
peace as a derivative value, 2
Peace Corps, 162
peasantry, the, reliance upon, 55–62
People's Republic of China, *see* China
Pijiguiti, strike at, 98
Pirow, Minister of Defence, Oswald, 132
political-military interaction, 62–67
political system based on degradation and exploitation, odiousness of, 154–155
political violence, definition of, 8; general words on African, 24–25; relation to guerrilla warfare of, 7; variables related to, 24
Pondoland (Transkei, the), 78; peasant uprising in, 113–114
popular attitudes, 38–39
popularization of nationalistic struggle, 174–175
Poqo, 78, 113
Portugal, 146, 147; attitude of South Africa toward, 132–133; "civilizing mission" in Africa of, 91–92; cost and importance of colonial possessions to, 105–106; significance of association with NATO of, 140–142; withdrawal from Mozambique and Angola (in scenario), 159
Portuguese, the, 35, 64; method of fighting revolutionary nationalists of, 69–70
Portuguese Africa, 14, 29; scenario of future events in, 185–187
"positive action," 30, 33
positive steps to assist nonwhites in Southern Africa, 161–164
PPA (*Parti Populaire Algérien*), 84
priorities, and ultimate ends, 2; and immediate ends, 3
Problems of War and Strategy (by Mao), 54
protracted war, effect on guerrilla thinking of, 67–68
pseudo-systems, 154

racial and cultural arrogance, institutionalization in Southern Africa of, 155
racism, 37
reeducating American and West European peoples, necessity of, 161–162

regime violence, 7–8
revolution, legacy of, 1–2
revolutionary situation in South Africa, question of existence of a, 63
Rhodesia, 14, 29, 50, 56, 69, 114, 132, 163; aid to Portugal by, 107; average annual earnings in 16; collapse in 1985 of (in scenario), 159; guerrilla movements and organizations in, 107–109, 193–194; question of intervention in, 179–180
Rhodesia/Zimbabwe, scenario of future events (1983–1985) in, 181–185
Rhodesian UDI, *see* UDI
Roberto, Holden, 94
Russia, *see* Soviet Union
Rwanda, 14

Salazar, Dr. António, 91
sanctions against Southern Africa, lowering of interest in, 171
Sakiet Sidi Yussef, bombing of, 85
Santos, *see* dos Santos
SATO, 142
Savimbi, Jonas, 192
Scandinavia, 124
Scandinavian opposition to apartheid, 170
scenarios (hypothetical): in chronological format (1983–1985) of overthrow of Rhodesian government, 182–185; in chronological format (1985–1991) of expulsion of the Portuguese from Portuguese Africa, 184–186; in narrative form of events in Southern Africa (Suid Afrika) in the 1990's, 155–161
Sekhukhuneland, resistance movement in, 114
Selected Military Writings (by Mao), 54
Senegal, 14, 102, 124
Senghor, 31
Sharpeville shootings, 112, 166
Shepherd Professor George W., Jr., on involvement with white Southern African states, 142–143n.21
Shona people, the, 109
Siddick, Secretary-General Dr. Abba, 192
Sierra Leone, 14
Simango, Reverend Uria, 64, 105
simbas, the, 61, 116, 117, 123
Sithole, Reverend Ndabaningi, 193
"slippery slope" syndrome, 142

Smith regime (Rhodesia-Zimbabwe), 69, 107, 181
social welfare as an immediate end, 3–4
Somalia, 14
Somali guerrillas, 58
South Africa, 14, 29, 35, 56, 63, 108, 179; aid to Portugal by, 107; effects of establishment of black governments adjacent to, 147–148; fear of black "terrorists" from neighboring states by, 71; guerrilla organizations in, 194; and nuclear power, 145; potential for urban-based uprisings in, 56–57; relations between the British Commonwealth and, 167–168; relation to guerrilla warfare in Africa of, 70–71; revolutionary nationalism in, 111–115; see also domino theory, sanctions, and United Nations embargo
Southern Africa, dependence on external environment by white governments of, 149–150; distasteful principles of white governments of, 154; domino theory of, 69; hypothetical description of, in the 1990's, 155–161; military force levels in, 134; prospects for guerrilla warfare in, 146–147; support given by the Western World to regimes of, 165
South Vietnam, 49
South West Africa (Nomibia), 29, 179; guerrilla activities and organizations in, 195
South West Africa National Union, see SWANU
South West Africa Peoples' Organization, see SWAPO
South West African National United Front, see SWANUF
Soviet Union, the, 142, 144; aid to African states or guerrilla organizations by, 102, 110, 111, 116, 124, 137, 191, 192, 193, 194; guerrilla training of Africans in, 51
Stanleyville rescue operation by Belgian-American paratroopers, 118, 136
Sudan, the 14, 59, 116, 124, 125, 192; Arab dominance in, 118–120; ethnic groups in, 118; guerrilla organization in, 195; guerrilla wars in, 117–118, 121–124
SWANU (South West Africa National Union), 111, 137

SWANUF (South West African National United Front), 111; factual summary of, 195
SWAPO (South West Africa Peoples' Organization), 78, 109, 110, 111, 130, 137, 174; factual summary of, 195
Swaziland, 14
Switzerland, 140; investment in South Africa by, 165, 166
Syria, 192
systemic frustration, conditions leading to, 13–24

Tambo, Oliver R., 194
Tanzania, 14, 56, 103, 104, 108, 163, 193, 194, 195
Tan-Zam railway project 163
target regimes, three types of, 76; cooperation among antiguerrilla, 132–133
technique of guerrilla movements, 77
technological change, effects on guerrilla movements of, 128–129
Tete province, 103
Togo, 14
"token" approaches toward South Africa, 170n.12
trade with South Africa, 167
traditional thought, influence upon individual and group performance of, 60–62
Transkei, the, 113, 114; see also Pondoland
Transvaal, northwest, 114
Tripoli, 192
Truon Chinh, see Chinh
Tshombe, Moise, 38, 96
Tunisia, 14, 85
typology of African guerrilla movements, 78

U. A. R., the, see United Arab Republic
UDI (Unilateral Declaration of Independence [by Rhodesia]), 79, 107, 163, 181
Uganda, 14; aid to the Anya'nya by, 122–123
Uigana wa Muingi, 79
Umkonto we Sizwe (Spear of the Nation), 112–113
UN, see United Nations
União dos Populações de Angola, see UPA
Unilateral Declaration of Independence by Rhodesia, see UDI

UNITA (*União Nacional para a Independência Total de Angola*), 96–97, 137; factual summary of, 192

United Arab Republic, the (U.A.R.), 14, 116; *see also* Egypt

United Kingdom, 165, 167, 172, 179; trade with South Africa by, 168; *see also* Britain *and* Great Britain

United Nations, the, 179; African leaders' different concepts of, 3–5; embargo by resolution of its Security Council on sale of arms to South Africa, 140; relation to African civil and guerrilla wars of, 138, 139; support of uprising in South Africa by troops of (in scenario), 160

United States, the, need of economic aid to black Southern Africa by, 163–164; investments in South Africa by, 165–166; joint interference with Belgium in the Congo by, 116, 118; intervention in Rhodesia (hypothetical) by, 180–181; involvement with Portugal and South Africa of, 140, 141, 142, 143; scientific and technological knowledge given to South Africa by, 169; relations between the Soviet Union and, 143–144; trade between South Africa and, 167–168

Unity of Opposites, Hegel's, 43

University Christian Movement, 162

UNOC (United Nations Operation in the Congo), 139

UPA (União dos Populações de Angola), 31, 78, 94, 96, 97, 102

UPA/GRAE, 56

UPC (*Union des Populations du Cameroun*), 78

Upper Volta, 14

urban areas, Africans in South African, 57

U.S. *see* United States

USSR, *see* Soviet Union

utopias, 28, 29

van Krimpen, Chr., on Portugal and NATO, 140n.18

variables in model of political violence, 24

Vattel, Emmerich de, 177

violence, cathartic quality in, 2n.1; as a "cleansing force," 65; determinants increasing or decreasing, 8–12; dichotomy between stability and, 3; as a

means to the achievement of social order, 4; natural resistance to, 37; reasons for adoption of, 35–36; role in Africa of, 30–33; *see also* political violence *and* regime violence

Vorster, Prime Minister J. B., 70, 133

war, elimination of causes of, 28–29; utility of absence of, 1–2

"warrior oath," *see batuni*

Waruhiu, Senior Chief, 80

weapons development, relation to guerrilla warfare of, 128–129

West Germany, 124, 140, 141; investment in South Africa by, 165, 166, 167; trade between South Africa and, 168

white governments of Southern Africa, future of, 149–150; *see also* scenarios

wilayas, 66, 89

Witzieshoek, resistance movement in, 113

World Bank, 166

World Council of Churches, 162

World Order Models Project of the World Law Fund, the, aims of, 2

Wretched of the Earth, 2n.1, 49n.17, 58, 58n.34, 59n.37, 61n.42, 65n.50

Young, Crawford, 16, 17, 58

Zambézia, unrest in, 94

Zambia, 14, 104, 107, 108, 163, 191, 192, 193, 194, 195; wage levels in, 15

ZANU (Zimbabwe African National Union), 49, 78, 107, 108, 109, 137, 174; editorial quoted in *Zimbabwe News*, 49, 73; factual summary of, 193–194

ZAPU (Zimbabwe African Peoples' Union), 28, 78, 107, 108, 109, 114, 130, 137, 174; factual summary of, 194

ZAPU/ANC Alliance, 194; operations in Rhodesia of, 50

Zimbabwe, 50, 52, 53, 69, 130, 138, 147; *see also* Rhodesia (Zimbabwe) under scenarios

Zimbabwe African National Union, *see* ZANU

Zimbabwe African Peoples' Union, *see* ZAPU

Zimbabwe liberation activities, 107–109

Zimbabwe News, the, quoted editorial in, *see under* ZANU

Zululand, resistance movement in, 114